Functional and Object Oriented Analysis and Design: An Integrated Methodology

Peretz Shoval
Ben-Gurion University, Israel

T0325218

IDEA GROUP PUBLISHING
Hershey • London • Melbourne • Singapore

Acquisitions Editor:	Michelle Potter
Development Editor:	Kristin Roth
Senior Managing Editor:	Jennifer Neidig
Managing Editor:	Sara Reed
Copy Editor:	Holly Powell
Typesetter:	Cindy Consonery
Cover Design:	Lisa Tosheff
Printed at:	Integrated Book Technology

Published in the United States of America by
    Idea Group Publishing (an imprint of Idea Group Inc.)
    701 E. Chocolate Avenue
    Hershey PA 17033
    Tel: 717-533-8845
    Fax: 717-533-8661
    E-mail: cust@idea-group.com
    Web site: http://www.idea-group.com

and in the United Kingdom by
    Idea Group Publishing (an imprint of Idea Group Inc.)
    3 Henrietta Street
    Covent Garden
    London WC2E 8LU
    Tel: 44 20 7240 0856
    Fax: 44 20 7379 0609
    Web site: http://www.eurospanonline.com

Shoval, Peretz.
  Functional and object oriented analysis and design : an integrated methodology / Peretz Shoval.
    p. cm.
  Summary: "The main objective of this book is to teach both students and practitioners of information systems, software engineering, computer science and related areas to analyze and design information systems using the FOOM methodology. FOOM combines the object-oriented approach and the functional (process-oriented) approach"--Provided by publisher.
  ISBN 1-59904-201-0 -- ISBN 1-59904-202-9 (softcover) -- ISBN 1-59904-203-7 (ebook)
  1. Object-oriented methods (Computer science) 2. Functional programming (Computer science) I. Title.
  QA76.9.O35S535 2007
  005.1'17--dc22
                                   2006010090

British Cataloguing in Publication Data
A Cataloguing in Publication record for this book is available from the British Library.

Functional and Object-Oriented Analysis and Design: An Integrated Methodology

Table of Contents

Preface

The main objective of this book is to teach students and practitioners to analyze and design information systems (IS) using the functional and object oriented methodology (**FOOM**),[1] which combines the functional (process-oriented) approach with the object oriented (OO) approach.

The **functional approach** to IS development (sometimes also termed the *traditional approach*) was popular in the 1980s and 1990s of the 20th century. The development life cycle of this approach is based on the *waterfall* model (or its variations), according to which the IS development is essentially a sequential process, with the possibility of repetitions and iterations, thus making it look more like a spiral process. This approach views the IS as made of functions (processes), interconnected in a complex manner. The analysis of the IS focuses on discovering and defining the functions which the system needs to perform, and the flow of data to and from those functions. Two of the notable methodologies supporting this approach are structure system analysis (SSA) and system structure design (SSD) (DeMarco, 1978; Gane & Sarson, 1979; Yourdon, 1989). The SSA methodology is based on the use of data flow diagrams (DFDs) which describe the various functions of the system; the data stores in which the data are saved; the external entities which are the source of data input to the system and the destination of output information; and the dataflows which connect all of these components. According to the SSD methodology, the DFDs created in the analysis phase are transformed into a modular description of application programs, expressed by structure charts (Yourdon & Constantine, 1979).

With the development of the relational data model on the one hand, and conceptual data models on the other hand, more emphasis was given to the analysis and design of the system's database. The entity relationships (ER) model and its entity relationship diagram (ERD) (Chen, 1976) had become a common mean for modeling the data and creating a conceptual data model, thus playing a complementary role to the role of DFDs in functional analysis. In the design phase, the ERD is mapped into a relational database schema. Simultaneously, the functional model is mapped, as mentioned previously, into structure charts of the application programs.[2]

One of the main problems with the traditional development methodologies such as SSA and SSD is the difficulty of transition from the analysis phase to the design phase. The transition is not smooth and causes difficulties because of the need to translate DFDs, which are a network structure, into structure charts, which are hierarchical. Another problem is the gap between the functional modeling aspect on one hand (leading to the creation of the application programs), and the data modeling aspect on the other hand (leading to the creation of the database schema of the application). In order to address these issues, Shoval developed the ADISSA methodology, which closes the gap between analysis and design phases and enables a smooth transition from the former to the latter phase (Shoval, 1988, 1991). The smooth transition from analysis to design is made possible by introducing a new construct in the DFDs: transactions. From a user's point of view, a transaction is a process performed by the IS to support a user's task, which is activated as a result of an event in the real (user) world. The transactions of the system are identifiable in the DFDs, and based on them it is possible to design all components of the system as a natural continuum of the analysis phase. The products of the design include, according to ADISSA, detailed descriptions of the application programs; a database schema; the user interfaces (menus trees) and the input/output screens; and reports.

The OO approach for IS development became popular in the early 1990s. The success of object oriented programming languages (OPL) motivated the penetration of the objects approach also to the area of analysis and design methodologies. In the last 15 years many OO analysis and design methodologies have evolved, and many techniques and diagram types which support these methodologies have been created, enabling the modeling of a system from various perspectives. Some examples of early OO methodologies can be found in Booch (1994), Coad and Yourdon (1990, 1991), Jacobson (1992), Martin and Odell (1993), Rumbaugh (1995), Rumbaugh, Blaha, Premerlani, Eddy, and Lorensen (1992), Shlaer and Mellor (1992), and Wirfs-Brock, Wilkerson, and Wiener (1990).[3]

The huge number of techniques and diagram types which evolved until the mid 1990s was a main driving force for proposing and adopting the unified modeling language (UML) as the "standard" for OO systems modeling.[4] UML is a collection of visual notation, that is, diagrammatic techniques. In spite of its great popularity and the advantage of having standardized techniques, UML has limitations. One of them is that UML includes many techniques with a certain degree of overlapping between them. Some techniques enable developers to achieve the same goal in different ways;[5] but it is not always clear which technique should be preferred. Clearly, multiplicity of techniques and notations makes learning UML difficult and complicates the development process because of the need to move from one model/diagram type to another while keeping all models consistent (Siau & Qing, 2001).

Ever since the use of development methodologies for the creation of IS, software developers had to deal with two main problems: (1) the gap between process and data; and (2) the gap between analysis and design. The gap between process and data was manifested in traditional methodologies by the fact that DFDs emphasize process (functional) modeling, neglecting somewhat the modeling of data. A remedy to this gap came with the introduction of conceptual data models, notably the ER model, which complement DFDs as tools for defining the users' requirements. In early OO methodologies, the gap between process and data modeling was manifested by putting most of the emphasis on data (objects) modeling, while process modeling played a minor role only. To compensate for this deficiency, various techniques were added over time to deal with the functional aspects; but the result was, as said, a multitude of techniques with no well-defined interconnection among them.

The gap between analysis and design is expressed by the fact that the transition from analysis to design is not always clear and natural. In the analysis phase we define what the system ought to do as based on the users' needs, while in the design phase we deal with *how* the system will do that. Although it is clear that the design should be a direct continuation of the analysis, analysis and design methodologies have not always succeeded in doing so; some methodologies do not make it clear what "belongs" to analysis and what to design, or when does one phase end and the other begins, or (especially) what to do with the products of the analysis phase in the design phase. A solution to this void was offered, as said, by the ADISSA methodology, which defines and derives transactions from the DFDs and uses them as the basis for designing the application programs, the user interface, and the inputs and outputs of the system (Shoval, 1988, 1990, 1991). Some OO methodologies have tried to bridge the gap between the analysis and design by making the borders between the two phases "fuzzy," that is, treating the design as a refinement of analysis (e.g., Coad & Yourdon, 1990, 1991). Some OO methodologies do not specify what activity belongs to which phase, or where one phase ends and the other begins, or which of the possible techniques should be used in each of these phases. Yet, some methodologies view design as a refinement of analysis.

FOOM methodology (initially presented in Shoval & Kabeli, 2001) combines the functional and objects approaches and gives them an equal stand in both phases. In the analysis phase, the users' requirements are defined by creating two complementary models: a data model, expressed in the form of an *initial class diagram*, and a functional model, expressed in the form of object oriented DFDs (OO-DFD). The two models are synchronized and used in the design phase in order to design the various components of the system. The design products include a complete class diagram; detailed descriptions of the class methods; user interfaces and input/output screens; and reports. The products of the design phase facilitate the construction (programming) of the system in an OO development environment.

Organization of This Book

This book is aimed for students of IS, computer science, management, and other fields which include a concentration on IS. It is intended to be a textbook of an advanced course (possibly in an undergraduate or graduate program), after the students have had at least one course in the fields of computer science or IS. In addition, it is recommended that the students take a course on databases (mainly being familiar with the relational model, data normalization, and the ER model). A course on IS analysis and design is not a prerequisite. However, familiarity with IS development methodologies, either from the functional or objects approach, is an advantage.

The book is divided into three learning sections, each consisting of three to five chapters. The first section deals mainly with the objects model and class diagrams; the second section deals with system analysis, and the third with system design. The material in each chapter includes many examples. At the end of each chapter there are review questions, which are meant to help the students in digesting and understanding the material. In some chapters there are also assignment questions which require solving practice-oriented problems. In addition to working on such assignments, it is recommended to include in the course a guided project, in which teams of two to three students perform the tasks of analysis and design of an IS for an organization in a real-world environment (as much as possible). If this is not possible an alternative is to perform a similar project on a case study that will be prepared for the students.[6]

The content of the book is as follows:

Section I (The Objects Model and Class Diagrams) provides a preview of the objects approach in general, and elaborates on the objects model and class diagrams in particular. The section consists of five chapters.

- **Chapter I (Introduction to the Objects Approach in Software)** presents the principles and characteristics of OO software in the objects approach, and common terms in OO programming.

- **Chapter II (The Objects Model and the Class Diagram)** describes in detail the components of the objects model (including objects, classes, attributes, relationships, and functions), and the class diagram which represents them.

- **Chapter III (Creating Class Diagrams)** discusses considerations and rules for identifying classes, attributes, relationships, and functions and presents case study examples (problems), that is, descriptions of users' data requirements, along with their class diagram solutions.

- **Chapter IV (Mapping Entity Relationship Diagrams to Class Diagrams)** explains why it might be preferred to first create an ERD and then map it to a class diagram. The chapter then describes the mapping rules and demonstrates the mapping process with several comprehensive examples.

- **Chapter V (Mapping Class Diagrams to Relational Schemas)** explains the need to map a class diagram to a relational schema. Most of the chapter is dedicated to presenting and demonstrating the mapping rules for converting a class diagram into a relational schema which is made of normalized relations. The mapping process is demonstrated with several comprehensive examples.

Section II (Functional and Object Oriented Analysis) starts with presenting a background for the development of UML, and then explains the motivation for the development of FOOM, which combines the objects and functional approaches. Most of the section is dedicated to learning how to analyze a system according to FOOM. The section consists of four chapters.

- **Chapter VI (Object Oriented Methodologies and UML)** reviews the evolution of OO methodologies and UML. Most of the chapter is dedicated to presenting and demonstrating the various techniques and diagrams which make up UML, and then it provides a detailed example of IS modeling using a UML-based methodology.

- **Chapter VII (Combining the Functional and Object Oriented Approaches: Introduction to FOOM)** starts by introducing the motivation for the development of a combined methodology. Then it presents the stages, substages, and products of FOOM.

- **Chapter VIII (Information Systems Analysis with FOOM)** elaborates on the activities and products of the analysis phase. The products of analysis include a data/objects model (in the form of an initial class diagram) and a functional model (in the form of hierarchical OO-DFDs. The two diagram types are synchronized in order to verify the correctness and completeness of the two models. The chapter presents various examples of diagrams of both types.

- **Chapter IX (Data Dictionary)** explains the roles of a data dictionary in the development of the IS and describes its components. The chapter presents a possible implementation of the data dictionary both with the relational and with the OO models.

Section III (Information System Design with FOOM) is about the design phase. The products of the design include: (1) a complete class diagram, containing (in addition to the data classes) the interface, inputs, outputs, and transactions class; (2) detailed descriptions of the various class methods; (3) the menus of the user interface; (4) the input and output screens and reports. The section includes three chapters.

- **Chapter X (Transactions and Their Top-Level Design)** describes what a transaction is and explains how to identify and extract the transactions from the OO-DFDs. Then it explains how to map transaction diagrams to top-level descriptions which details their components and process logic.
- **Chapter XI (Designing of the Man-Machine Interface: Menus, Inputs, and Outputs)** presents a method for the design of user interfaces— menus trees—for the entire system as well as for its subsystems. Then it describes how to design the inputs and outputs/reports of the systems.
- **Chapter XII (Detailed Design of the Transactions and Class Methods)** describes how to map top-level descriptions of transactions to detailed descriptions, and then how to "decompose" these detailed descriptions into various methods, which are attached to proper classes. Two equivalent techniques for the description of methods are provided: pseudo code and message charts. The chapter ends with a review on the products of the design phase, which serve as input to the system construction (programming) stage.

References

Avison, D., & Fitzgerald, G. (1988). *Information systems development: Methodologies, techniques and tools.* Oxford, UK: Blackwell.

Booch, G. (1994). *Object-oriented analysis and design with applications* (2nd ed.). Redwood City, CA: Benjamin/Cummings.

Chen, P. (1976). The entity-relationship model—Toward a unified view of data. *Transactions on Database Systems, 1*(1), 9-36.

Coad, P., & Yourdon, E. (1990). *Object oriented analysis.* Englewood Cliffs, NJ: Prentice Hall.

Coad, P., & Yourdon, E. (1991). *Object oriented design.* Englewood Cliffs, NJ: Prentice Hall.

DeMarco, T. (1978). *Structure analysis and system specification.* Englewood Cliffs, NJ: Prentice Hall.

Gane, C., & Sarson, T. (1979). *Structured systems analysis, tools and techniques.* Englewood Cliffs, NJ: Prentice Hall.

Jacobson, I. (1992). *Object-oriented software engineering: A use case driven approach.* New York: Addison Wesley.

Jayaratna, N. (1994). *Understanding and evaluating methodologies: NIMSAD, a systematic framework.* London: McGraw Hill.

Martin, J., & Odell, J. (1993). *Object-oriented analysis and design.* Englewood Cliffs, NJ: Prentice Hall.

Olle, W., Sol, H., & Verrijn-Stuart, A. (Eds.). (1986). *Information system design methodologies—Improving the practice.* North Holland: Elsevier Science Publishers; IFIP.

Rumbaugh, J. (1995). OMT: The dynamic model, the functional model, the object model. *Journal of Object-Oriented Programming, 7*(9), 6-12; *8*(1), 10-14; *7*(8): 21-27.

Rumbaugh, J., Blaha, M., Premerlani, W., Eddy, F., & Lorensen, W. (1992). *Object-oriented modeling and design.* Englewood Cliffs, NJ: Prentice Hall.

Shlaer, S., & Mellor, S. (1992). *Object lifecycles—Modeling the world in states.* Englewood Cliffs, NJ: Yourdon Press, Prentice Hall.

Shlaer, S., & Mellor, S. (1992). *Object-oriented systems analysis: Modeling the world in data.* Englewood Cliffs, NJ: Yourdon Press, Prentice Hall.

Shoval, P. (1988). ADISSA: Architectural design of information systems based on structured analysis. *Information System, 13*(2), 193-210.

Shoval, P. (1990). Functional design of a menu-tree interface within structured system development. *International Journal of Man-Machine Studies, 33,* 537-556.

Shoval, P. (1991). An integrated methodology for functional analysis, process design and database design. *Information Systems, 16*(1), 49-64.

Shoval, P. (1998). *Planning, analysis and design of information systems* (Vols. 1-3). Tel-Aviv, Israel: Open University Press. (Original work published)

Shoval, P., & Kabeli, J. (2001). FOOM: Functional and object-oriented analysis and design of information systems—An integrated methodology. *Journal of Database Management, 12*(1), 15-25.

Shoval, P., & Kabeli, J. (2005). Essentials of functional and Object-oriented methodology. In M. Khosrow-Pour (Ed.), *Encyclopedia of information science and technology* (pp. 1108-1115). Hershey, PA: Idea Group.

Siau, K., & Qing, C. (2001). Unified modeling language (UML)—A complexity analysis. *Journal of Database Management, 12*(1), 26-34.

Wieringa, R. (1998). A survey of structured and object-oriented software specification methods and techniques. *ACM Computing Surveys, 30*(4), 459-527.

Wirfs-Brock, R., Wilkerson, B., & Wiener, L. (1990). *Designing object-oriented software.* Englewood Cliffs, NJ: Prentice Hall.

Yourdon, E. (1989). *Modern structured analysis.* Englewood Cliffs, NJ: Prentice Hall.

Yourdon, E., & Constantine, L. (1979). *Structured design.* Englewood Cliffs, NJ: Prentice Hall.

Endnotes

[1] FOOM was developed by Peretz Shoval, the author of this book, with the assistance of his doctoral student Judith Kabeli (Shoval & Kabeli, 2001, 2005). FOOM is based on and expands the ADISSA methodology, which Peretz Shoval has developed as a functional development methodology (Shoval, 1988, 1991, 1998).

[2] More background and surveys of traditional IS development methodologies can be found, among others (in Avison and Fitzgerals (1988), Jayaratna (1995), Olle, Sol, and Verrijn-Stuart (1986), and Wieringa (1998)).

[3] For a survey of both structured and early object-oriented methodologies see Wieringa (1998).

[4] UML Web sites are detailed in the References.

[5] For example, sequence diagrams and collaboration diagrams.

[6] It is also recommended that the students will build (program) the system (or parts of it) in a proper development environment. This can be done in a follow-up course or exercise.

Acknowledgments

This book is the outcome of many years of work, research, and teaching in the areas of information systems analysis and design, as well as data modeling. Many of the ideas regarding functional and object oriented methodology (FOOM), which are the core of this book, originated from the Architectural Design of Information Systems based on Structures Analysis (ADISSA) methodology, a functional-oriented methodology which I developed in the late 1980s. Some of those ideas include the method to design transactions (processes) and the method to design menus-tree interfaces. FOOM can be viewed as an enhancement of ADISSA with object oriented ingredients, notably the use of class diagrams for data modeling, and the method for designing class-methods from the transactions.

The development of FOOM was done in cooperation with Judith Kabeli, my doctoral student at the time of its development. I am especially thankful for Judith's contributions in utilizing the methodology in several case studies and projects, as well as in conducting experimental evaluations of the methodology. The fruits of our cooperation are reflected in many papers we have jointly published in journals, books, and conference proceedings. I am also thankful to the many students at the Department of Information Systems Engineering of Ben-Gurion University, as well as students of other departments, who took part in the various experiments and who utilized the methodology in their graduation projects.

This book was first published in Hebrew by the Open University. I would like to acknowledge the help of Dr. Ilan Ben Ami, the head of academic development unit, and his staff, as well as the staff at the graphics unit. Special thanks go to Irit Asher who worked "around the clock" preparing the figures.

I appreciate the work done by the reviewers: Dr. Micha Hanani, Dr. Arieh Nachmias, and Dr. Bracha Shapira, for their constructive comments on the Hebrew version of this book.

Thanks go to the publishing team at Idea Group Inc., in particular to Kristin Roth, Development Editor, for her guidance and for keeping the project on schedule.

Finally, I thank my wife Sara for her patience, understanding, and love throughout all our years together, and my children and their families for their love.

Peretz Shoval

Section I:
The Objects Model and
Class Diagrams

The objects model had become dominant in the field of programming languages, and from this field it has spread to other fields of computing, including analysis and design of information systems. Alongside with the traditional analysis and design methodologies, which are based on the functional approach (also termed process-oriented, or traditional methodologies), object oriented methodologies have and are still evolving. This unit provides a preview of the objects approach in general, and elaborates on the objects model and class diagram in particular. The unit contains five chapters.

Chapter I (Introduction to the Objects Approach in Software) presents the principles and characteristics of object oriented software and the common terms in object oriented (OO) programming.

Chapter II (The Objects Model and the Class Diagram) describes in detail the components of the objects model (including objects, classes, attributes, relationships and functions), and the class diagrams which represent them.

Chapter III (Creating Class Diagrams) discusses considerations and rules for identifying classes, attributes, relationships and functions; and presents case study examples (problems), i.e., descriptions of user data requirements, along with their class diagram solutions.

Chapter IV (Mapping Entity Relationship Diagrams to Class Diagrams) explains why it might be preferred to first create an ER diagram and then map it to a class diagram. The chapter then describes the mapping rules, demonstrating the mapping process with several comprehensive examples.

Chapter V (Mapping Class Diagrams to Relational Schemas) explains the need to map a class diagram to a relational schema. Most of the chapter is dedicated to presenting and demonstrating the mapping rules based on which a relational schema (made of normalized relations) is created. The mapping process is demonstrated with several comprehensive examples.

Chapter I

Introduction to the Objects Approach in Software

This chapter presents the principles and characteristics of software in the objects approach, and the common terms in object oriented (OO) programming.

Principles and Characteristics of the Objects Approach

The term "object oriented" spread in the last decade and a half, throughout many fields of computing, including the analysis and design of information systems (IS). The use of the OO approach began in the early 1970s in fields such as computers architecture, operating systems, and artificial intelligence. But the main field to which the approach penetrated was programming languages, beginning with *Simula* and then with *Smalltalk*. Some years passed by until the approach became popular in the programming field. Reasons for the vigorous penetration of the approach include the emergence of the windows-based graphical interfaces technology, the desire to economize development costs by reusing existing software, and the transition from centralized computing to distributed- and Internet-based computing. As aforesaid, the approach penetrated into other fields of computing due to its success in the field of programming, including the field of analysis and design of IS.

OO analysis and design may be viewed as an extension of OO programming. This extension may be considered as analogous to a former extension in the field of structured programming: In the same manner that the success of the structured programming approach was followed by the development of system analysis methodologies such as structured system analysis (SSA) (DeMarco, 1978; Gane & Sarson, 1979) and system design methodologies such as structured system design (SSD) (Yourdon & Constantine, 1979), so was the success of the OO approach in programming followed by development of OO analysis and design methodologies (Sumit, Srifdhar, & Radhakanta, 2001; Wieringa, 1998).

Another source, from which the OO approach nourished, is conceptual data models, notably Chen's (1976) entity relationship (ER) model and Smith and Smith's (1977) database abstractions. As known, the ER model describes reality using entities, attributes, and relations, distinguishing between entity types and entity occurrences. The OO approach also describes reality by entities that have attributes; only here, instead of the terms *entity type* and *entity occurrence*, the OO approach uses the terms *class* and *object*, respectively; that is, a class consists of objects which are characterized by the same attributes. Different relationship types between the object classes are also observed. Hence, there is a lot of similarity between the OO and the ER approach with regard to how they model the data structure of reality.

However, the OO approach models not only the data structure but also their "behavior," that is, the functions that can manipulate the data. In IS that are developed in the traditional approach (meaning pre-OO era) there is a separation between the structural component, that is, the database schema, and the functional component, that is, the programs which perform various functions on the data. The database schema is defined by a data definition language (DDL) of the database management system (DBMS), and the functions are defined separately from the database schema. These are expressed by application programs, written in some high-level programming language, which embed data manipulation language (DML) commands of the DBMS, or by queries written in a fourth generation language (4GL) or a query language which is part of the DBMS.[1] In contrast to that, in an IS which is developed according to the OO approach, the components are connected: The software system is a collection of objects that are classified in classes; each class includes definitions of the objects structure as well as of the functions which can operate on the objects during their lifetime in the system.

Among the justifications for the development of the OO approach is the growing need for developing more complex IS than the ones which were developed in the previous decades. Indeed, most of the organizational or business-oriented IS can be implemented with traditional software tools, because such IS are characterized by a database that can be represented as tables or relations (according to the relational model) and by relatively simple application programs which perform queries and update the data in the tables. However, in the last years there has been a growing demand to develop IS in new fields which were not handled in the past, such as systems for engineered design and manufacturing (CAD/CAM), geographical information systems (GIS), computer aided software engineering (CASE), and multi-media systems. Such systems are characterized by complex data structures and complex functions which are hard to implement in traditional programming languages and relational DBMSs.

The relational model is simple and easy to apply, but it has limitations: tables assume "horizontal" homogeneity (i.e., every record in a table has the same attributes) and "vertical" homogeneity (i.e., every attribute has the same data type for all records in the table). A relation does not enable direct representation of multiple valued attributes (sets). Sometimes an entity in reality cannot be represented as a holistic unit, that is, in one relation, and must be artificially decomposed into several relations, causing inefficient retrieval of data.[2] In complex applications such as CAD there are complex objects which can not be represented as rows of tables. In multi-media systems there are graphics, pictures, sound, and so forth. Such data are usually held in different length series of bytes with different relationships between them. These can not be represented by relational tables. It is expected that in the future there will still be a wide use of relational DBMSs in application domains where they are effective. But in order to allow application development in complex domains such as previously stated, there is a need for an approach which enables representation of complex data structures.

The terms which the OO approach uses differ from the terms used in the traditional programming world. Those who support the OO approach claim that the basic terms in this field are "natural," as they are based on terms known from childhood. From childhood we know that the world consists of objects which have attributes. For example, the human body consists of body parts; people have similar attributes/characteristics, but there are different groups/types of people, and so forth. The first thing children learn is to identify objects (such as people); later on they learn to identify the body parts from which they are assembled; then they distinguish between different groups (classes) of people (objects).[3]

Many claim that the OO approach to software development has advantages compared to the traditional approach. Here are some advantages which are attributed to OO software development:

- **OO programming is simpler than traditional programming:** As aforesaid, there is a separation in traditional programming between data and functions. Different functions can access and manipulate the same data and the programmer must know the data structure well and plan the programs well in order to ensure data completeness and correctness. In OO programming, the data and behavior (functions) are integrated. An object is like a box containing its structure (the data) and its behavior (the functions which can operate on the data). Whoever is outside the object does not need to know how the data and functions are defined. He/she only needs to know what the object is and what it can do. OO systems development includes mainly the definition of objects and their functions; they can be built without the need of thinking of loops and complex branching, as in traditional programming. Usually the programs are smaller and simpler than in traditional programming; therefore the chance of an error is smaller. Once an object is built and functions well, the developer considers it as a "closed box" that can be used without knowing how it is built. Hence, software engineering resembles hardware engineering. Each object is independent; therefore entire classes of objects can be changed independently. Since changing a class can be done easily, maintenance of OO systems is considered easier than that of traditional systems.

- **The OO approach can encompass many phases of the system's development process:** For instance, the system's analysis is done by OO analysis yielding an objects analysis model; the system's design is done by refinement of that model and adding design artifacts yielding a design model; the implementation of the system is done by OO programming; CASE tools, which support the development, utilize the OO approach; and the data are stored using an object oriented database management system (OO-DBMS). That is, the same approach can be used in nearly all stages of the system's development and life cycle, and there is no need to mix different approaches. That is unlike other development approaches which may require a combination of a variety of methods; that is, a combination of functional analysis using data flow diagrams (DFD) with data analysis using entity relationship diagrams (ERD). Some claim that combining different methods is unnatural and causes difficulties to developers. In contrast, the OO approach represents data, processes, people, and so forth—all as objects.[4]

- **The OO approach supports reuse of software; therefore new software development is faster and more reliable:** An organization dealing with software development can maintain a software library of objects of certain application domains. If such a library exists, the development of a new application turns into a matter of choice and connection between existing objects. Since the existing objects were already tested and examined independently, when connected they provide an application within a short time. Only entirely new objects need to be developed or acquired. Some claim that eventually there will be global object libraries, and software developers will only need to search and choose what they need for the new applications. Since the objects in these libraries will be reliable (having been tested in the past) the development of a new application and the modifying of an existing application will be easy to perform. Therefore, software development will not only be cheaper and faster, but also more reliable and error free.

Terms in OO Programming

An **object** is a thing for which data is saved and actions (functions) are performed. An object is an abstraction of something in the real world that we need to represent in the system. An object has **attributes** which are a collection of data which describe it. An object's **state** is the values which its attributes possess in a certain moment. In addition, an object has a **behavior**; that is, the various **functions** which can operate on the object. Other common terms for functions are **services** and **methods**.

A **class** is a collection of objects of the same kind; that is, an object is an instance of the class to which it belongs. All objects belonging to a specific class have the same attributes and behavior. Classes can be organized in **superclass** and **subclass** hierarchies. **Inheritance** means that a subclass inherits attributes and behavior from its superclass. **Multiple-inheritance** means that a subclass can inherit from more than one superclass.[5]

We shall demonstrate now the terms introduced so far. Assume there is an object which is a certain student. The student has attributes such as: *student ID* (Identification Number), *name, birth date,* and *average grade.*[6] The student's state is the values of his attributes in a certain point of time. For example, *student ID*: '12345678', *name*: 'John Doe', *birth date*: '22/07/1985', *average grade*: '87.4'. The state of an object may change over time, according to various events which cause appropriate actions to be performed on an object throughout its lifetime in the IS. For example, adding a new student to the system, locating a student, and displaying some of its attributes (i.e., its state), updating values of the student's attributes (such as changing the address or calculating the average grade), and so forth. The IS contains many students; each student is an object (instance) of the **class** of students, assuming all the students have the same attributes and behaviors. In our example we name the class **Students** (but it may also be in singular: **Student**).[7]

As aforesaid, classes are organized in a hierarchy. In our example, the **Students** class can be a subclass of the superclass **People**. This superclass can have other subclasses, such as **Lecturers** and **Administrative Employees**. A subclass can be in itself a superclass of subclasses. For example, **Lecturers** can be a superclass of **Senior Staff** and **Junior Staff**. The hierarchy is expressed by inheritance of attributes and behaviors: The superclass's attributes and behaviors are inherited to its subclasses. In addition, each subclass may have specific attributes or behaviors which its superclass does not have. For example, the class **People** may include general attributes that all people have (and which are relevant to the IS) such as: *name, birth date,* and *address*, as well as general behaviors (functions) such as: *add a new person, locate a person, display a person's details, change a person's details,* and *delete a person*. The class **Students** (as well as all other subclasses of **People**) inherits **People's** attributes and behavior, meaning that every attribute and every function that are defined for every person are applicable to every student as well. In addition, specific attributes (e.g., *average grade*) and specific functions (e.g., *calculate average grade*) can be defined for students.

The advantage of inheritance is that existing software code can be reused if one needs to implement similar functions, rather than writing new code. For example, if a **Student's** class needs to be implemented in a new system, there is no need to define and code it from scratch; rather, existing code (in a software library or in another IS) which includes a **People** class can be used as a superclass, so that only specific attributes and functions need to be coded. Reuse of code saves development time, prevents errors in the new software, and contributes to the standardization of the software.

Note the difference between reusing code in an OO programming environment and reusing code in a traditional programming environment, in which code is also reused in different programs. Organizations possess program files which can be used in different applications, according to the application's needs. This reuse may save time and development effort as well; however, the difference is that in traditional programming there is no return to the original code. It means, once the program code is copied, there are two different programs (software entities): the original and the new one; each can develop separately and independent of the other. If an error is discovered in the original program or some change to it is required, the change is not applied in the new program. Contrarily, in OO programming with inheritance, a superclass can be changed and the subclass inherits its new behavior by simply recompiling it. The specific functions of the subclass are not affected. For example, we may change the superclass **People** by adding an attribute, say *address*; then we can compile the subclass **Students**, meaning that the subclass will now have the new attribute *address*. That is, the change is done only once and applied to all subclasses, thus truly obtaining the advantage of software reuse.

It needs to be clarified that inheritance does not occur by itself; it has to be well planned. That is, appropriate classes and hierarchy relations must be constructed, so that the general attributes and functions of objects will be defined in the classes at the higher level of the hierarchy, while the specific attributes and functions will be defined in the classes at the lower levels. In our example the attributes: *name, birth date,* and *address* are defined in the general class **People**, and its subclasses (at some level of the hierarchy) inherit these attributes without the need for redefining. This applies to the general functions as well, such as locating a certain person or updating a person's details. In contrast, it is obvious that an attribute such as *research name* is specific to the **Research Student's** class. As we will see later on, one of the main issues in the OO approach is to plan correctly the classes and their attributes, behaviors, and inheritance relationships.

OO software is a collection of cooperating object classes. In OO software, the objects simply exist and await activation. Activation occurs when an object (belonging to a certain class) receives a **message** from another object. Hence, there is a **sender** object who delivers a message to the **receiver** object. The message includes the name of the function which the sender asks the receiver to perform. A message may include **parameters** (also termed arguments) which are the data needed by the receiver's function to perform. The receiving function performs the function it was asked to perform on its object in the way it was defined (i.e., coded) while using the data handed with the message—if needed. The function may be, for example, locating/retrieving the object, updating its state (i.e., changing one or more of its attributes), doing some calculations based on the object's data, and so forth. At any rate, the sender does not know **how** the function is performed; it is internal to the receiver. The object is viewed as a "closed box," or a capsule, which can perform certain functions (identified by its functions names), but no one outside must know how it performs its functions.

A function's code may include messages to other objects. A message asks an object to perform a certain function that it knows to perform. Hence, a "chain reaction" may occur due to further activation of objects by messages sent from already activated objects.

The following example demonstrates the activation process (see Figure 1[8]): An IS includes a class **Students** (as described earlier) and a class **Registrations** whose objects are the events of all students' registrations to courses. **Registrations** class includes the attributes: *student ID, course code, registration date (year, semester), grade,* and *date of grade*; and a function named *update course grade*. A process of reporting a course grade is activated due to an event in the real world; for example, a teacher sends a grade report at the end of the semester to the department secretary who is in charge of updating the system. Assume that system includes a class named **Forms**, and one of its objects is a grade report form designed to input course grades. The secretary starts the process by making certain menu selections (which can be viewed as sending messages to a function of a class **Menus**, which is not shown in the figure). As

Figure 1.1. Update grade event

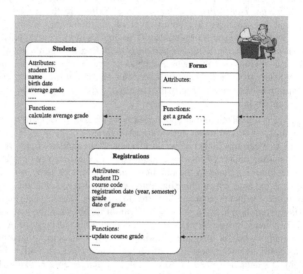

a result, the desired grade report form is presented on screen; the secretary fills in the necessary details (*student ID, course code, grade,* and *date of grade*), and then hits a "send" button. This can be viewed as sending a message to the function *get grade.* Assume that this function, besides doing some internal activities (e.g., checking the correctness of the input data) sends a message to the class **Registrations** to its function named *update course grade,* along with the parameters: *student ID, course code, grade,* and *date of grade.* Based on that, the receiving function locates/retrieves the specific object of **Registrations** and starts its internal process. Assume that the function's code includes the following two procedures: (1) registering the new grade and date and saving the updated **Registrations** object; and (2) sending a message to the function *calculate average grade* of class **Students**, with the parameters *student ID* and *grade;* this will enable the receiving function to locate the specific student object and update its *average grade* according to the new course grade. The receiving function retrieves the student object, recalculates the new *average grade,* and saves the updated student object.[9] At the end, the function sends the sender (in **Registrations**) a confirmation status, and this function can in turn send to its sender (in **Forms**) some text confirming the update.[10]

An object is independent of other objects. As aforesaid, the way in which an object performs its role (meaning the way the method is implemented) is unknown to other objects. That means that the internal structure of an object or its implementation can be changed without causing problems to other objects. The external world can approach an object using its **interface**. An object's interface includes the names of the functions that it can perform. A function has a **signature** which includes: (1) the function name; (2) parameters for the data it will get (as input) from the sender; and (3) the data it will return (as output). As aforesaid, not all functions must have parameters or return data.

Note again that the system's data and function are defined within class objects and not outside of them. The internal structures of objects and of the functions that can operate on them are concealed from the external world. The sender only needs to know which function can provide the required service, and on which object the function should be applied; it is not supposed to know how the function is implemented and how it performs. This is termed **encapsulation**.

OO software is therefore a collection of objects of various types, which may be connected by messages sent to functions aimed to perform certain operations on the objects. Usually, a certain function of a certain class is initiated due to an event in the real world, which causes a user of the system who is in charge of handling the event to act (but sometimes a function can be initiated automatically, for example, as based on predefined time or by a certain device). The triggered function may operate on an object or objects of the class, or send a message to another function of the same or another class, to operate on respective objects, and so on.

An object is, as we already know, an instance of the class to which it belongs. All objects of the class are identical in structure and behavior, but differ only in their identity and state, but the same function can operate on the different objects of the class. Therefore, it is clear that the functions' code is not stored separately within each object; rather, the code of each function is written and stored once for all objects of the class; in other words: the functions belong to the class. An object is simply a data structure holding its data values. When a function is triggered by a message, the software system binds the function code (which is stored in one location) to the object on which the function needs to be performed.

Summary of Characteristics of OO Software

We recount the advantages of software in an OO approach as appose to traditional software.

- **Abstraction of reality:** The OO software system is built according to a model which is more adaptable to reality than in the traditional approach, because in the OO approach, the reality is represented as it is, meaning as objects, which makes the system more comprehensible.

- **Encapsulation and information hiding**: A definition of a class includes its objects' data structures and behavior. The object's definition is "private" and concealed from the external world. Outside the object, what is known is only "what" the object can do, but only "inside" it is specified "how" the object does it. The object has a public interface through which it allows whoever is outside to know what it can do. These attributes allow developers: (1) to change the objects inner definitions without changing its external appearance and without affecting other objects; and (2) to easily use existing objects, because whoever develops a new application only needs to know what an object can do, not how it does it. If anyone (say a user or another object) needs to know or change anything in a certain object, he/she needs to approach the object (by sending a message) and ask it to perform the needed function. The way in which the function performs is hidden from any external object.

- **Inheritance:** The existing definitions of object classes can be used as is or changed according to specific needs using the inheritance principle. Inheritance creates hierarchies among classes and makes it easier to design the system, because existing attributes and functions do not have to be redefined. This way, redundant definitions are prevented, development effort is spared, and complicated object classes can be easily built.

- **Reusability**: Due to abstraction, encapsulation, and inheritance, object classes originally built for other systems can be reused. Reuse saves costs, shortens development time, and improves system's reliability. This enables easy changing and expanding of the existing system.

- **Creating new software markets:** Due to reusability, software companies can supply class libraries to the use of many organizations in various domains.

- **Easier programming:** The programs are built in small parts, which are easier to make. The programmer builds one class function at a time, thus avoiding complicated programming.

- **Easier software maintenance:** Each class can be maintained separately, because each class is independent of other classes.

- **Improved communication between developers and users:** The developers and users think in the same terms: objects having attributes and functions that are performed in response to events. Therefore, the OO approach encourages understanding between users and developers.

Review Questions

1. What has motivated the development of the OO approach?

2. In what way is the objects model similar to a conceptual model, and in what way are they different?

3. What types of applications are suitable to develop with the objects approach rather than the traditional approach?

4. What are the main advantages of the objects approach to IS development?

5. Explain and provide examples for the following terms: object; attribute; state; behavior; function/service/method; class; superclass and subclass; inheritance; message; parameter; interface; signature; and encapsulation.

6. What is reuse in software, and why is it more associated with OO development than with traditional development?

References

Chen, P. (1976). The entity-relationship model—Toward a unified view of data. *Transactions on Database Systems, 1*(1), 9-36.

DeMarco, T. (1978). *Structure analysis and system specification.* Englewood Cliffs, NJ: Prentice Hall.

Elmasri, P., & Navathe, S. (2003). *Fundamentals of database systems* (4th ed.). Boston: Addison Wesley.

Gane, C., & Sarson, T. (1979). *Structured systems analysis, tools and techniques.* Englewood Cliffs, NJ: Prentice Hall.

Garcia-Molina, H., Ullman, J., & Widom, J. (2002). *Database systems—The complete book.* Upper Saddle River, NJ: Prentice Hall.

Smith, J., & Smith, D. (1977). Database abstractions: Aggregation and generalization. *ACM Transactions of Database Systems, 2*(2), 105-133.

Sumit, S., Srifdhar, P., & Radhakanta, M. (2001). Revolution or evolution? A comparison of object-oriented and structured systems development methods. *MIS Quarterly, 25*(4), 457-471.

Wieringa, R. (1998). A survey of structured and object-oriented software specification methods and techniques. *ACM Computing Surveys, 30*(4), 459-527.

Yourdon, E., & Constantine, L. (1979). *Structured design.* Englewood Cliffs, NJ: Prentice Hall.

Endnotes

[1]   To be more precise, in some DBMSs it is possible to define functions as part of the database schema. These are sometime termed *database procedures* or *stored procedures*, but their use is limited usually to perform checks of completeness or constraints on values of fields/attributes.

[2]   For more information on databases and the relational model, see for example, Elmasri and Navathe (2003) and Garcia-Molina, Ullman, and Widom (2002).

[3]   Indeed, *Smalltalk* was developed originally for children.

[4]   In spite of what is said here, we shall see that in the OO approach too, different techniques are combined in the development process.

[5]   Hence, in multiple-inheritance, the data model is actually a directed graph of classes rather than a hierarchy.

[6]   Attribute names are written (here and in the rest of the book) in *italics*. Values of attributes are written within ' ' signs.

[7]   Class names are written in **Bold**; initial letter capitalized.

[8]   At this stage, the reader can understand the figure intuitively; in the following chapters, more detailed explanations will be given.

[9]   This is an informal description of the function; actually it may get assistance from other functions of this class to perform tasks of retrieving the object or saving it. These details are not important at this stage.

[10]   The figure does not show arrows returned to senders because these are not considered messages but rather confirmations. By the way, it is not necessary for a receiver to return a confirmation or any data to the sender; it depends on the specific application needs.

Chapter II

The Objects Model
and the Class Diagram

*This chapter describes in detail the components of the objects model
(including objects, classes, attributes, relationships, and functions), and
the class diagram which represent them.*

Similarities and Differences Between
the Objects Model and the
Entity Relationship Model

The objects model (or object oriented [OO] model) is a conceptual-application
model that is used to define a database schema representing a certain reality. The
model views the world as consisting of objects belonging to classes. The objects
of these classes have attributes, behavior (i.e., functions), and various relationships with other objects.

The objects model can be presented as a class diagram (also termed OO diagram
or objects diagram). Like an entity relationship diagram (ERD), the class
diagram has two main goals:

1.   To serve as a communication medium between the developers (analysts/
     designers) and the users or their representatives. The diagram is created
     as a result of the interactions between the two parties, during which they

discover and define the users' information needs; the diagram serves like a contract between these two sides which summarizes the users' needs.

2.   To be the basis for further development of the information system (IS). Based on the diagram, it should be possible to design the database schema of the application, and (partially) the functions that it will have to perform. For that, it is necessary to transform the class diagram into an equivalent verbal description—an objects schema. This is done using an object definition language (ODL), similar to data definition language (DDL) in the relational model. In principle, all components of the class diagram are mapped to the objects schema. However, the objects schema includes more details which are not included in the diagram. For example, in the diagram each attribute has a name, and some attributes may have specific constraint definitions (e.g., key, unique); in the objects schema there are more detailed definitions, including the attributes' domains or data types (e.g., numeric, char., real, etc.) and lengths. Another example, in the class diagram, we only write the names of the classes' functions, while in the objects schema we specify the parameters of the functions.

As aforementioned, there is a great deal of similarity between the OO and ER models and diagrams, since the ER model is one of the sources from which the objects model originated. But there are differences between the two models, which we will review later on. One of these differences is that the ER model is "static," that is, it only deals with the data structure, while the objects model also includes "behavior," that is, the functions that operate on the data.

The rest of this chapter is dedicated to describing the components of the objects model and the class diagram. The description is organized in four main categories: objects and classes, attributes, relationships, and functions.

Objects and Classes

Object

An object represents a thing that exists in the real world, tangible or intangible. In the real world there are many different things, but we are only interested in those which are relevant to the business or the organization, and for which data needs to be stored in the IS, as based on the users' needs.

An object can be tangible, for example, a student, an employee, an item or a book. But it can also be an intangible thing, for example, a purchase order, a delivery of goods; or it can be an event that has to be recorded, for example, a student registers to a course, a reader lends a book. The thing all objects have in common is that they all contain data which need to be saved, updated, or retrieved and presented to users. They are sometimes termed data objects or entity objects. The process of creating an objects data model includes the discovering and identification of the types of objects that exist in the reality and on which data needs to be kept in the system. This is done, as said, in cooperation between analysts and users or their representatives (e.g., experienced users or managers who are familiar with the organization, the existing IS, the problems caused by that system, and the needs from the future IS). Based on the types of objects, the database schema and other components of the IS will eventually be built.

In addition to the data objects, there are those who distinguish other kinds of objects, such as interface objects, which are used to enable communication between the IS and external entities or users, for example, windows, input screens, icons, buttons, and other accessories known as the graphical user interface. Such objects do not originate from the reality being modeled and do not contain real-world data; they are used as a means to build the system in its development environment. In the system analysis phase, when we build models of the reality according to the users' needs, we deal only with data objects, while other kinds of objects are dealt with in the following phases of development.

An object is characterized by attributes, which have values. The values of the attributes are the object's data. For example, the object **student** can be characterized by these attributes: *student ID, first name, last name, birth date, city,* and *average grade.* The values of these attributes for a certain student may be: '1234567' for *student ID,* 'John' for *first name,* 'Doe' for *last name,* '22.07.1985' for *birth date,* 'New York' for *city,* and '87.4' for *average grade.* The values of these attributes determine the state of the object. It is obvious that the state of an object can change from time to time. For example, John might move to a different city, or his average grade may change.

In addition to attributes, an object has "behavior," which means all the actions or functions that can operate on the object or its attributes during its lifetime in the system, for example, adding a new student, displaying the state of a student, updating a student's address, calculating the average grade, and so forth. The various functions can be performed on an object in response to events in the real world. For example, the function *add student* is activated when a new student is admitted; the function *update address* is activated when a student moves to a different city; the function *calculate average grade* is activated when a new course grade is reported. At this point we do not explain who and how a function is activated, nor how the function performs its task. We only say that a function is activated by a message sent to it from an object, asking it to do what it ought to do. Usually, a message arrives with parameters containing data which the function needs in order to do its task. For example, in order to activate the function *update address*, the message sent to the function should include the object's (student's) identifier and the new city. To conclude this introductory discussion on "behavior," we note that like objects and their attributes, the functions too must be defined and based on the users' needs.

Objects in the real world are not "independent"; they usually have relationships with other objects. For example, a student may belong to a certain department, be registered to certain courses, and have certain classmates. Just like the need to keep data on the object (i.e., its attributes) and define its behavior (the functions that operate on it), it is also important to know are other objects to which it is related. Sometimes an action performed on an object will affect other objects related to it. Sometimes it is necessary to display data of objects which can be found based on predefined relationships. For example, if a student is admitted to a certain department or moves to a different department, a record of the event should be kept in the student object (for example, by changing the value of a certain attribute), and this will be done by an appropriate function. Additionally, this should also be recorded in the respective department object, using its proper function, to enable finding the department's students. In order to allow all of this to happen, a relationship must be defined between each student and his/her department. Similarly, if a student registers to a course, the event should be recorded in both the student and course objects. Another example of enabling one to produce a report providing some details about the students who registered to a course, one needs to find the specific course object and the respective (registered) student objects. In general, many relationships of different types may exist between different objects. The various relationship types need to be defined in the course of creating the objects model.

Class

A class is a collection of objects of the same type, that is, objects having the same attributes, behavior (functions), and types of relationships. For example, assuming that all students have the same attributes, functions, and relationship types, we may say that the students belong to a class **Students**.[1]

When we say that the objects of a class have the same attributes we do not mean, of course, that they have the same values; every object has its own attribute values, for example, every student has its own *student ID*, *name*, and so forth. The same is true for relationships: All objects of a class have the same types of relationships, but obviously every object has its specific relationships with other specific objects. For example, a certain student may be registered to certain courses, belong to a certain department, and so forth. When it comes to behavior,

Figure 2.1. An object's class

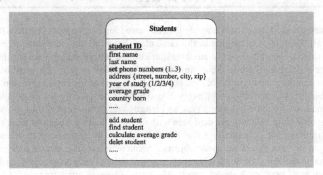

things are different: The functions which can operate on an object (that until now we considered as belonging to the object) actually belong to the object's class. When a certain function needs to act on a certain object, a message is sent to the function of the class, while one of the parameters sent with it is an identification of that object. Hence, we may assume that all the functions of a class are located in one place (say attached to their class); when a function needs to be executed, it is called (triggered) by a message which includes the necessary parameters. The function operates on the object (perhaps changes its state); eventually the object and the function return each to its place.

Sometimes, objects can be very "similar" to one another, but not entirely; there may be differences in some attributes, functions, or relationships. For example, in the case of student objects, there may be graduate students, who are indeed students, but they also have specific attributes which are not shared by other students (such as supervisors and thesis topic), or specific functions (such as a function for assigning a supervisor or recording a thesis topic), or specific relationship types (such as being supervised by supervisors). In such case we may define a specific class **Graduate Students** as subclass of **Students**. We will elaborate on classification later on, in the section on relationships.

In a class diagram, a class is represented by a rectangle divided into three parts, as shown in Figure 2.1. In the upper part we write the class name, in the middle— the attribute names, and in the lower part—the function names.

Attributes

An attribute is a type of data that needs to be stored for every object. As already said, all the objects belonging to the same class have the same attributes. The data, that is, the values of the attributes, are stored within each object (in the system's database), while the definitions of the attributes (e.g., the attribute names and their data types) are kept separately, as part of the class definition.[2] Attribute names are unique for every class (but not necessarily for the whole schema). An attribute has a data type and length, which determines the type of data it may store. We will not deal here with the specific data types and lengths of attributes;[3] we only mention that these details are not defined in the class diagram anyhow, but rather in the objects schema which will be generated from it. Even in the objects schema it is not necessity to define the data type and length of each and every attribute separately. If a certain type of attribute appears in several classes, even if having different names but the same data type, it may be defined once only under a category of "data type definitions" (also termed "domain definitions"), while within each class the respective attribute will just reference to its data type definition. For example, within "data type definitions" we may define:

- Type name: 'ID'; data type: 'numeric' (9)
- Type name: 'Name'; data type: 'characters' (30);

while within the class **Students** we may define the following attributes:

- Attribute *student ID* type *ID*
- Attribute *last name* type *Name*
- Attribute *first name* type *Name*
- Attribute *department* data type characters (20)

The latter is an example for an attribute definition whose data type is not defined separately but rather within its class definition.

Types of Attributes

Simple/Atomic Attributes

A **simple/atomic** attribute may have a single value of the certain data type. For example (see Figure 2.1), *student ID, first name, last name, average grade*. Sometimes we want to limit or constrain the possible values of an attribute. Here are some common constraints:

- **Default:** The attribute of an object is assigned a default value. The value may be assigned either at creation of the object or due to some operation on it some other time, unless a different value is assigned due to a certain function operating on the object. For example, the attribute *country born* of class **Students** may be defined as follows: Attribute *country born* type *country* default 'USA'. This definition may be useful if many students were born in the USA, for it allows time to be saved when inputting the data of new students: Only for those born in different countries will we need to input different values.

- **Not-Null:** The attribute must have a value. It means that when the object is created the attribute must be given a value; the value may be changed later on, but it may not be nullified. Hence, in case one wishes to change the attribute a new value must be provided. Here is an example for Not-Null definition: Attribute *last name* type *name* not-null.

An attribute may be defined as both 'default' and 'not-null'. For example, in class **Students** we may define: attribute *department* not-null default 'Software Engineering', meaning that it if no other value is assigned, the student's department is software engineering. A student may move to another department, but may not be without a department.

- **Unique:** The value of the attribute must be unique among all objects of the class. For example, Attribute *department* unique. It means that there may not be two departments having the same name. A unique attribute may be null, unless it is additionally define as not-null.

- **Enumerate:** The attribute can have one of the enumerated values. The values are listed within parentheses, separated by a '/'. For example, Attribute *day* enumerate (Sun/Mon/Tue/...)

Tuple

Tuple (sometimes also called structure or group) is a group of (two or more) attributes that appear together. For example, an address may be defined as Attribute *address* tuple *{Street, Number, City, Zip}*. For short, the word "tuple" may be left out, because the "{ }" parentheses indicate that the attributes within are a tuple.

Key

A key is an attribute whose value is unique among the class' objects, and therefore enables to identify an object in the class. Obviously, a key may not be null. A key is often used for searching/locating or storing an object in the database. The key name is underlined, as can be seen in Figure 2.1 for *student ID*. A key may sometimes consist of more than one attribute (because no single attribute alone can identify an object). For example, assume a class **Course Offerings,** where each of its objects includes details of a specific course offered in a certain year and semester. In this case, the key would be *tuple {course code, year, semester}*. Instead of underlining the key, or in addition to it, it is possible to write 'key' after the attribute name(s).

A class may have more than one key (while each key may consist of one or more attributes). For example, a student may have two keys: *student ID* and *student number* (a number assigned to each student by the university). In this case, each of these is considered a candidate key; one of them is defined as 'key', while the other is defined as 'unique'. It is better to choose as key the shorter attribute (field lengthwise), or the more useful one, since the user may be using it to search desired objects.

It is not always possible to find a key which can uniquely identify an object of a class. For example, assume a class **Registrations**, in which every object includes data on the registration of a certain student to a certain course offering. It is possible to define the key: *{student -ID, course code, year, semester}* but this would require including these attributes in the class. This is not necessary; we may save "space" by only including the attribute *course grade* because the other details may be found in related objects (i.e., of the student and the course offering objects). But obviously *course grade* cannot be defined as a key (as many students may obtain the same grade). So how can we tell who is the student and which is the course? For this, we need to define proper relationships between each student's object (in **Students** class) and his/her specific registration objects in **Registrations**, as well as between each Course Offering's object and its specific registration objects. We should not be bothered by the "technical" aspects of the realization of these relationships; suffice it to understand that by defining proper relationships it is possible to locate an object even if it cannot be identified by its own key attribute(s). We will discuss more on relationships and how we use them to refer to objects later on in this chapter.

Anyway, whether a key is defined for the class or not, one must assume that when an object is stored in a database, it is given an object identification number (OID) by the database management system. This unique, internal ID serves the system for the purpose of identification and location of objects, and it cannot be change by a user.[4] In the registration example, for instance, when a registration of a student to a course is reported, the system will create a new object of **Registrations** (assume it would be done by *add a registration* function). Upon creation, it is assigned an OID which the system can use for various purposes, for example, to determine its physical location in the database, to add it to the student's object as a new member of its *set registered to courses*; as well as to add it to the course offering's object as a new member of its *set registered students*. This will enable a user to find the registration object in order to report its course grade at the end of the semester. For that, the user will only need to provide the keys of the student (*student ID*) and the course (*course code*), and the system will be able to find (using the right functions) the registration object.

Set Attribute

A set attribute, also termed multi-valued attribute, may have multiple values. The number of values may vary from one object to another. In some cases there is no limitation on the number of values; in other cases it is possible to limit the number by specifying a min or max number. For example, in Figure 2.1 we have *set phone numbers (1...3)* meaning that each student must have at least 1 phone number but not more than 3. The min number of values may sometimes be zero (meaning no values) or any positive number. If there are no limitations, nothing is written after the set name; if there is only a min limit, we write '*' or 'N' instead of a specific max value. It should be noted that the values within a set must be unique, that is, no duplicate values are allowed.

A set may consist of tuples of attributes, for example, *set address {street, number, city Zip}*, or *set grades {course code, grade}*. Sometimes we may be willing to constrain one or more of the member attributes of the tuple to be unique in the set. In the previous example, although the combination of course code and grade must be unique, each of the member attributes is not necessarily unique; hence it is possible to have two tuples such as '{CS, 85}, {CS, 95}' (as if there are two grades for the same course). To prevent such possibility we must specify a partial-key constraint on the respective attribute(s) within the set. This is done by a broken underline of the partial key, for example, *set grades {course code, grade}*. Here is another example: consider a set in **Students** class named *set annual average grade {year, average grade}*. This definition enables storing multiple grades for a certain year, for example, {2006, 85}, {2006, 95}. In order to make sure that there is only one average grade per year, we must specify *set annual average grade {year, average grade}*.

Reference Attribute

A reference attribute refers to another object (in the same or a different class). A reference attribute does not contain a value, but rather the OID of the referenced object. More on reference attributes will be discussed later in the context of relationships between objects.

Combinations of Attribute Types

Attributes can be combined and nested in various ways. For instance, a tuple may consist of a simple attribute and of sets; a set may consist of tuples (as already seen) and of other sets. Here are a few examples of possible combinations of attribute types, all dealing with the class **Students**.

- set tuition-fees tuple {date-paid, bank name, sum}
- total-grades tuple {total grade average, set annual average grade tuple {year, average grade}}
- *set course-achievements {course code, year, semester, set grades {final grade, exam grade, set assignment-grades {assignment#, weight, grade}}}*

(Note that the word tuple was left out in the last example.)

In spite of the possibility to combine and nest sets within sets, this is not recommended because it complicates the data structure and comprehensibility of the class diagram. Such situations can be simplified by defining separate classes instead of nested attributes. This will be elaborated later on in this and in the next chapter.

An Attribute or a Class?

Sometimes we are faced with the dilemma of deciding whether something is an attribute of a class, or entitled to be a class of its own, having relationships with other classes. For example, let us assume that we need to know which vehicle a student owns. We could define an attribute of class **Students** named *car plate number*. If we also need to know the year the car was made we could define another attribute for it, and so on. However, we may consider defining a class **Cars** which will have certain attributes, for example, *plate number* and *year made* (and perhaps also *manufacturer name, set repairs made*, etc.), and also define a relationship between the classes **Students** and **Cars**. Which is better, then: to keep the car's details as attributes of the student object, or create a class **Cars**? This question does not have only one right answer; it may depend on, for example, the number of attributes of cars: The more things we want to know about cars the more justification we have to define a class **Cars**. In that case, we will of course have to define a relationship between each student object and his/her car object (or objects), a relationship that will replace what was originally considered an attribute of **Students**.

It is obvious that if we make changes in classes and attributes, it may also require making changes in the class functions. For example, if the *plate number* and *year made* attributes are part of the **Students** class, this class might have a function named *display student's car details* that will enable retrieving this information from a student object. However, if cars are defined in a class of their own, and we still need to find information about a student's cars, we will not be able to find what we are looking for in the student's object only. Hence, the aforementioned function will have to change somehow including sending a message to a function of class **Cars**, and the latter function will retrieve the car's information. (We will discuss functions later on as well.)

To conclude the discussion on classes, we would like to mention again that a class is not a "normalized" structure (in the relational model sense). It is possible for a class to be normalized in the sense that it has a key, and all its other attributes functionally depend on it; but, as we already know, a class does not have to have a key (only an OID), and even if it has a key, it may contain attributes of various kinds, including sets and combinations of simple attributes, tuples, and sets. One can see advantages and disadvantages in a class structure compared to a normalized relation. Generally, a relational (normalized) structure has less duplicity of data, and is easier to update. However, the retrieval of data is more complicated and may require more time (because of the need to perform joint operations in order to find data that might be spread across various relations). The opposite is true for the objects model: Generally there are more data duplicities, which make updating more difficult, but it might be easier to retrieve desired data because of the higher chances of finding it in one class.[5]

Relationships

As we already know, objects are not necessarily "independent," but can be related to other objects (either in the same class or in other classes). We distinguish between three kinds of relationships: ordinary relationships, aggregations (whole-part relationships), and inheritance (class-subclass relationships).

Ordinary Relationships

An ordinary relationship (or association), like a relationship between entities in the ER model, means that an object in a certain class can be related to one or more other objects. In the objects model only binary and unary relationships are allowed.[6] Unlike the ER model, ternary or higher order relationships are not allowed. When a relationship of this kind needs to be expressed, it is done by defining a "relationship class"—as will be elaborated later on.

In the class diagram, a relationship is specified by a line connecting the respective classes (unlike the ER model, where a diamond shape is used to emphasize the relationship). The relationship name is written above or under the line. Next to every class participating in the relationship we write the multiplicity of the relationship, that is, how many objects may participate in that type of relationship. A simplistic way to define multiplicity is one-to-one (1:1), one-to-many (1:N)[7] or many-to-many (N:N or M:N). In this notation '1' or 'N' mean how many objects at most may participate in a relationship type. For example, a 1:N relationship *belongs to* between **Students** and **Departments**, where the '1' is next to **Departments** and 'N' is next to **Students**, means that a student may only belong to one department, while a department may have many students. This definition does not tell us if a student must belong to any department or if a department must have any students. A more precise way to define multiplicity is by distinguishing between the min and max number of participants in the relationship. We will use the example shown in Figure 2.2 to explain the matter.

The relationship *belonging* between **Students** and **Departments** is generally many-to-one. But more precisely, the (1,1) next to **Departments** means that a student must belong to one department, no less and no more; the (0,N) next to **Students** means that a department might not have any students (this may be true for a new department), but there is no limitation on the number of students it may

Figure 2.2. Ordinary relationships between classes

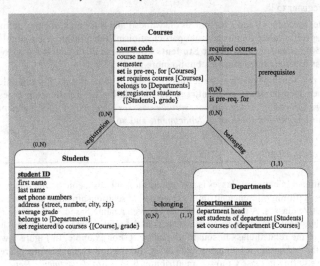

have. The 1:N relationship between **Departments** and **Courses** can be interpreted in a similar way.

The unary relationship *prerequisites* in class **Courses** is (0,N) in both sides of the relationship, meaning that a course may (but must not) require many prerequisite courses; similarly, a course may (but must not) be required (as prerequisite) for many other courses. Since a course may play two different roles in this relationship type, we write on the relationship line, next to each of its ends, the role it plays in the relationship. In this example, the multiplicity of the relationship is symmetric, so apparently there is no importance to mentioning the roles, but this would not be the case in nonsymmetric relationships. For example, if we assume that a course may only have one prerequisite, but can be a prerequisite for several other courses, in that case we need to write (0,1) next to one end of the line, and the role 'required courses', and write (0,N) next to the other end, and the role name 'is prerequisite for'.

Registration is a many-to-many relationship between **Courses** and **Students**. The (0,N) next to **Courses** means that a student does not have to register to even a single course (say a new student), but he/she may register to many courses. The (0,N) next to **Students** means that a course may have no students registered to it (say a new course), but there is no limitation on the number of students who may register to it.

Besides the values 0 and 1 for min, or the values 1 and N for max, we may define other specific values for min and max participation in a relationship. For example, (10,150) instead of (0,N) next to **Students** would mean that a course must have at least five registered students but no more than 150.

Many relationship types may be defined between the same classes. For example, between **Departments** and **Courses** we may define the relationship types: *courses offered by a department, service courses received by a department, the most popular course of a department*, and so on.

Reference Attributes

A relationship between classes is not represented only by a connecting line, but also by defining reference attributes (also called relationship attributes) of the respective classes. A reference attribute is given a name based on the name of the relationship or on the role of its objects in the relationship, followed by the name of the related class in square brackets [..]. For example, in Figure 2 we have the *belonging* relationship between **Courses** and **Departments**; therefore we define in class **Courses** an attribute: *belongs to department [Departments]*. (It is possible, but not mandatory, to write 'rel' or 'ref' before the [..].) Note that a reference attribute does not contain a value, but rather the OID of the related object—as if it is a pointer to that object. In our example, assume that every course object contains in its attribute *belongs to* the OID of its department. Note that due to the min 1 multiplicity of the relationship there must be an OID for every course. A min 0 (meaning that there may be courses which do not belong to any department), would mean that a course which does not belong to a department has no OID of a department but rather a null value. Note the inverse reference attribute of **Departments**: *set courses of department [Courses]*; it is a set reference attribute because a department may have many courses. So, assume that the members of the set are the OIDs of the respective courses.

In general, for a one-to-one relationship, a referenced attribute is defined in each of the involved classes; for a one-to-many relationship, one for the reference attributes—that of the class which is in the "one" side of the relationship—is a set attribute; for a many-to-many relationship, both reference attributes are sets.

In an objects schema (but not in the class diagram) we further clarify the relationship between objects by adding to each reference attribute—next to the name of the referenced class—the name of the "inverse" attribute, that is, the attribute in the other object which refers to this object. For example, in class

Courses we will define the reference attribute: *belongs to [Departments]
inverse courses of department*, while in **Departments** we will define the
reference attribute: *set courses of department [Courses] inverse belongs to.*

All the aforementioned material on reference attributes also applies to unary
relationships. For example, in Figure 2.2, due to the *prerequisites* relationship,
there are two reference attributes in the class **Courses**, one for each of the roles
a course can have: one set reference attribute for the prerequisite courses: *set
required courses [Courses]*, and the other for the courses this course is a
prerequisite for: *set is pre-req. for [Courses]*. Of course, the name of the
referenced class in both attributes is identical, but each attribute has a different
name.

Attributes of Relationships

A many-to-many relationship may have attributes. In Figure 2, for instance, there
is a many-to-many relationship *registration* between classes **Courses** and
Students. Assuming that a student obtains a course grade, the grade is an
attribute of the *registration* relationship. It is not an attribute of a student only
or the course only, but of the relationship between the two. In the ER model, the
grade would have been marked as an attribute of the relationship diamond. In the
relational model, a new, "relationship relation" would have been defined and the
grade would have been included (with *student ID* and *course code* as key). In
the objects model, we specify the relationship attribute(s) together with the
respective reference attributes. This forms a tuple whose components are the
reference attribute and the relationship attribute(s). In our example, we define
in class **Courses** the attribute: *set registered students tuple {[Students],
grade}*, and in class **Students** we symmetrically define the attribute: *set
registered to courses {[Courses], grade}*.

As we can see, relationship attributes may cause duplicity of data, because the
relationship data are written in both related objects. (Each grade, in our example,
is written/stored in both the student objects and the course object.) On the other
hand, it allows us to efficiently find the grades obtained by a student, as well as
the grades given in a course. This is so if we need symmetric access to the data—
and this is the way we define the relationship attributes in the class diagram
which we create in the analysis phase; but it is not necessarily the way it will
eventually be implemented in the database. If, for example, we will find out that
no one (i.e., no user of the system) needs to know the students' grades in a
certain course (but say only the student names and their average grade), then the
attribute *set registered students* of class **Courses** will not include the grade, so
it will be defined as: *set registered students [Students]*. Moreover, if we will
find out that no one needs to know which students took the course (but say only

their average grade), then there is even no need to implement the set attribute *registered students*. In other words, there is no must to implement all reference and relationship attributes symmetrically. The decision whether to do so (or whether or not to implement them at all) depends on the users' needs, which must be defined separately (in the functional analysis process). However, while building the class diagram, if opt to model a M:N relationship between two classes directly, we write the reference and relationship attributes symmetrically—with duplicities.

The more relationship attributes we have in a many-to-many relationship, the bigger the amount of duplicities. The problem can be avoided by defining a "relationship class" between the M:N related classes. That class will hold the data of the relationship attributes. In our example, instead of defining a direct relationship between **Courses** and **Students** we may define a relationship class **Registrations**, as presented in Figure 2.3. The attributes of this class include a key tuple consisting of two reference attributes, one referring to **Students** and one to **Courses**. In addition, it has a simple attribute *grade*. Note how the key tuple is written: Being a key of the class it is given an attribute name; for simplicity the key name may be identical or similar to the class name, and it is underlined. We term it "key tuple." This key does not contain values but rather OIDs of the referenced objects (obviously, the combination of two OIDs of an object must be unique).[8] The attribute names *the student* and *the course*, preceding the

Figure 2.3. Representing a many-to-many relationship via a relationship class

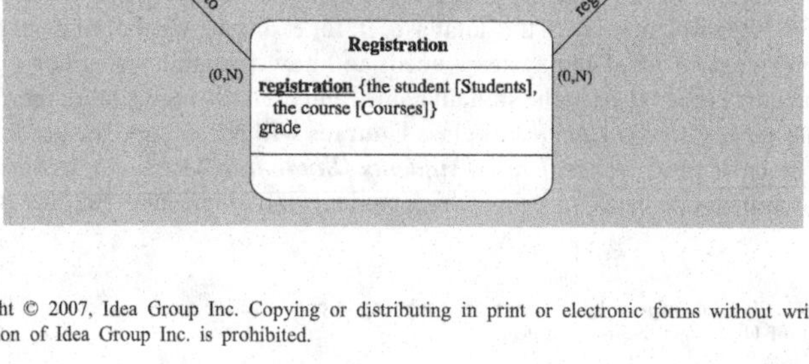

respective class names, are not mandatory and are written only for clarity; suffice it to specify only the referenced class names, that is, *registration {[Students], [Courses]}*. Viewing the two reference attributes within the tuple, following the underlined key, makes it clear that this is a relationship class, representing a many-to-many relationship between the referenced classes. Note that in each of the "parent" classes, **Courses** and **Students**, there is a set reference attribute to class **Registration**. Using one of these sets, it is possible to find the courses a student is registered to and his/her grades, or the students registered to a certain course and their grades.

As we have seen, a many-to-many relationship may be represented by direct relationships between the involved classes, or by a relationships class. The more relationship attributes there are, the more justifiable it is to adopt this solution. By the way, even if the many-to-many relationship is unary, we can still define a relationship class, assuming there are relationship attributes. Let us assume, for example, that the *prerequisites* relationship (Figure 2.2) has the following relationship attributes: *date set* and *min qualifying grade*. In that case, instead of keeping these attributes within the two set reference tuples, it seems preferable to define a relationship class **Prerequisites** (see Figure 2.4), in which each object is a prerequisite relationship between two courses: the required (termed *pre*; may be termed "parent course") and the requiring (termed *post*; may be termed "child course"). Note that the key of this class is a tuple with two

Figure 2.4.

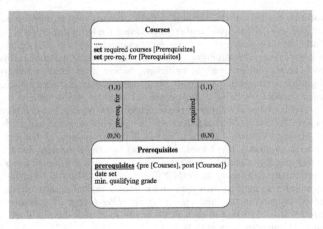

references to class **Courses**: one to the "parent" course object and the other to the "child" course object.[9] Note that in the class **Courses** we define two set reference attributes: *requires courses* and *pre-req. for courses*; the inverse reference attributes enable finding the respective course objects.

Up until now we have been discussing many-to-many relationships having relationship attributes. Generally, one-to-one relationships too may have relationship attributes. For example, assume a one-to-one relationship named *management* between two classes **Employees** and **Departments**. This relationship may have an attribute *date appointed*. A one-to-one relationship with attributes can be treated just like a many-to-many relationship, including the possibility to define a relationship class; but this solution is rare because in reality such cases (namely of 1:1 relationships having many relationship attributes) are rare. The case of one-to-many relationships is a bit different; if there are relationship attributes in such a case, they may be considered as attributes of the class in the "many" side of the relationship. For example, consider the one-to-many relationship *belongs to* between classes **Students** and **Departments** (see Figure 2), and assume that we need to know the date each student was admitted to his/her department. Although some may claim that this date is an attribute of the relationship, it is more correct to say that it is an attribute of **Students**, because every student belongs to just one department. Therefore, in such case we only have to add to class **Students** a simple attribute *date admitted*—with no changes in the reference attributes of the two classes.

Dealing with Ternary Relationships

It has already been said that in the objects model, ternary relationships are not defined, nor are relationships of higher order. If such a relationship exists in the real world, the relationship itself is considered an object; thus a class is defined whose instances are the relationship occurrences. For example, assume a reality in which agents sell products to customers, hence, there exists a ternary relationship involving three participants: an agent, a product, and a customer. In the objects model we define a relationship class **Sales**, whose objects are actually events of sale, in addition to classes **Customers**, **Agents**, and **Products** (see Figure 2.5). Every object of **Sales** refers to three objects, one in each of the related classes. Assuming an agent may sell many products to the same customer, that a product may be sold by an agent to many customers, and that a customer may buy a product from many agents (perhaps at different times), we define a many-to-many-to-many (M:N:P or N:N:N) relationship. Therefore, the key of **Sales** is a tuple consisting of three reference attributes, each referring to one of the aforementioned classes: *sale {[Products], [Customers], [Agents]}*.[10] It is clear that in each of the involved classes there is a set of reference attributes to the **Sales** class.

Figure 2.5. Representing a many-to-many-to-many relationship

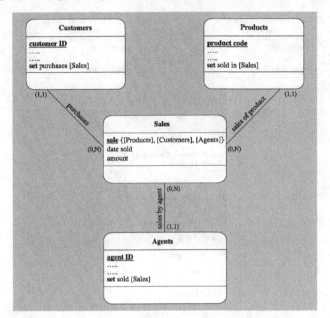

Now let us analyze the case of a many-to-many-to-one (M:N:1) relationship. Assume that the policy of the previous company is that a certain product may be sold to a certain customer by one agent only. In other words, if a customer buys a product from a certain agent, he may not buy that product from another agent, but he may buy other products from that agent, not to mention that the agent may sell the same product to other customers. The class diagram depicting this situation is shown in Figure 2.6. It looks very similar to the former example where we had a M:N:P relationship, and we still see similar relationships and cardinalities, because each of the involved classes is still in 1:N relationship with the class **Sales**. The difference can be seen in **Sales**: Its key is a tuple of two reference attributes only: *sale {[**Products**], [**Customers**]}*, while the reference attribute *the agent [**Agents**]* is not part of the key. It means that a certain sale event, which is identifiable by a certain customer and a certain product, has (i.e., refers to) just one agent.

Figure 2.6. Representing a many-to-many-to-one relationship

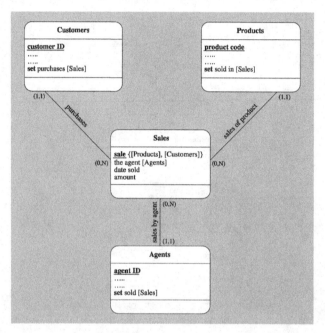

It should be mentioned that a ternary many-to-many-to-one relationship is rare in the real world, and the previous example was only invented to demonstrate the way such a relationship can be represented in a class diagram. An even rarer relationship is many-to-one-to-one (N:1:1). Let us assume in accordance with the previous example that in addition to the aforementioned constraint that a customer may buy a certain product from one agent only, a customer may only buy one product form a certain agent. There are two alternative ways of defining the attributes of **Sales**:

Alternative 1:
- *sale {[Customers], [Agents]}*
- *the product [Products]*

Alternative 2:
- *sale {[Customers], [Products]}*
- *the agent [Agents]*

Aggregation

Aggregation is a structural relationship between objects from different classes that "come together." In most cases we are dealing with a relationship between one object which is the "whole," and other objects which are its "parts." That is why aggregation is also called "whole-parts" relationship. For example, a car is made of an engine, a body, wheels, and so forth. Each of these is an object of a respective class, while the relationship enables finding the parts (components) of the whole object (car). Another kind of aggregation is "container-contained" relationship. For example, an office contains chairs, tables, shelves, phones, and so forth. Another kind is "collection-member" relationship. For example, an organization is made of departments, workers, buildings, offices, machines, laboratories, and so forth.

Figure 2.7 demonstrates a "whole-parts" aggregation. We have a class **Airplanes** (the "whole"), and classes **Engines** and **Gears** (the "parts"). A "whole-parts" relationship is marked by a line with a diamond next to the "whole" class.

Figure 2.7. A whole-parts relationship

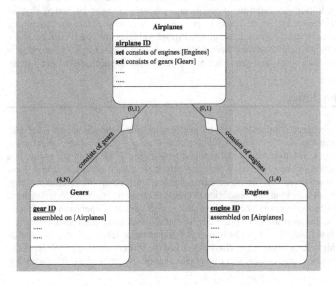

We also write the multiplicities of the relation similar to an ordinary relationship, but here the multiplicity at the "whole" side must be (0,1) or (1,1). The max is always 1, meaning that a certain part (engine or gear) must be installed (at a certain point in time) in one airplane only. The min may be 0 or 1: min 0 means that a part may not be installed on an airplane (e.g., when an engine or a gear is in repair); min 1 would have meant that the "part" cannot be disconnected from the "whole." In such case, the diamond is shaded (not shown in this Figure). In the "part" side, there can be any min and max numbers. In our example, an airplane must have at least one engine but no more than four; and at least four gears without any limitation on the max number.

Besides the slightly different symbol, an aggregation is not much different from a one-to-many relationship between the class in the "whole" side and each of the classes in the "parts" side. Like an ordinary relationship, a "whole-parts" relationship is defined by reference attributes (see Figure 2.7). Actually, many objects in reality may be defined as aggregations, but they are not modeled as such, but rather as ordinary relationships. For example, we may say that a university consists of departments, students, professors, buildings, and so forth, but still it is not customary to define an aggregation relationship between university and the latter. Instead, ordinary relationships are usually defined between them. Only when indeed the "parts" cannot be removed from the "whole" there may be an advantage in modeling such relationships as an aggregation, because in such cases the addition or deletion of the "whole" implies also addition or deletion of its parts. Anyway, it must be stated that an aggregation is not an inheritance relationship; the "whole" and the "parts" are different types of objects, belonging to different classes, the "parts" do not inherit from the "whole" and they have different keys. In our example, an airplane is made up of engines and gears, but an engine or a gear are not kinds of an airplane.

Inheritance

An inheritance relationship, also termed "generalization-specialization" or "is-a" relationship, enables us to distinguish superclasses from subclasses that inherit attributes, relationships and functions from them. A class, as we know, is a collection of objects sharing the same attributes, relationships, and functions. However, there may be objects of a certain kind which are similar to other objects in their kind, but in addition having some specific attributes, relationships, or functions. In cases like these we distinguish between super- and subclasses. This is demonstrated in Figure 2.8, which shows a superclass **Students** and a subclass **Undergraduate Students**. The inheritance relationship is marked by a semicircle (a triangle can also be used) on the line connecting the classes. The distinction is made since, according to the example, an undergraduate student has

Figure 2.8. Inheritance with one subclass

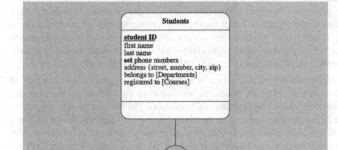

specific attributes (*average grade* and *sport club*) that other students do not have. (Other students may include, e.g., graduate students, external students, and others). It is obvious that an undergraduate student is first of all a student, and has the same attributes as the other (in the superclass)—*student ID, name, phone numbers*, etc.) However, undergraduate students have additional, specific attributes (possibly also specific relationships and functions—not shown in this figure).

We should consider this question: How do we know when it is necessary to distinguish between super- and subclasses? In the previous example, is it not enough to define just a class **Students** and include in it the two specific attributes of undergraduate students? In such case only undergraduate student objects will have values in those two specific attributes, while for all other student objects these attributes will be null. If the majority of students are undergraduates, then indeed there might be no justification for making the distinction. But if only some of the students are undergraduates, it would mean that for many objects there will be null values. Hence, the more distinct attributes we have—not to mention distinct functions and relationships—the more justification there is for subclassification.

As we already know inheritance enables us to use the definitions (code) of existing classes to create new ones with minimal effort. Let us assume that there is an application in which a **Students** class is already defined (There may be a software library which includes many classes, brought from other application.). Now, assume that we want to devote special attention to undergraduate students. So we only need to declare a new class named **Undergraduate Students**, and define that it "inherits" the (existing) **Students** class.

One might ask: Where is the data of undergraduate students stored? Is part of the data stored in class **Students** and another part (data of the specific attributes) in class **Undergraduate Students**? The answer to this cannot be found in the model (meaning in the class diagram); it depends on the way the system will be implemented. There are many possible ways to implement the system, on which we will not elaborate here. At the conceptual model level we are not concerned with implementation issues; we only need to know and specify that every undergraduate student is also a student, and therefore the data saved on such student includes all the data we would save on an ordinary student, and the specific data as an undergraduate. Generally, we say that every object of the subclass is also an object of its superclass, and a superclass contains all the objects, including those of the subclasses.

Figure 2.9. Inheritance with two subclasses

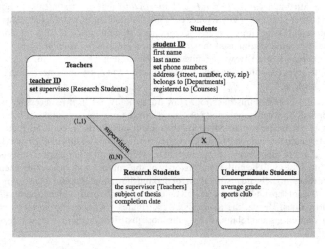

Figure 2.9 shows a superclass **Students** with two subclasses: **Undergraduate Students** and **Research Students**. We can see that each of the subclasses have their own specific attributes and may also have specific relationships, other than those of the superclass. In general, the superclass may have many subclasses, depending on the specific attributes and relationships of its objects. A subclass may itself be a superclass for subclasses. For example, the subclass **Research Students** may have a subclass **PhD Students**, assuming such students have specific attributes, relationships, or functions that are not shared by all other research students.

If there is a structure where the superclass has more than one subclass, we may also define participation constraints on objects of the subclasses, as follows:

1. **Exclusiveness: 'exclusive' or 'overlapping'** participation. Exclusive means that an object may belong to only one subclass, while overlapping means that an object may belong to more than one subclass. Figure 2.9 shows an example: A student may be only an undergraduate **or** a research student, but not both. Exclusiveness is indicated by '**X**' within the inheritance symbol (X stands for exclusive). In case overlapping is allowed, nothing is signified. In other words, the default case assumes that subclasses may overlap.

2. **Totality: 'total'** (also **'cover'**) or **'not-total'** (**'non-cover'**) participation. Total means that there are no more objects other than those defined by the subclasses; hence, all objects of the superclass belong to the defined subclasses. Not-total means that there may be objects in the superclass which do not belong to any of the subclasses. For example, if there are only undergraduate and research students (and no other types), it is a 'total' situation. Such case would be marked by '**T**' within the inheritance symbol (T stands for total). If other types of students may exist, such as external students or alumni, we have a 'not-total' situation. Not-total is not signified. In other words, the default case assumes that subclasses are 'not-total'. Note that the other possible types of students are not subclassified because they have no specific attributes, relationships, or functions; these students are members of the superclass only.

In the case of totality, where all objects of the superclass belong to any of its subclasses; it means that the superclass itself has no objects—it is considered an **abstract class** that only includes definitions of attributes and functions, which are inherited to the subclasses. (We will elaborate on abstract classes later on.)

Following the aforementioned participation constraints, the following four combinations of exclusiveness and totality are distinguished:

- **Overlapping and Not-Total:** this is the default situation; no symbol needed.
- **Exclusive and Not-Total:** marked by X.
- **Overlapping and Total:** marked by T.
- **Exclusive and Total:** marked by XT.

In conclusion of this subject we provide a more comprehensive example of a class diagram (Figure 2.10). The superclass **University Workers** has three subclasses: **Teachers, Students** and **Administrative Workers**. The subclass **Students** is also a superclass of **Undergraduate Students** and **Research Students**. All the university workers are identifiable by an *ID* number. The

Figure 2.10. A class diagram with inheritance and ordinary relationships

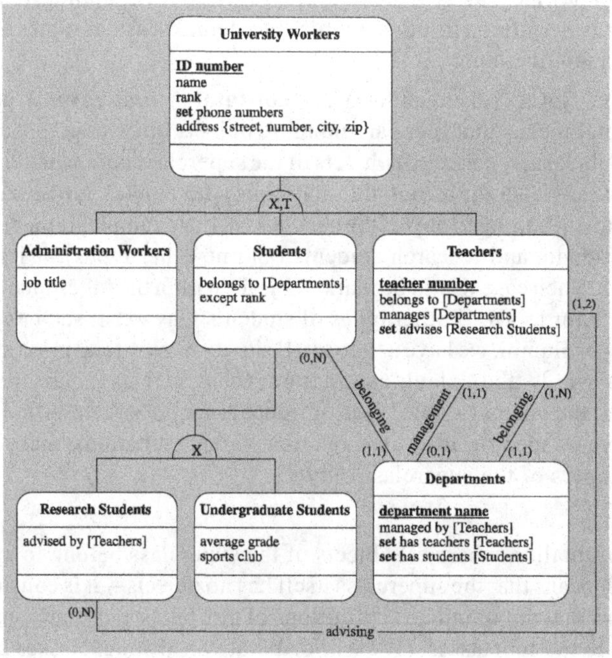

participation constraint on the subclasses of **University Workers** is 'XT', that is, there are no other subtypes but the previously mentioned three, and an object can belong to one of the three only. The subclass **Teachers** has several specific attributes, in addition to the attributes inherited from **University Workers**. Note that **Teachers** has an additional key: *teacher number*. We can also see that **Teachers** has two relationship types with **Departments**: a one-to-many relationship *belonging*, and a one-to-one relationship *management*. While every teacher must belong to one department, only some teachers manage any department. A department may have many teachers, but at least one; and it must have one manager (who is a teacher). A student must belong to one department, but there may be departments with no students. Each of the two subclasses of **Students** has its specific attributes (in addition to the attributes inherited from **Students**). A research student is related with one or two supervisors (teachers), but not all teachers must supervise research students. It should be noted that there may be other types of students besides the above two (because no 'T' constraint is specified) but a research student cannot be at the same time an undergraduate student ('X' is specified). At any rate, each and every student, no matter of which type, must *belong to* a department.

Polymorphism

A subclass can inherit the attributes from its superclass as they are; the names of the inherited attributes are not written in the subclass. But it is possible to change the definition of inherited attributes in some way. For example, it is possible to change data types or lengths. In such a case, the name of the inherited attribute needs to be written in the subclass, and it must be redefined in the objects schema (where data types of the attributes are defined). Obviously, the original name of the attribute must be used; otherwise the system will assume that the original attribute is inherited and there is an additional specific attribute.

A subclass may also inherit all the functions of the superclass as they are (and then there is no need to write the function names in the subclass) but it is possible to change specifications of inherited functions. For example, assume that in the **University Workers** class there is a function named *add new employee*. Now assume that the procedure for adding a new student is different from that of adding a new employee (who is a teacher or an administrative worker); this means that we have to define (and then code) a specific procedure for this function, replacing the original one. Hence, there will be two functions named *add new employee*: a general one for all workers excluding students, and a specific one for students only.

The aforementioned cases are examples for **polymorphism**: using the same name of attribute or function, but implementing it differently for different types of objects in an inheritance hierarchy. Hence, every attribute or function defined in the superclass is inherited to the subclasses, but if an existing name of attribute or function appears also in a subclass, it is assumed that they are redefined (in the objects schema, not in the class diagram); the definitions of attributes or functions in a subclass **override** the definitions given in the superclass.

Multiple Inheritance

Multiple inheritance means that a class may inherit (attributes, relationships, and functions) from more than one superclass. In the class diagram, multiple inheritance is marked by two or more semicircles, one for every superclass (see examples in Figures 2.11 and 2.12).

We distinguish between two types of multiple inheritance: multiple inheritance from different sources and multiple inheritance from one source. In **multiple inheritance from different sources**, the subclass inherits its attributes and functions from all of its superclasses, when none of the superclasses share an "ancestor" (no two classes originated from the same class). This case is demonstrated in Figure 2.11: A caravan is both a private home, which is a type of building, and a wheeled vehicle, which is also a type of vehicle. Therefore, a caravan inherits all the attributes, relationships, and functions of its different

Figure 2.11. Multiple-inheritance from different sources

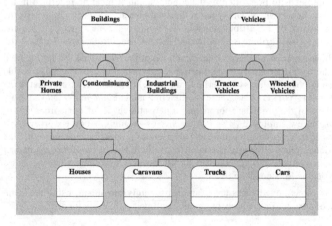

Figure 2.12. Multiple-inheritance from the same source

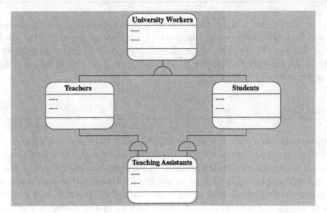

superclasses. In **multiple inheritance from the same source**, the "chains of inheritance" originate from the same ancestor class. In Figure 2.12 we see that **Teaching Assistants** (TA) inherit both from **Students** and from **Teachers**, but both of them inherit from **University Workers**; that is, TAs actually inherit attributes from the same superclass.

Multiple inheritance can be problematic if the superclasses of a certain class have attributes or functions with identical names; the problem is this: Since different superclasses may have attributes and functions with the same names but different data types or functionality, how can we know which of the different attributes or functions to inherit? The problem becomes more acute when dealing with multiple inheritance from different sources, because the sources' attributes and functions may be substantially different (while in multiple inheritance from the same source there is a chance that many attributes and functions are inherited from the same ancestor with no changes, and each of its subclasses has only a smaller number of specific attributes or functions having the same names). There are ways to overcome the problem, like using polymorphism (changing the definitions of the problematic attributes and functions), or specifying the name of the class from which we wish to inherit a specific attribute or function. This can be done by writing the superclass name before the attribute or function name (i.e., superclass name.attribute/function name).

Selective Inheritance

Selective inheritance is used when we wish to prevent certain attributes or functions from being inherited to a subclass. This can be done by writing the word "except" followed by the name of the attribute or function which we **do not** wish to inherit. An example for this can be seen in Figure 2.10, where the attribute *rank* is not inherited to **Students**.

Abstract Class

An abstract class is a class that has no objects, but it has attributes, functions, and subclasses which inherit from it. The definition of such an "empty" class enables us to save the time needed for defining attributes and functions in various classes. For example, in Figure 2.10 we defined the **University Workers** class. At first glance, it appears that we could have done without it, since every person at the university is one of the three: teacher, student, or administrative worker. However, in this case we would have had to define the shared attributes, relationships, and functions in each of the three classes; the definition of the **University Workers** as their superclass saves time and prevents duplicities.

The state of abstract class can easily change to an ordinary one (i.e., a class that has objects). In our example (Figure 2.10), the **University Workers** class can be considered abstract only because of the 'T' constraint, meaning there are no other kinds of employees in the university but those defined in the subclasses. However, had we chosen to allow other kinds of employees (who have no specific attributes and relationships) their objects could only exist in the superclass. Of course, in that case the 'T' constraint must be removed.

An abstract class does not have to have a key (since it does not have objects to distinguish between). This is true only if the subclasses have keys of their own, which are different from one another. For example, if a teacher is identified by *teacher number*, a student by *student ID,* and an administrative worker by *emp-ID* (and the 'T' constrain holds), then there is not a necessity to define a "super key" for **University Workers**. If, on the other hand, all types of workers are identified by a universal (national) ID number, it would be preferred to define this attribute as key of the superclass—as demonstrated in Figure 2.10.

Functions

A class has functions which can perform actions on its objects. All the functions that can be performed on an object during its lifetime in the system define the object's "behavior." Recall that while the objects of a class are assumed to be stored in a database, it may be assumed that the functions of a class (more precisely, the code of the functions) are stored separately, along with other definitions of the class (especially its attributes). This place is usually called the catalog.

As we know, a function has a name. The function's full name, by which it can be identified, is the name of the class it belongs to, and the function's name within the class (it means, of course, that the function's names within a class are unique). A function may also include an output variable, by which the outcome of the operation will be returned to the function that called it, and a list of parameters (arguments) by which the function receives values needed for the execution. We call this part of the function (i.e., the function name and its parameters) **signature**. The main part of a function is the **method**, that is, a detailed specification of how the procedure will perform the function. A method can be viewed as a small program, made up of specific commands which are organized in proper process logic, using patterns of structured programming (i.e., sequences, branches, or loops). In addition to ordinary commands which a method performs by itself, it may include messages to other functions, whether belonging to the same class or to other classes. A message includes, as we know, the name of the receiving function (and its class), and it may include parameters through which the function will receive data needed to execute, or an output variable in case the sending method needs to get a result from the receiving message.

As an example we bring here the definitions of a class **Student** and its subclass **Graduate Student**, each including several attributes and functions. The example is written in C++; it is not the intention to get into the code details, only to demonstrate how functions and methods can be defined.

The **Student** class has several attributes defined as "private." It means that they cannot be accessed from outside the class; they are hidden. On the other hand, the functions are defined as "public," which means that the class objects are accessible through them. Generally, functions too can be defined as private, but only if they may be activated by other functions of that class. The function *student*, whose name is the same as the class name, is a constructor function, which can create/add a new student object and initialize its attributes. (Similarly, we can also define a destructor function, capable of deleting a student object.)

The other function, *show student*, can present a student's details. In the parentheses following the function's name, the parameters and their data types are listed. The code of the method is written separately. It starts with the class name followed by the name of the function (and in parentheses the names and data types of the parameters, as before). Without getting too deep into the matter, the code of the method includes the following commands: receive a name, ID, and average grade, verify that the average is between 0 and 100, and if it is— create a new student object. The function *show student* has no parameters; its task is to display the state of the student (i.e., the values of its attributes *name, ID,* and *average grade*).

The subclass **Graduate Student** has three specific attributes: *salary, advisor name,* and *thesis title*. It also has two functions: a constructor and a display (*show student*) function. We can see that the constructor has a list of parameters which includes *student*, and that the code of the method includes a message to the constructor *student*. The function *show graduate student* calls the function *show student*—which belongs to its superclass (and which, as we know, displays three student attributes), and also includes commands to display the specific attributes of the graduate student.

```
#include <iostream.h>
#include <string.h>

class student {
   private:
      char s_name[30]
      long s_id;
      float avg_grade;
   public:
      student (char *s_name, long s_id, float avg_grade); (This is the signature of the function.)
      void show_student (void)
};

student:: student (char *s_name, long s_id, float avg_grade)        (and here is the method)
{
   strcpy (student::s_name);
   student::s_id - s_id;
   if (avg_grade > 0.0 and avg_grade < 100.0) student::avg_grade = avg_grade;
   else // invalid average grade
   student::avg_grade = 0.0;
}

void show_student (void)
{
   cout << "Student name is  " << s_name << endl;
   cout << "Student ID is   " << s_id << endl;
   cout << "Average grade is  " << avg_grade << endl;
};
```

```
class graduate_students : public student  {        (This is the way to specify inheritance.)
    private:
      float salary;
      char advisor_name [30];
      char thesis_title [60];
public:
    graduate_student (char *, long, float, float, char *, char *)          (constructor)
    void show_graduate_student (void)                    (another function)
};
                                            (code of the constructor method)
graduate_student::graduate_student (char *s_name, long s_id, float avg_grade,
    float salary, char *advisor_name, char *thesis_title) : student (s_name, s_id, avg_grade)
{
    strcpy(graduate_student::advisor_name, thesis_title);
    graduate_student::salary = salary;
}
                                            (code of the other method)
void graduate_student::show_graduate_student (void)
{
    show_student ();
    cout << "Advisor name is " << advisor_name << endl;
    cout << "Thesis title is " <<  thesis_title << endl;
    cout << "Salary is " << salary << endl;
}
```

In the phase of system analysis, when we define the objects model and create the class diagram, we do not deal with definitions of the parameters and the methods of the function and certainly not with the writing of code; these things will be done in the design and programming phases, respectively. In the analysis phase, our main goal with respect to functionality of the sought system is to decide which functions are needed and to which class each function belongs. This will be discussed in detail later on. At this stage we concentrate on the class diagram and how the functions are defined within, assuming that we already know which are the functions of each class. In the class diagram we write only the names of functions in the lower part of the class rectangle. Figure 2.13 demonstrates two classes with their functions (For the sake of simplicity, the names of the attributes are not shown.) At a later stage, when we will create the objects schema, we will be more specific and add for each function its parameters and their data types and then detail the methods. Methods can be described using various techniques, including in natural language, pseudo code or specific types of charts—as will be detailed in further chapters of this book.

Figure 2.13. Examples of class function

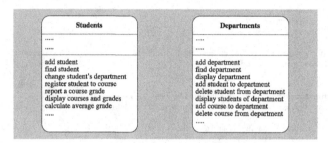

Types of Functions

We distinguish between three types of functions: basic functions, application-specific functions, and application programs.

Basic Functions

It is assumed that every data class has basic functions which enable us to perform the four basic operations: create, read, update, and delete—in short: CRUD.

- **Create:** This function adds a new object. It is possible to set the attribute values of the created object in several ways: some will have default values (if such values were predefined); some will get values while being created, through user input; some may remain null until they are updated by some other function. For example, assume that the function *add student* of class **Students** receives, when activated,[11] the parameters: *student ID, name,* and *address*, but not a department code, which at that time is unknown. The department code might be updated by another function some other time (say when the student will be assigned to a department).

- **Read:** This function finds/retrieves an existing object of the class. The function will receive (as a parameter) the identification of the sought object (for example, student ID) and will return the object or a message saying that the object does not exist. In addition to the basic Read function, there may be specific functions to find one or many objects according to certain search criteria, depending on the specific application and its users, for example, a function to find and display the codes and names of courses which a certain student has taken, and the grades received.

- **Update:** This function changes values of attributes of an existing object. Generally, a class may have different specific update functions, if it has attributes which have to be updated in different manners or at different times. For example, the **Students** class may have an update function to change some attributes of a student, such as, address and phone numbers; another to change his/her department; yet another to add or update a course grade, and so forth. Each of these functions might be activated, most likely, in response to an event occurring in the real world. It should be noted that every attribute of a class must be updatable by a function.

- **Delete:** This function deletes an object from the class. The function needs to receive a value that will enable it to identify the object to be deleted. It also should be able to return a message informing the user whether the object has been deleted or not found.

We also assume that a basic function performs checks and other "standard" actions, such as:

- **Checking the validity of the message:** Every function checks its activation message and verifies its correctness. The message arguments are compared to the definitions of the matching attributes. If an error is found, a message is sent to the function that sent the original message.

- **Confirmation message:** An activated function may return (to the function that sent it) data, or a confirmation that it performed its task, or an error message. There is no necessity for the receiving function to return any message to the sender, although it is reasonable that doing so will be done in many cases.

Dealing with Relationships Between Objects

The addition, change, and deletion functions need to take into account the relationships of their target object with other objects and perform referential integrity checks. For instance, an addition function needs to check the types of relationships and their cardinality—as defined in the class—to make sure the addition is allowed. For example (see Figure 2.2), when we wish to add a new student object, the addition function needs to check the definition of two relationship types: *registration* to **Courses** and *belonging* to **Departments**. As for the former, the multiplicity defines that a student does not have to be registered to even a single course, so everything is fine; as for the latter, the multiplicity states that a student must belong to a department, so the addition function needs to get (from the sender function) a name of a department. In addition, the addition method should include a message to the function *add a student to department* of class **Departments**, with a department name as parameter. This function, in turn, will check whether that department exists. If it does, the function will check the multiplicity of the *belonging* relationship. Since the maximum is 'N', there is no reason not to add the student to the department. Therefore, it will end its task by adding the new student's OID to the reference attribute *set students of department [**Students**]* and send a confirmation to the **Students**' addition function. That function, in turn, will complete its task by adding the department's OID to the reference attribute *belongs to a [**Departments**]* of the new student object.

In a similar way, the delete function needs to check whether the deletion is allowed, and if it is, to complete the necessary actions that might be needed due to the object's relationships and their multiplicities. For example, let us examine the delete function of the class **Departments** (see Figure 2.2). The function needs to check the relationships of **Departments** with **Courses** and **Students** to verify that if the department is deleted no constraints are violated. In our example a department does not have to have any courses or students, so it may be deleted. However, we still may have a problem because if a department has at least one course (this can be verified by looking if there are any OIDs in the *set courses of department [**Courses**])* or at least one student (this can be verified similarly in the respective reference attribute), then the question is what to do with those courses and students (because according to those classes' definitions, each course and each student must belong to a department. Before demonstrating how this problem can be solved, we only mention that a change function too may have to perform similar checks. For example, if we wish to transfer a student to another department, we have to make sure the other department exists, that the number of students in the student's current department may be reduced by one (if there is a min constraint on the number of students in a department), and that the student can be added to their new department (if there is a max constraint).

Addition, deletion, or update of an object may have side effects, due to its relationships with other objects, the types of those relationships, and their multiplicities. Side effects may be: (1) preventing the change because it violates a certain constraint, or (2) approving the change but applying other changes as well, according to the predefined constraints. Whether to prevent or approve a change which may violate constraints is a matter of organization policy (rules). We can distinguish between several kinds of policies which it is possible to apply in different cases. Here are some examples of policies for a 'Delete' function:

- **Delete is restricted:** This is considered a default option, meaning that one cannot delete an object if it will cause violation of a constraint. For example, if we wish to delete a course and there are students registered to it (at least one), the deletion is not allowed (so the problem might be overcome by first canceling the registrations of those students to that course).

- **Delete cascades:** This means that not only the deletion is allowed but it will also cause deletion of a related object which can cause the violation of the constraint. For example, if we wish to delete a department which has students, they will be deleted too. This policy is, certainly, "destructive" and should be applied carefully.

- **Delete nullifies:** This means that the delete is permitted, but the related objects will have to be changed too, so that they will not refer to the deleted object. For example, if we wish to cancel a course, in addition to the deletion, any students who registered to the course will be unregistered (i.e., the reference to the course will be nullified).

Until now we have explained and demonstrated several types of referential integrity checks which should be performed by Add, Update, and Delete functions.[12] The checks may be part of those basic functions or be defined as separate functions, which will be activated by the aforementioned basic functions. This way, the basic functions become simpler, and the referential integrity check functions can be changed with greater ease, according to the organization's policy.

Since we assume that every data class has CRUD basic functions, and in order to simplify the class diagram, there is no need to write the names of these functions in the class diagram. Due to inheritance, it may be assumed that all classes inherit the basic functions from a superclass where these functions are defined.

Application-Specific Functions

Specific functions are defined according to the needs of the application (i.e., of the users). Such functions may perform various specific tasks, beyond what can be achieved with the CRUD basic functions, for example, a function that calculates a student's average grade, a function that displays a student's list of grades per academic period, or a function that displays details on a department's students or teachers. It is reasonable for an application-specific function to include messages to basic functions to perform basic CRUD operations. For example, a specific function that calculates a student's average grade may include a message to a 'Read' function of **Students** class that will retrieve the student's object, including the grades, and then another message to an 'Update' function to store the calculated average.

One of the main issues in the objects model is to find out which are the application-specific functions and to which class to attach each of them. This issue is part of the system's analysis phase. In that phase, analysts cooperate with users (or their representatives) in order to elicit and define the various user requirements from the system. The main products of this phase are a functional model and a data model (i.e., a class diagram). The functional model will enable us to define the functions, while the data model (class diagram) will assist in determining to which class to attach each function. Many more details on the analysis phase will be provided in Unit 2 of this book. Meanwhile, we bring here several more detailed examples of application-specific functions and their process logic.

Example 1: An Extracting and Reporting Function

We need to produce a report providing details of students who belong to a certain department. For this we define an application-specific function that belongs to the class **Departments**. Once activated by a user (at this stage we do not detail how it can be done), the function will first find the specific department object; this will be achieved by sending a message to the basic function 'Read'. The returned department object includes a set reference attribute *students of department,* which includes OIDs of students (see Figure 2). The function will perform a loop on this set; within the loop there will be a message to the class **Students** to its basic 'Find' function, which will find an object of a student (according to the current OID) and return it to the sender. Other commands in the loop will include sending the student's details to print. At the end of the loop there may be other commands, for example, summarizing the number of students in the department, and so forth.

Example 2: An Update Function

We need to register a student to courses. Assume that the registration takes place at the beginning of every semester, and that a student may register to one course or more.[13] The application-specific function will belong to the class **Students**. Note that a student object includes the set reference attribute: *set registered to courses {[Courses], grade}* (see Figure 2). The objective is to add tuples to this set, one per each course that he/she registers to. At this stage only the courses' OIDs will be added, but the grade will be null. The function will be activated through the user interface. First, it will find the student's object using the basic function 'Read'. Then it will perform a loop as long as there are more courses the student wants to register for. In every iteration of the loop, the function will send a message to the user (imagine that it is done through a message to a function of a class **Forms** which presents a form on screen) requesting the user to input a course code. Once the course code is returned to the update function, it will send a message to the 'Read' function of the class **Courses** in order to verify that the course exists. If the 'Read' function returns an error message the update function will send an error message to the user (via the aforementioned form) requesting the user to reenter a course code. If the search function finds the course object it returns its OID to the update function. Now the update function needs to make sure that the student is not already registered to this course, so it will run a search **inside** the set reference attribute. If it finds the aforementioned course's OID in the set, the function will send an error message to the user, but if not, it will perform the addition to the set. It will then send a message to the class **Courses**, to its specific function *add a student to course*; the message will include, of course, the course OID (by which the course object will be found) as well as the student's OID, so that, that function will be able to add the student's OID to the set reference attribute: *set registered students {[Students], grade}*. Every iteration of the main loop of the update function (of **Students**) will end with a message to the user (on screen) asking whether he/she wants to register for more courses. If the answer is yes, a new update loops will begin; otherwise the update will terminate.

Here is a short (and abbreviated) description of this update function in pseudo code:

```
Begin function "Register student to courses"
Student-OID = Students.Read(student-ID)          (this is a message to the basic function)
Do while the student wishes to register to more courses:
     Course-code = Forms.present form Course-Registration       (the form will return a course
                        •                                        code entered by the user)
     course-OID = Courses.Read(course-code)       (a message to Courses to find the course
                                                   object)
     If error then Forms.error message: "no such course";
            Course-code = Forms.present form Course-Registration
     Else For i=1 to end of set registered to courses
            If course-OID = [Courses] then Forms.error message: "already registered
                  to this course"; Error = "yes"
            Else;
          Next i
          If Error <> "yes" then append the tuple {course-OID, Nill} to set registered
                  to courses; Courses.add a student to course (course-OID, student-OID)
                                       (this is a message to a specific function of Courses)
          Else;
          Forms.ask user if continue registration
End while
End function.
```

We have seen that the update function which belongs to the **Students** class has also updated the lists of students registered to a course by activating the respective update function of **Courses** class. The update could have been implemented in a different way, such as defining a function in **Courses**: *Register a student to course*. This way, every activation of the function would have caused the addition of a student's OID to the set *students registered to course"* of **Courses**. But in order to register the certain student to several courses, we would have had to run this update function several times. Using the function presented previously, we only have to activate it once, no matter to how many courses the student wishes to register for. From this we can learn that there is more than one way to implement a function, and that various options should be considered carefully in order to find the most appropriate.

The messages sent from one function to another could also be described by a diagram, in which message lines connect the involved classes. As you can imagine, an attempt to draw such a diagram for a system with many functions would result in many intersecting lines and a diagram would not be comprehensible. However, it is reasonable to draw such a diagram for a single application-specific function, where only the relevant classes and the functions that are called by that function are displayed. In our last example, such a diagram would include the three involved classes: **Students**, **Courses**, and **Forms**, a message line from **Students** to **Forms** (with the name *present form Course Registration* on it), and two message lines from **Students** to **Courses**, with the function names *Read (course-code)* and *add a student to course*, respectively.[14]

Application Programs

In principle, we could implement every task of the IS using application-specific functions or basic functions, where an application-specific function may include messages to other application-specific or basic functions. If we choose to implement all of the IS tasks this way, we might end up with long "chains" of functions and messages. This might raise problems of comprehensibility and maintainability. Moreover, if we will assign many specific functions to a certain class, its "independence" may be harmed: It might become "tailored" for a specific application and will not be reusable for other applications. By doing so, we will be defeating one of the main objectives of OO development.

According to this, there might be functions which we would prefer to implement using an application program which will not be attached to "ordinary" data classes. Consider the following examples: (1) We need to produce a report showing the details of certain departments, and for each department we need to detail the courses it offers in each of its degree programs, and the teachers who can teach these courses; (2) We need to display the details of the students in all departments whose average grade in a certain year and semester is above a certain value, and send them a message; and (3) We need to cancel certain course offerings, void the registration of students to those courses, and the assignment of the teacher and TAs to those courses. In such cases, many objects from different classes are involved, and many application-specific and basic functions need to be activated in order to complete a task. An IS may have many such "complex" functions. Such a function need not be attached to a certain class; it might not even be clear to which class such function should be attached. Instead, we may opt to separate such a function from any ordinary data class and attach it to a specific abstract class, which will contain no objects—only such functions. Such functions may be termed application programs. Actually, the abstract class will not include the entire application programs, only their "main" parts, because each "main" program will contain, besides "ordinary" commands or procedures, messages to basic and application-specific functions of various classes.

Review Questions

1. What are the two main roles of a class diagram?
2. What is the difference between a class diagram and an objects schema?
3. What are the differences and similarities between a class diagram and an ER diagram?
4. Explain the difference between class and object.
5. What is the relation between 'class' in the objects model and 'entity' in the ER model?
6. What is the difference between 'data object' and 'interface object'?
7. What parts of the definition of an attribute are included in the class diagram and what parts are included in the objects schema?
8. Give an example for each of the following (non-key) attributes: a simple/atomic attribute; a tuple of simple attributes; a set of simple attributes; a reference attribute; a tuple consisting of a reference attribute and a simple attribute; and a tuple consisting of two reference attributes and a simple attribute.

9. Give an example for each of the following keys: a key consisting of one simple attribute; a key consisting of two simple attributes; a key tuple consisting of a reference attribute and a simple attribute; a key tuple consisting of two reference attributes; a key tuple consisting of two reference attributes and a simple attribute; and a key tuple consisting of three reference attributes.

10. What is OID and what is it used for?

11. Show an example in which a thing can be defined as an attribute of a class, or alternatively as a class related with another class. What is the dilemma?

12. What is the meaning of min '0' or '1' at the "one" side of a relationship? Show examples.

13. What is the min possible value at the "many" side of a relationship? Explain.

14. Show examples for each of the following types of relationships: one-to-one; one-to-many; and many-to-many. For each case, show examples with min values of '0' and '1'.

15. What is the problem with relationship attributes in a many-to-many relationship between two classes? What can be done about it? Show examples.

16. How do the objects model and class diagram deal with ternary relationships in reality? Compare to how it is done in the ER model.

17. What is the difference between an aggregation and an ordinary relationship between classes?

18. Show examples for the following types of inheritance: inheritance with one subclass; inheritance with two subclasses with "exclusive' constraint; inheritance with two subclasses with "total' constraint; a subclass with multiple inheritance from one source; and a subclass with multiple inheritance from different sources.

19. What are the considerations for or against subclassification? Show examples for and against subclassification.

20. What is an abstract class and what can it be used for?

21. What is polymorphism? What is it good for, and which problems may it cause?

22. Clarify the difference between 'function' and 'method'. Where are each of them defined?

23. What are basic functions? Show examples for each type.

24. Which checks need to be performed upon activation of a function that attempts to delete an object having relationships with other objects? Distinguish between different types of relationships that object may have.

25. Explain the difference between an application-specific function and a basic function. Explain and exemplify the relationship between the two types.

References

Elmasri, P., & Navathe, S. (2003). *Fundamentals of database systems* (4th ed.). Boston: Addison Wesley.

Garcia-Molina, H., Ullman, J., & Widom, J. (2002). *Database systems—The complete book*. Upper Saddle River, NJ: Prentice Hall.

Endnotes

1   A class name may be in plural or singular, so we may as well say class **Student**.

2   We may assume that the database schema of a certain application is kept in a dictionary or catalog of the system.

3   We do not deal with such details at the stage of data modeling. Generally, there is no difference between the definition of data types of object attributes and data types of variables in programming languages or in Data Base Management Systems (DBMS). Sometimes data type definitions depend on the specific software used to implement the system.

4   Although we do not deal with physical aspects of the system and the database, we may assume that an OID acts like a pointer to a certain place where the object is stored.

5   A deeper discussion about these issues is beyond the scope of this book and can be found in books dealing with relational and object oriented databases (e.g., Elmasri & Navathe, 2003; Garcia-Molina, Ullman, & Widom, 2002).

6   A binary relationship relates two objects, each belonging to a different class; a unary relationship relates two object both belonging to the same class.

7   1:N or N:1 are identical, only the order of the related objects is switched.

8   A DBMS which would implement this model may use this key to avoid object duplicity, like an ordinary key which contains data.

9   Here too we give names to the reference attributes, preceding the referenced class names. However, we may abbreviate by writing only the names of the

referenced class (within square brackets). This will be shown in further figures.

[10]   Note that in this example we omitted the names of the reference attributes within the key tuple.

[11]   Recall that a function is activated by a message sent to it by another function. Here, assume that the message was sent from the function named *input student details* which belongs to a class **Forms**.

[12]   More detailed explanations are beyond the scope of this book; they can be found in books on databases.

[13]   You may assume that the registration can be performed by a clerk/ secretary using a manual form which includes the details of the student and of the courses to register; or directly by the student through the Internet. These options do not affect the logic of the required function.

[14]   This is only an intuitive description of such a diagram; more details will be provided when dealing with methods in the final unit of this book.

Chapter III

Creating
Class Diagrams

This chapter discusses considerations and rules for identifying classes, attributes, relationships, and functions; and presents case study examples (problems), that is, descriptions of users' data requirements; along with their class diagram solutions.

Rules for the Creation
of Class Diagrams

In the previous chapter, we have come to know the components of the objects model and the class diagram. When the problem is small, there seems to be no problem to identify the object classes, attributes, and relationships and present them properly in a class diagram. However, in reality things are (usually) not simple, the problems with the existing system and the needs from the new system are usually not well defined.

The study of the problems users have with an existing system and their requirements from the new system, is carried out using common information gathering techniques, such as: (1) interviews with various users in different management levels; (2) brainstorming with the users' representatives; (3) observations on how certain workers are performing their jobs or how certain processes are carried out; (4) study and analysis of documents describing the organization and the existing business processes; (5) distribution of questionnaires and the conducting of polls among users (customers, suppliers); and (6) the study of other organizations and systems which bear resemblance to the studied organization. All these techniques have shortcomings. For example, documents may not be accurate or up-to-date; users are not homogenous; there may be many different users who function in different organizational units and ranks, with different experience and different acquaintances with the existing system and its problems and with different preferences. Hence, the different users may understand the situation and problems with the existing system differently and pose different, sometimes even conflicting, requirements from the new system.[1]

Unlike functional analysis, which concentrates on identifying and defining the functions of the information system (IS), data analysis concentrates on identifying the object classes, their attributes, and relationships among them. Some claim that data analysis is easier than functional analysis because it is easier to identify objects than to identify functions, since objects are usually more tangible and stable, while functions are intangible, vague, and changing artifacts. However, there are those who claim it is the opposite, that is, that functional analysis is easier because users tend to describe what they do and what they want the system to do for them in terms of functions, not objects. There is no clear answer which task is easier.[2] At any rate, here we concentrate on data analysis with the objective to create a class diagram representing the data structure of the reality being modeled.

It is obvious that the construction of a class diagram is not a structured, algorithmic, sequential process, which ensures one "correct" solution. Rather, it is an iterative process, which involves a lot of trial and error. It relies on work practice, experience, intuition, and requires close collaboration between the analyst and the users.

As was mentioned before, one of the first and main problems in creating a class diagram is identifying the objects and classifying them. There are various guidelines as to how this should be done. For example, Coad and Yourdon (1990) suggest the following guidelines (among others) for the identification of classes:

- Examine what are the facilities, instruments, organizational units, and so on, which the system needs to keep information about.
- Examine what are the events in reality which need to be remembered and stored in the information system.
- Examine the various roles performed by people working in or for the organization.
- Examine other system connected to the system in question (or systems that bear resemblance to it).

- Coad and Yourdon (1990) also suggest different criteria in order to help the analyst decide if something is an object, that is, if it deserves to be defined as an object. Here are a few of the criteria:

  o **The need to remember:** is there any information that needs to be kept on the object in the information system? If not, there is a good chance it is not an object.

  o **The need to behave:** is there any behavior that needs to be saved? i.e., is there a need to process or use functions on it? If there is no behavior, it is probably not an object. If no information needs to be saved on it, and it has no behavior, it is certainly not an object.

  o **More than one attribute:** an object has usually more than one attribute; if this is not the case, one should examine if it is an object, or just another object's attribute.

  o **More than one object:** a class usually includes several objects. If a class has no instances, then the designer should reconsider whether this class has a place in the system. However, the possibility of an abstract class should be considered, if other classes inherit from it.

  o **The attributes are always applicable:** it is best if all objects in a class have values in all their attributes. If this is not the case, splitting of the class into super and subclasses should be considered, so that the attributes defined in the superclass would characterize all the objects, while specific attributes would apply to the respective subclasses only.

  o **The relationships are always applicable:**[3] As with attributes, it is best if all the objects in a certain class have the same types of relationships with other objects. If this is not the case, splitting of the class into subclasses should be considered, so that relationship types which may apply to all objects will be of the superclass, while specific relationship types will be of the respective subclasses.

  o **The functions are always applicable:** As with attributes and functions, if there are functions that are not applicable to all the objects in class, splitting of the class should be considered. This way the right functions would be assigned to the super and subclasses.

  o **Thing are within the scope of the problem:** One has to assure that all the object classes included in the model are relevant. However, one should not stick too heavily to the present condition, for it may lead to mistakes. For example, if a certain organization uses a certain form to make purchase orders, it does not mean that a "purchase order form" class needs to be defined. The present orders system represents the present conditions and technology, but not necessarily of the new system. It is better to define classes with a high abstraction level, which are less bound to the present conditions. Therefore, instead of defining a "purchase order form" class, it is better to define a "purchase order" or "order" class.

The division to super and subclasses can be done in two ways: top-down and bottom-up. According to the top-down approach, the general classes are located and classified, and then objects having specific attributes, relationship types, and behaviors are identified. Based on it, **specialization** of the classes takes place—subclasses are defined, with specific attributes, relationship types, and behavior. According to the bottom-up approach, "independent" classes are first identified, without any connection to other classes. Afterwards, similar classes (which have similar attributes, relationships, and behavior) are identified and **generalization** is performed—a superclass is defined, and it receives the shared attributes, relationship types, and behavior. It is obvious that in reality it is impossible (and not necessary) to use only one approach; the process is iterative and involves both specialization and generalization.

A possible work order of creating a class diagram is first to identify and define the classes, their attributes, and relationship types, and then to define the behavior, that is, their functions. A different work order may be to first perform the task of functional analysis and create a functional model of the system; then use this model to identify the classes and their attributes and relationship types. Another possibility is to work concurrently on the two tasks of data analysis and functional analysis. There are many different development methodologies which offer different orders of activities. We will be dealing with these issues in Unit II of this book. At this stage we concentrate on creating class diagrams only, without considering the system's functionality.

Examples and Exercises on the Creation of Class Diagrams

In this section, we present examples for the creation of class diagrams.[4] Each example consists of a problem statement and its solution—a class diagram. Each problem statement can be viewed as a data requirements document, which represents the users' data-related needs. (As already discussed, in reality one may not assume that the users' requirements are already predefined and given in a "clear" and easy to read description. Obviously, in reality the problems are much more complex. But such real-world examples cannot be provided in a textbook.)

The reader is asked to treat the examples as self practice exercises. This means: first, read the problem statement; based on it, create your class diagram; only then look at the provided solution and the explanations that accompany it.

As said, in this chapter we deal with data modeling, not with functionality. Therefore functional requirements are hardly mentioned in the problem statements, and hence, names of functions are specified in a few cases only.

Example A: Research Proposals

You need to create a data model for an IS that will manage information regarding research proposals submitted by university researchers to research funds (i.e., organizations funding academic research). The system will serve the Research Contracts division of the university and the researchers.

A researcher belongs to a department and occasionally submits research proposals. A researcher has an ID number and name and works for one department of the university. A department is identified by a department name and is managed by one researcher. A research proposal may be submitted by one or several researchers (principal investigators [PIs]). A research proposal has a title given to it by the researcher, but since a title may not be unique, the university's Research Contracts division assigns each proposal a unique research code. The proposal is submitted to a research fund (identified by a fund name). When a proposal is first submitted, the PIs specify how many years the research is supposed to take (between 1 to 4 years), and for every year they specify: how much money they request, who will be the coinvestigators (CIs) (i.e., other university researchers who work on the research), and how many months will each of the CIs work on the research. The research fund may approve or disapprove the request, or approve a different amount of money. At the end of every year, the PIs have to resubmit their request of funding for the next year, and the research fund may disapprove or approve any amount of money. The status, amount, and date of approval must be registered.

A class diagram for this example is presented in Figure 3.1. Here are a few explanations regarding this diagram:

- The problem description makes it clear that there is a need to define classes for researchers (**Researcher**), academic departments (**Department**), and research proposals (**Research**, in short).5 However, it may not be clear at first glance that there is a need of a class **Research Year**, and

Figure 3.1. Class diagram of the research proposals example

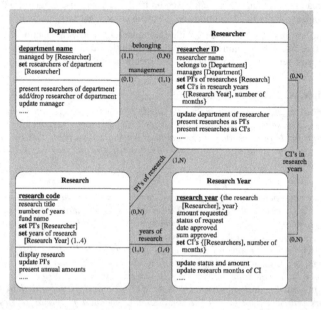

some may define a set attribute in the **Research** class instead. However, a more in-depth examination reveals that we need to save data for each research year separately. Hence, each research year is an object, which is different from the research object. Obviously, there is a 1:N relationship between the two classes, with the specified multiplicities, because every research will last between 1 and 4 years, while every year of research is associated with exactly one specific research.

• Each of the classes **Researcher**, **Department**, and **Research** has a simple key attribute. However, **Research Year** is identifiable by a tuple made up of two attributes: one is a reference attribute *the research [Research]*, and the other is *year* (i.e., the calendar year of the research). Note that the name of the key of **Research Year** is identical to the class name, as we do in most cases where a key is constructed of several attributes. Note also the inverse reference attribute of class **Research**: *set years of research [Research Year]*.

- In this solution we define a **Researcher** class without distinguishing PIs from CIs. It means that every researcher has a set reference attribute of research proposals submitted as a PI, and a set reference attribute of researches on which he/she had worked each year as a CI. But there may be researchers who are PIs only or CIs only (or even researchers who are neither). Figure 3.2 presents another possible solution to the problem, in which the two subtypes of researchers are distinguished. The class **Researcher** retained the attributes shared by all researchers (and the relationships with **Department**), while each of the subclasses has a respective set reference attribute: *set PI of researchers [Research]*, and *set CI in research years {[Research Year]*, no. of months}. Therefore, in the **Research** and **Research Year** classes, the reference sets refer to the respective subclasses.

- There is a many-to-many relationship between **Researcher** and **Research Year** (as well as between **CI** and **Research Year** in the alternative

Figure 3.2. Alternative class diagram with subclasses

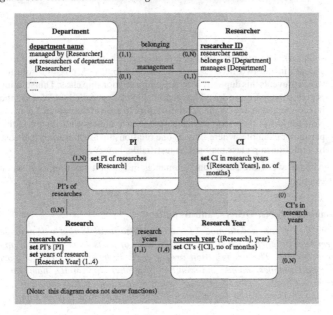

Copyright © 2007, Idea Group Inc. Copying or distributing in print or electronic forms without written permission of Idea Group Inc. is prohibited.

Figure 3.3. Alternative class diagram with a relationship class

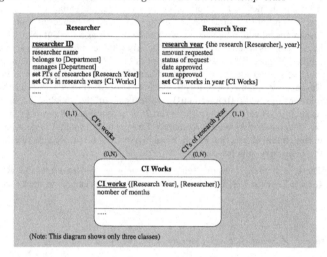

(Note: This diagram shows only three classes)

solution). The relationship has a relation attribute *no. of months* which appears in the two inverse set reference attributes. A possible solution which prevents this duplicity is by defining a relationship class. This solution is presented in Figure 3.3.[6] The relationship class is called **CI Works**, and it is connected in one-to-many relationships to each of the "parent" classes. Note the key of this class: It consists of the two reference attributes. In this particular example, where there is one relationship attribute only, this use of a relationship class may not be justifiable, however.

• As said, we wrote some function names in the first solution, only as an example.

Example B: Parts, Orders, and Suppliers

You need to create a data model for an organizational IS that will manage information on parts (items), suppliers, orders of parts from suppliers, and their deliveries. The organization orders parts using order forms. A part has a part number, name, and weight. A supplier has an ID, name, and address. An order is identified by an order number, and it lists the parts and quantities ordered. An order is sent on a certain date to a certain supplier.

Suppliers deliver parts which have been ordered along with a delivery certificate. The certificate is identified by a number on which the delivery date is also written. A delivery may contain parts from different orders, and it specifies the order according to which a part is supplied and the quantity supplied, per order. (Hence, a delivery may contain a certain part which has been ordered in different orders and specifies the quantities per each order.) A delivery may contain only some of the parts and quantities which have been ordered in a certain order. Records must be kept of the parts, suppliers, orders, deliveries, and parts outstanding (i.e., ordered parts not yet supplied).

The class diagram in Figure 3.4 presents a solution to this problem. Here are a few clarifications:

Figure 3.4. Class diagram of the parts, orders and suppliers example

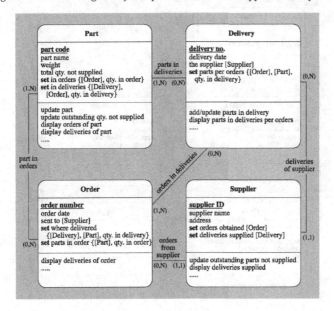

- There is a many-to-many relationship between the **Part** and **Order** classes. While a part does not have to be present in even a single order, an order must include at least one part.

- Each of the set reference attributes: *in orders* of class **Part**, and its inverse attribute *parts in order* of class **Order**, include, besides a reference to a class, the relationship attributes *qty. in order*. This duplicity can be avoided by creating a relationship class, as shown in Figure 3.5.

- The relationship between **Order** and **Supplier** is many-to-one: An order is sent to one supplier, while a supplier may get many orders or none at all.

- Every object of the **Delivery** class, which is identified by *delivery no.*, also includes a reference attribute to its supplier and a set reference attribute *parts per orders,* which is a tuple made of three attributes: reference to **Order**, reference to **Part** and *quantity in delivery*. Each such can be viewed like an "item row" in the delivery certificate, specifying the quantity

Figure 3.5. Alternative class diagram with a relationship class

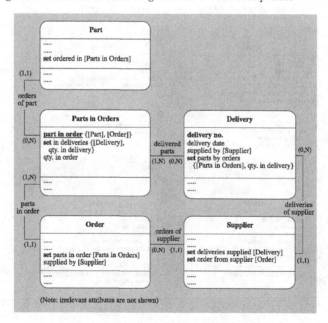

of each item sent per its order. Note a similar set *where delivered* in **Order** class, which also includes a triplet: a reference to **Delivery**, a reference to **Part**, and *quantity in delivery*. The set *in deliveries* of **Part** also includes such a triplet: a reference to **Order**, a reference to **Delivery**, and the quantity in delivery. This means that either by looking at **Order** or **Part** we can tell in which orders and deliveries a certain part appears. The relationship attribute *qty. in delivery* can be found in three different places in this solution.

- Figure 3.5 presents another possible solution, which appears to be easier to understand and also eliminates some of the duplicities in the previous solution. In this solution, the many-to-many relationship between parts and orders is expressed using the **Parts in Orders** relationship class. The key of this class includes reference attributes to **Part** and **Order**. The class also includes the relationship attributes *qty. in order*, and the set *in deliveries* which is made of two attributes: a reference to **Delivery** and *qty. in delivery*. The inverse set in **Delivery**, named *parts by orders*, is also made of two attributes: a reference to **Parts in Orders** and *qty. in delivery*. Note that **Delivery** is only linked to **Parts in Orders** and not to **Part** and **Order**. The set reference attributes in the two classes are "simple" and include less duplicity compared to the set attributes in the previous solution.

Figure 3.6. Alternative class diagram with another relationship class

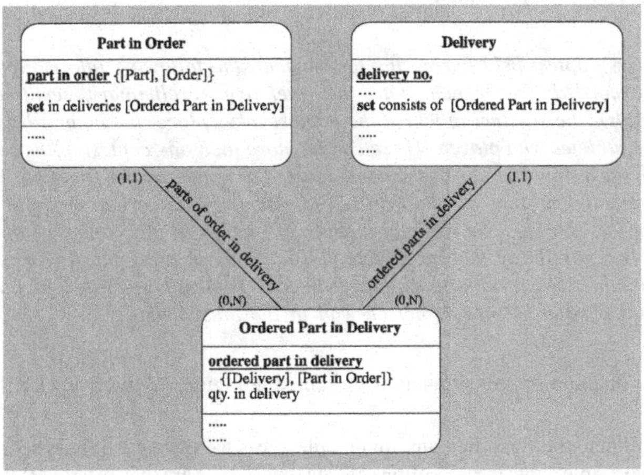

- There is another possible solution to this problem, which "decomposes" the many-to-many relationship between **Part in Order** and **Delivery** by using a relationship class. Figure 3.6 presents only that part of the solution: The additional class **Ordered Part in Delivery** includes a key made of two reference attributes: one to **Delivery** and one to **Part in Order**. In addition it has an attribute *qty. in delivery*. Each of the referenced classes includes a set reference attribute to **Ordered Part in Delivery**. In this solution there is no duplicity of data; the "cost" of this solution is an increase in the number of classes (because we are actually "normalizing" the classes, similar to normalized tables in the relational model). The objects model does not answer the question which is the best solution, and leaves that to the discretion of the designer.[7]

Example C: Sport Tournament

In an athletics sport tournament, athletes from various countries take part in various contests. The IS manages information on the participants, that is, athletes, coaches, and managers; and on the contests. Each participant is given an ID number, and his/her name, country, and birth date has to be recorded. Each athlete's blood type is also recorded. Every athlete can only play in one branch of a sport. Throughout the tournament, every athlete undergoes drug tests; for every test the test code, date, and result are recorded. The same test can be taken several times but on different dates. Every coach has one branch of sport he/she coaches; he/she may coach several athletes (but at least one). An athlete has one coach only. A coach cannot be an athlete.

For every contest held during the tournament, the following information is being recorded: the branch, date, the level (e.g., preliminary, semifinals, and finals), the stadium in which the contest takes place, the hour it began, and the athletes who played. There can be more than one contest of the same branch each day, but not in the same level. For example, it is possible that a basketball semifinal will be held in the morning of a certain day and the final in the evening. The minimal number of players in any contest is three. There is a possibility that an athlete will not play in any contest (e.g., due to an injury). The result of each player in each contest is recorded, and also the total number of medals he/she won in the tournament.

A class diagram for this problem is presented in Figure 3.7 (with no clarifications).

In addition to the class diagram, for completeness we show the objects schema of this example. Note the definitions of data type, which are then referred to from

Figure 3.7. Class diagram of sport tournament example

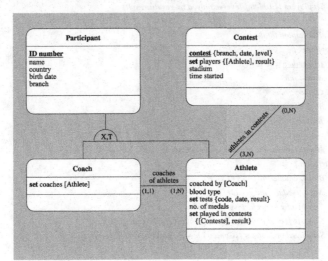

the attributes' definitions within the classes. In some cases the data types of attributes are defined within their classes. Note also that class **Participant** is defined *total-cover*, standing for the T sign in the class diagram; similarly, subclasses **Athlete** and **Coach** *exclude* each other.

Objects Schema of Sport Tournament

    Data type definitions {

        Type ID: numeric (9)

        Type name: char (30)

        Type date: dd/mm/yyyy

        Type time: hh/mm

        Type result: decimal (3.2)

    }

Class Contest

    Attributes {

        Contest {branch: name, date of contest: date, level: numeric (2)}

        Stadium: name

> *Time started: time*
> *Set players {[Athlete] inverse played in, result: result}*
> *}*

Class: Participant total-cover
  Attributes {
    <u>*ID number*</u> *type ID*
    Name: name
    Country: name
    Birth date: date
    Branch: name
  }

Class Athlete inherits Participant excludes Coach
  Attributes {
    Blood: enumerate (A, A+, A-, B)
    No. of medals: integer (2)
    Coached by [Coach] inverse coaches
    Set tests {code: char (3), date: date, test result: char (10)}
    Set played in contests {[Contest] inverse players, result: result}
  }

Class Coach inherits Participant excludes Athlete
  Attributes {
    Set coaches [Athlete]
  }

End of Sport Tournament schema.

Example D: Library

A book in the library has an international standard book number (ISBN), title, publisher, year of publication, and one or more authors. (For sake of simplicity assume that author names are unique.) In order to assist with book selections, each book is characterized by a few key words. There are books of which the library has several copies. Each copy can be shelved in a certain place in the library. A place is identified by a hall name and shelf number. The library lends books to readers. Each reader has a reader ID, name, and address. The book's lending out and return dates are recorded. It is impossible to lend out the same copy of a book to the same reader more than once on the same day. However, it is possible to lend it out on the same day to different readers (for example, one reader checks out the book in the morning, returns it in the afternoon, and then another reader checks it out).

Figure 3.8. A class diagram of the Library example

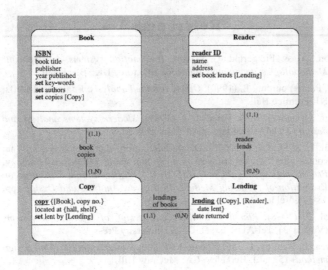

A solution for this problem is presented in Figure 3.8.

Review Questions

1. Which techniques can be used when studying the users' requirements prior to creation of the objects model?

2. What criteria and guidelines can be used to discover objects and classes?

3. What is the difference between division of classes into superclasses and subclasses according to the top-down approach compared to the bottom-up approach?

4. Discuss the possible work orders for identifying functions and defining the "behavior" of a system.

References

Avison, D., & Fitzgerald, G. (1988). *Information systems development: Methodologies, techniques and tools*. Oxford, UK: Blackwell.

Coad, P., & Yourdon, E. (1990). *Object oriented analysis*. Englewood Cliffs, NJ: Prentice Hall.

Hoffer, J., George, J., & Valacich, J. (1999). *Modern systems analysis and design* (2nd ed.). Reading, MA: Addison Wesley.

Kabeli, J., & Shoval, P. (2003). Data modeling or functional analysis: What comes next? An experimental comparison using FOOM methodology. *Proceedings of the Eight CAISE/ IFIP8.1 International Workshop on Evaluation of Modeling Methods in Systems Analysis and Design* (pp. 48-57). Velden, Austria.

Shoval, P. (1998). *Planning, analysis and design of information systems* (Vols. 1-3). Tel-Aviv, Israel: Open University Press.

Whitten, J., Bentley, L., & Dittman, K. (2000). *Systems analysis and design methods* (5th ed.). Berkeley, CA: McGraw Hill.

Yourdon, E. (1989). *Modern structured analysis*. Englewood Cliffs, NJ: Prentice Hall.

Endnotes

[1]   More on these problems can be found in the literature on systems analysis and design. See, for example, Avison and Fitzgerald (1988), Hoffer, George, and Valacich (1999), Shoval (1998), Whitten, Bentley, and Dittman (2000), and Yourdon (1989).

[2]   More on this debate can be found in Kabeli and Shoval (2003).

[3]   This criterion is not one of those proposed by Code and Yourdon (1990). It is added in the interest of completeness.

[4]   The examples are based on similar examples brought in Chapters 9.1 and 9.2 in Shoval (1998).

[5]   In this and the following class diagrams all class names are in singular.

[6]   This solution shows only the relevant parts of the diagram, and refers to the solution shown in Figure 3.1, which only has a **Researcher** class; a similar solution could be provided for the case shown in Figure 3.2. The reader may create the equivalent diagram for this case.

7   Other solutions, a little different from those presented here, are also possible. The reader is welcome to try and find them.

Chapter IV

Mapping Entity Relationship Diagrams to Class Diagrams

This chapter first explains why it might be preferred to first create an entity relationship diagram (ERD) and then map it to a class diagram. The chapter then describes the mapping rules, demonstrating the mapping process with several comprehensive examples.

Why Map an ERD to a Class Diagram?

We have already seen that there is a great deal of resemblance between the objects and entity relationship (ER) models.[1] The main difference between the two is that the ER model does not deal with functionality of the system. But there are some other differences. One of the main differences is that in the objects model there are only unary and binary relationships, while in ER there are also ternary relationships. This means that a ternary relationship between objects in reality, which can be represented as such in an ERD, is represented in a class diagram as a (separate) class. Another difference is that in ER there may be weak entity types, signified by a special symbol (a dotted rectangle for the weak entity type and dotted diamonds and connection lines for the relationships to the respective "strong" entity types). In the objects model there are no "weak" classes, but there may be classes whose key includes reference attributes to other classes. Of course, there are some differences in notations; the most visible is that in the ERD a relationship is signified by a diamond, while in the class diagram there is simply a connection line; in the ERD attributes are presented in ovals connected to their entity or relationship types; in the class diagram the attributes are listed inside the rectangle of the class. In almost any other sense, the models are very similar.

In the previous chapter we have learned how to create a class diagram based on the users' needs. However, there is an alternative way—to first create an ERD (based on users' needs) and then map it into an equivalent class diagram. There are several reasons to pursue this course of action: Some analysts may prefer working with an ER model, either because of having more experience with ER or due to personal preference. Moreover, there is research which shows that an ERD is in some cases more comprehensible by users (Shoval & Frumermann, 1994), and that analysts create more correct data models when using ERDs rather than class diagrams (Shoval & Shiran, 1997). The main reason for these two phenomena is the advantage of ER in dealing with ternary relationships: The ER model is capable of representing such relationships "directly," using the diamond symbol, while the objects model represents such relationships as "relationship classes." Because of this it is sometimes difficult to understand whether a class represents a "simple" thing or a complex one. Indeed, a "relationship class" can be identified by looking at the key: It consists of two or three reference attributes (depending on the specific type of ternary relationship which it stands for), but this form of identification is not clear enough compared to the "direct" representation of a ternary relationship in ERD.[2]

Whether we agree with these claims or not, it is important to remember that there may be users who prefer ERDs or understand them better than class diagrams, and that there may be analysts/designers who prefer ERDs or produce more correct schemas when using them rather than class diagrams. Hence, given an ERD, we must provide a precise method for mapping it to an equivalent class diagram. Equivalent means that they bear the same meaning (semantics). Once the target class diagram is created, it is of course possible to add the functional dimension (i.e., to define the functions and attach them to the proper classes).

The Mapping Rules

We present the mapping rules according to the following categories: (1) mapping of simple entity types and their attributes; (2) mapping of relationships between simple entity types; (3) mapping of weak entity types; and (4) mapping of structural relationships.

Figure 4.1. Mapping of entities and relationships

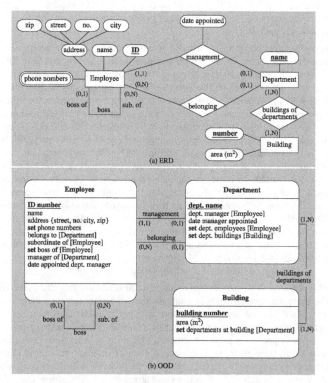

Mapping of Simple Entity Types and Their Attributes

Every simple entity type (i.e., not a weak or a subentity type) is mapped into a class. Its attributes are mapped as follows:

*   A simple attribute is mapped to a simple attribute.
*   A complex attribute is mapped to a tuple made of the respective attribute.

- A multi-valued attribute is mapped to a set attribute.
- The key of the entity type (one attribute or more) is mapped to a key of the class.

Example: The ERD in Figure 4.1(a) includes three simple entity types with several attributes and relationships. The object oriented design (OOD) in Figure 4.1(b) demonstrates the mapping of those entities and their attributes into classes. Note the mapping of the attributes *ID, name, address,* and *phone numbers* of the **Employee** entity type; the mapping of *name* of **Department**, and the mapping of *number* and *area* of **Building**. (At this point ignore the mapping of the relationships.)

Mapping of Relationships Between Simple Entity Types

We distinguish the mapping of unary and binary relationships from the mapping of ternary relationships.

Mapping of Unary and Binary Relationships

The relationship between the entity types is mapped to an equivalent relationship between the classes created from those entity types. In addition, a reference attribute is added in each of these classes. If the relationship is unary (meaning only one class was created), two reference attributes are added in the class, and each is given an appropriate name.

The type of relationship dictates the following types of reference attributes:

- **1:1 relationship:** The reference attribute in each class is singular (meaning reference to a single object). If the 1:1 relationship has attributes, they are mapped to simple attributes of each of the classes. (Note the duplicity; as we know, at a later stage such duplicity may be removed—depending on the users' needs, as would be determined in the functional analysis process.)
- **1:N relationship:** The reference attribute from the "1" side of the relationship is defined **set** (meaning, referring to several objects); the reference attribute from the "N" side of the relationship is singular. (Recall that a 1:N relationship has no attributes.)

- **N:N relationship without attributes:** Each of the reference attributes is defined **set**.

  Example: In Figure 4.1 we can see relationships of the various types:

  o The **unary relationship** *boss* of **Employee** is one-to-many, and therefore it is mapped into two reference attributes of class **Employee**: one *subordinate-of [Employee]* for the employee's boss, and the other *set boss-of [Employee]* for the employee's subordinates. Note the role names written next to the ends of the relationship line.

  o The **binary relationship** *management* is one-to-one; it is mapped to a single reference attribute in each of the involved classes, while the relationship attribute *date appointed* is mapped to a simple attribute in each of the two classes. Note that for brevity, the name of the attribute in each class is slightly different: *date manager appointed* in **Department** and *date appointed dept. manager* in **Employee**.

  o The **binary relationship** *belonging* is a one-to-many; it is mapped to *belongs to [Department]* of **Employee**, and to *set dept. employees [Employee]* of **Department**.

  o The **binary relationship** *buildings of department* is many-to-many; it is mapped to a set of reference attributes in each of the two classes.

- **M:N relationship with attributes**—there are two mapping options:

  1. **Mapping to set reference attributes:** This option is similar to the previous case of N:N relationship without attributes. But in this case each of the set reference attributes is a tuple consisting of a reference attribute along with the relationship attributes. (Again, note the duplicity of relationship attributes in the two classes.)

     Note that if a relationship attribute is multi-valued, it is mapped to a set. This means that in such cases, the set attribute in each of the involved classes contains a set for each multi-valued attributed of the relationship.

  2. **Mapping to a *relationship class*:** According to this option, the relationship is mapped to a new, relationship class. The name of this class can be identical or similar to the relationship's name. In addition, a one-to-many relationship is defined between each of the regular classes and the relationship class. The multiplicity of each of these relationships is as follows: At the end next to the regular class it is $(1,1)$,[3] while at the end next to the relationship class it is identical to the multiplicity in the "many" side of the original relationship. The at-

Figure 4.2. Mapping of M:N relationships with attributes

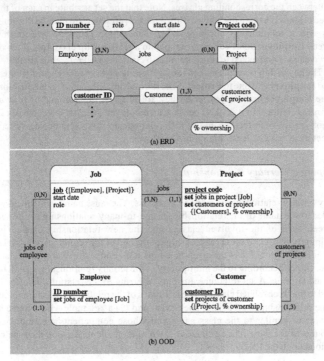

(a) ERD

(b) OOD

tributes of the relationship class are as follows: (1) its key is a tuple, whose name may be identical or similar to the class name, and whose components are a pair of reference attributes to the two related classes; and (2) its other attributes are the attributes of the original relationship. In each of the two related classes, a set reference attributes are defined, referring to the relationship class. Note that in this mapping there is no duplicity of attributes. The more attributes a N;N relationship has, the greater justification is for opting this solution.

Example: Figure 4.2 includes two many-to-many relationships with relationship attributes. We demonstrate the two mapping options. The *customers of projects* relationship between **Project** and **Customer** is mapped to a respective relationship between the corresponding classes. Note that the set attribute in each of the related classes is a tuple made of two attributes: a reference attribute to the other class and a relationship attribute *% of ownership*. The *jobs* relationship between **Employee** and **Project** is mapped to a relationship class **Job**. Each of the two classes connected to this relationship class has a set reference attributed to it. The key of **Job** is a tuple named **job** containing a pair of reference attributes, one to **Employee** and one to **Project**. Note the multiplicities of the relationships: At the **Employee** and **Project** ends they are (1,1); at the **Job** end of *jobs of employee* relationship it is (0,N) because an employee does not have to work in any job (project); at the *Job* end of *jobs* relationship it is (3,N) because every project must have at least three jobs (employees).

Mapping of Ternary Relationships

Every ternary relationship is mapped to a class. The class name is identical or similar to the name of the relationship. A one-to-many relationship is defined between each of the involved classes and the new relationship class. The multiplicity of each of these relationships at the end of the regular class is (1,1). The multiplicity of each of these relationships at the end of the relationship class is determined according to the multiplicity of the ternary relationship, as will be detailed later on. A set reference attribute referring to the relationship class is added to the three related classes. The attributes of the relationship class include: (1) the relationship attributes, if such exist; and (2) a key tuple whose name is identical or similar to the class name and whose components are reference attributes to the three related classes or two of them, depending on the type of relationship in the ERD:

1. If the relationship is N:N:N, the key tuple consists of three reference attributes, one for each of the connected classes.

   Example: Figure 4.3 presents a N:N:N relationship *sales*, where a sale involves a product being sold by an agent to a customers, and there are no constraints on who may buy or sell products. The relationship is mapped to the relationship class **Sale**. Note the set reference attributes in each of the three regular classes, and in particular note the key of **Sale** which includes three reference attributes to the three classes. The relationship's attributes appear in the relationship class only.

2. If the relationship is N:N:1, the key tuple consists of two reference attributes only—referring to the two classes that are at the "N" sides of the relationship. In addition, there is another reference attribute (not part of the key) referring to the class in the "1" side of the relationship.

Figure 4.3. Mapping of a N:N:N relationship

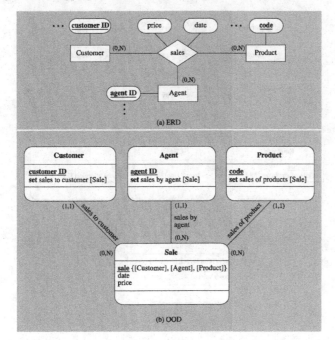

Example: Figure 4.4 presents an N:N:1 ternary relationship *jobs*. The relationship defines that a certain employee may work on a certain project in one city only[4] (while he may work in a certain city on many projects; and a project in a city may involve many employees). The relationship is mapped to a class **Job** whose key contains reference to **Employee** and **Project** only, while the reference attribute to **City** is not part of the key.

3.   If the relationship is N:1:1, the key structure consists of two reference attributes—one referring to the class at the "N" side of the relationship, and the other, to **one** of the other two classes (at the "1" side). In addition, there is another reference attribute (not part of the key) referring to the other class (at the "1" side) that is not referenced from the. The choice of which of the classes in the "1" side in the key is arbitrary.[5]

Figure 4.4. Mapping of a N:N:1 relationship

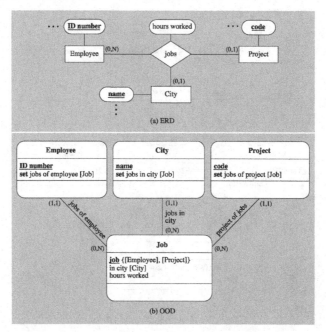

Example: Figure 4.5 presents an example similar to the former one, except for the fact that here there is an additional constraint: not only that a certain employee may work on a certain project in one city only, but he may work in a certain city on one project only.[6] According to the mapping demonstrated in this example, the key of **Job** includes references to **Employee** and **City**, and an additional reference to **Project**. An alternative mapping could be identical to the one presented in Figure 4.4.

Mapping of Weak Entity Types

A weak entity type may be mapped to attributes of the class created for its strong entity type, or to a class of its own—depending on other relationships it may have.

Figure 4.5. The mapping of an N:1:1 ternary relationship

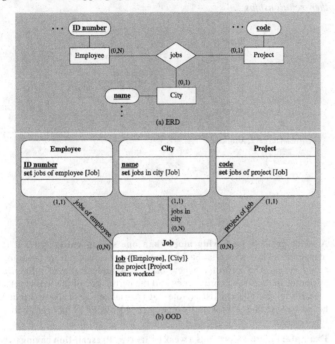

Here are the rules for the different cases:

1. **A weak entity type having one strong entity type and no other relationships:** It is mapped to a set attribute of the class created from its strong entity type. That set may be a tuple if the weak entity type has several attributes. Moreover, it may even include sets it if the weak entity type has multi-valued attributes.

    Example: Figure 4.6 presents a weak entity type **Assignment**, which is linked to the strong entity type **Doctor**. Note the partial key attribute *day* indicating that a doctor may have only one assignment (actually work shift in any day he works). The weak entity type is mapped to *set assignments of doctor {day, from hour, to hour}* in class **Doctor**.[7]

Figure 4.6. Mapping of a weak entity type having one strong entity type and no other relationships

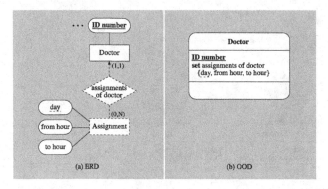

2. **A weak entity type having more than one strong entity type:** It is mapped to a class with relationships to the classes created from its strong entity types. The key of the new class is a tuple made of reference attributes to the strong entity types **and** the partial key of the weak entity type, if such partial key exists. (Note that a partial key is not always needed because sometimes a weak entity type can be identified by its strong entity types only.)

    Example: Figure 4.7 presents a weak entity type **Prescription** having two strong entity types **Patient** and **Medicine,** and a partial key *date*. It is mapped to a class **Prescription** whose key is a triplet: two reference attributes to the respective classes, and the attribute *date*. In addition, the class includes the attribute *quantity*. The multiplicities of the relationships between the new class and the two other are identical to the multiplicities of the relationships in the ERD. (Note that we would have reached the same mapping had the prescription been an N:N relationship between **Medicine** and **Patient**.)

3. **A weak entity type which is also a strong entity type or having also ordinary relationships:** It is mapped to a class, like an ordinary entity type. Its key is a tuple including a reference to the class created from the strong entity type **and** the partial key attributes. If the weak entity type has also ordinary relationships with other entity types, these relationships are mapped just like any other relationship. The weak entity type at the lower level is mapped like any other weak entity type.

Figure 4.7. Mapping of a weak entity having two strong entity types

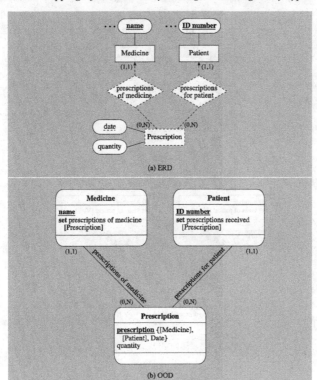

(a) ERD

(b) OOD

Example: Figure 4.8 exemplifies the case of a weak entity type having also a regular relationship. The weak entity type **Visit** is identified by its strong entity type **Patient and** its partial key *date*. In addition it has an ordinary N:1 relationship with **Doctor** (which means that every patient's visit is treated by one doctor only). It is mapped to **Visit** class whose key consists of a reference to Patient and the attribute *date of visit*. In addition, the class has a reference attribute to **Doctor**. Obviously, in class **Doctor** a new set reference attribute is added referring to his/her visits.

Figure 4.8. Mapping of a weak entity type having an ordinary relationship

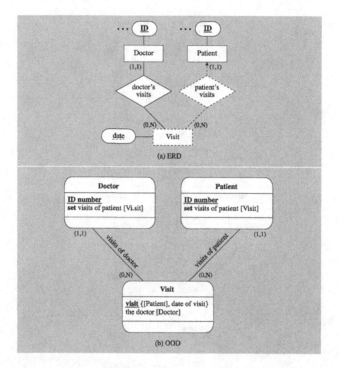

Mapping of Structural Relationships

This section deals with mapping of inheritance and aggregation relationships. Actually, there is no difference between the two models and diagram types in these cases, except for a slight difference in the symbols. Hence, the mappings are straightforward.

1. **Mapping of inheritance relationships:** A subentity type is mapped into the subclass of the class created from the super entity type. An inheritance relationship is defined between the respective classes. If 'Total' (T) or

'Exclusion' (X) constraints are defined in the ERD, they are copied to the class diagram.

2. **Mapping of an aggregation relationships:** An aggregative relationship is dealt with just like any ordinary relationship: The class created from the entity type at the "whole" side of the aggregation contains a set reference attribute for each of the classes created from the entity types at the "parts" side of the aggregation. Similarly, each "part" class contains a reference attribute to the "whole" class.

Due to simplicity of these mappings, no examples are shown.

Examples and Exercises on the Mapping of ERDs into Class Diagrams

In this section we present examples for the mapping of ERDs to class diagrams. For each example we show: (1) a narrative description of the users' requirements; this description is brought only to ease comprehension of the ERD; (2) the ERD created for these requirements. It must be noted that we present only one possible ERD for any given example; as we know, sometimes more than one (correct) ERD is possible;[8] and (3) the class diagram obtained according to the mapping rules.

The reader is asked to treat the examples as self-practice exercises. This means that before looking at the class diagram of each example, the reader is expected to review the ERD and create his/her own solution by applying the mapping rules; and only then compare his/her solution with the one presented in the book.

Example A: Clinic

We have to create a data model for a clinic information system (IS) that will record and provide information of the clinic employees, patients, visits of patients in the clinic, and treatments given to them.

The clinic's employees are doctors, nurses, and administrative workers. Each worker is identified by an ID number and has a name, address, and phone number. A doctor has also a license number (in addition to his ID number as any other employee) and one or more specializations. A nurse has a specialization classification and a role he/she performs in the clinic.

Doctors are assigned to treat patients in the clinic on certain days and hours; a doctor may work only one shift per day (i.e., from an hour to an hour).

For each patient, we record his/her ID number, name, address, and one or more phone numbers. A patient may visit at the clinic no more than once a day and is being seen by a doctor; not necessarily the same doctor in different visits. The doctor who treats the patient writes a diagnosis. As a result, the doctor may prescribe medicines for the patients, including the medicine name, daily dose, and the number of days each medicine should be taken. (Assume that each medicine has a unique identification name.) The doctor may also send the patient for additional examinations (tests) to be performed on certain dates. Each test has a code, description, and a location where it takes place. (Assume that a certain test can only be performed in one place only.)

- **ERD:** The ERD of the clinic is presented in Figure 4.9.
- **OOD:** Figure 4.10 presents the class diagram created according to the mapping rules. Note the way the following issues were dealt with:
  - The ordinary entity types **Employee**, **Patient**, **Medicine**, and **Test** were mapped to respective classes; the subentity types **Doctor** and **Nurse** were mapped to subclasses of **Employee**. (Note that on both the ERD and the OOD there is an exclusion constraint on the participants of **Employees**, but not a total constraint, because there are other types of employees who are neither doctors nor nurses.)
  - The weak entity type **Assignment** was mapped to a set attribute of the subclass **Doctor**. This set is a tuple made up of the three attributes of the weak entity type.
  - The weak entity type **Visits** was mapped to a class because it has ordinary relationships with other entity types. Note that the key of **Visit** contains a reference to **Patient** and *date of visit*. In addition, this class has a reference attribute to the **Doctor** who treats the patient, and two set reference attributes: one to **Medicine** and the other to **Test**.
  - The weak entity type **Visits** has two many-to-many relationships with relationship attributes. We demonstrate the two options of mapping such relationships: The *subscriptions* relationship was mapped to a relationship class **Subscription**, whose key refers to both **Visit** and **Medicine**, and it includes the two relationship attributes *number of days* of *daily dose*. The *examinations* relationship, on the other hand,

Figure 4.9. ERD of the clinic example

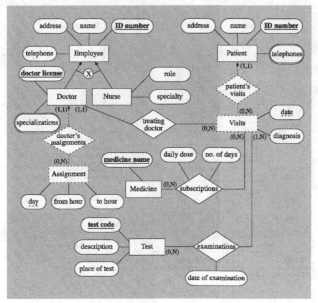

was mapped to set reference attributes of **Visit** and **Test**, each including also the relationship attribute *date*.

Example B: Archeological Excavations and Exhibitions

An IS for the Archeological Commission is needed in order to manage information on excavation sites, discovered artifacts, their maintenance treatments, and museum exhibitions.

Each discovered artifact is given a unique ID number, a description, and a type (category). In addition, the date when the artifact was discovered is also recorded. Over time, an artifact undergoes certain treatments. The treatments' dates and types need to be recorded. An artifact can undergo the same treatment on several occasions and several treatments on each occasion.

Figure 4.10. Class diagram of the clinic example

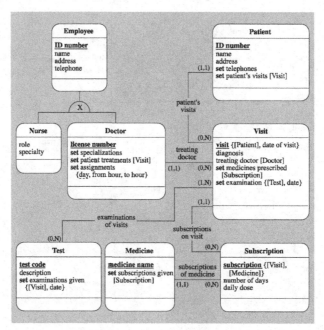

Every excavation site has a unique name and the date in which the excavation had begun. A site is located in a certain region and has a researcher who is in charge of the site. Each researcher has an ID, a name, a degree, and an academic institute to which he/she belongs. From time to time, excavations are carried out in the sites. The date of each excavation needs to be recorded, along with the number of artifacts found. Many researchers can take part in every excavation, and the number of hours each researcher worked needs to be recorded.

The found artifacts are presented from time to time in various museums. Each museum has a unique name, an address, and a manager (assume that he/she is identified by name). An artifact may be presented in a museum for a while. It may be presented in the same museum several times, but it can

Figure 4.11. ERD of the archeological excavations and exhibitions example

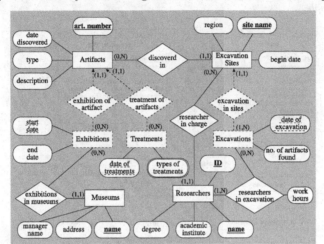

only be in one place at a time. The start and end dates of each presentation of an artifact in a museum need to be recorded.

- **ERD:** Figure 4.11 presents the ERD.

- **OOD:** The class diagram created by mapping the ERD is shown in Figure 4.12. Here are several clarifications:

    o   The ordinary entity types **Artifacts, Excavation Sites,** and **Researchers** are mapped to classes, with their corresponding attributes.

    o   The weak entity type **Treatments** has no relationships with the other classes, so it is mapped to a set attribute *artifact treatments* of class **Artifact**. The set contains two components; one is *date of treatment* and the other is *set types of treatment*. Hence, we have a set within a set; this enables recording several types of treatments on the same date.

    o   The weak entity type **Exhibitions** has a regular relationship with **Museums**. Therefore, it was mapped to a class. Its key consists of two attributes: a reference to **Artifact**, and *start date*: These two are

Figure 4.12. Class diagram of the archeological excavations and exhibitions example

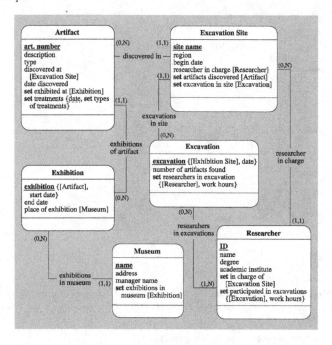

sufficient to identify each exhibition of an artifact, no matter where it is. The class also has a simple attribute *end date* (hence each exhibition has one beginning date and one end date associated with it), and a reference attribute to **Museum**.

o   The way of dealing with the weak entity type **Excavations** is similar to the case of **Exhibitions**. Note that the type of relationship between Excavations and **Researchers** is many-to-many, and therefore we get sets (*took part in excavations* and *participants*) in each of the respective classes, referring to the other class. In addition, the relationship attribute *work hours* also exists.[9]

Figure 4.13. ERD of the travel agency example

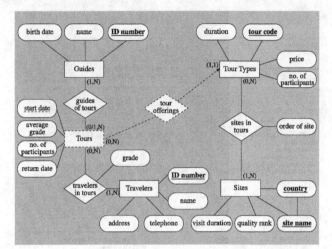

Example C: Travel Agency

A travel agency needs an IS to manage information on its guided tours, guides, and travelers. The agency plans different tour types. Each trip type is identified by a code, and it has duration (number of days), a price (per traveler), a max number of participants, and a list of sites that will be visited in the tour, including the order of their visit (e.g., 1ˢᵗ, 2ⁿᵈ, etc.). A certain site may be included in various tour types. Each site is located in a certain country and has a name which is unique in its country (but in different countries there may be sites with the same name). Each site also has a recommended duration of visit (hours) and a quality rank.

The agency offers tours throughout the year. The same tour type may be offered many times, but no more than one tour of a certain type may commence on the same day. Several guides may be assigned to guide each tour. A guide has an ID number, name, and birth date. For each participant (customer) of a tour the following details need to be recorded: ID number, name, address, and phone number. At the end of a tour, each participant is asked to grade his/her level of satisfaction from the tour. Each participant's grade and the average grade of all participants are recorded.

Figure 4.14. Class diagram of the travel agency example

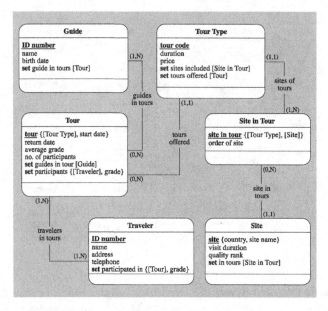

- **ERD:** Figure 4.13 presents the ERD.
- **OOD:** The class diagram created by mapping the ERD is shown in Figure 4.14.

Example D: Parliament

An IS needs to be created for a Parliament, purposed to manage information on parliament members (PM), parties, parliament committees, governments, coalitions, parliament sessions, and committee meetings. The system will not only serve the present Parliament, but also those to come.

A PM has an ID number, a name, a birth date, a profession, and a party to which he/she belongs. A certain individual may be a PM for several terms. He/she may be a member of only one party while being in a certain parliament, but he/she may change a party when a new parliament is elected. A record of the number of parliament sessions each PM attends is kept, along with the total number of bills he/she presented and the number of queries he/she submitted. The information on the participation and activity of each PM is kept until a new parliament is elected. At that point this information is erased, and recording of participation and activities for PMs in the new parliament begins.

Each party has a code, name, and establishment date. A party has a chairman who must be also a member of the present parliament. A party can be represented in many parliament terms. A record of the PMs of every parliament and their parties is kept. A record is also kept of the number of PMs of each party in every parliament term, along with the number of the registered party members and the number of votes the party received in the elections.

A parliament is identified by a number, and it also has a date when it is sworn in and a speaker (chair or parliament). The speaker may be replaced during the parliament's term, and records need to be kept on the beginning and end date of each speaker's term. (Assume that a speaker cannot serve more than once during the same term.) The Parliament holds sessions; each session is held at a certain date, and there cannot be more than one session on the same date. Every session has one chair of session.

Several committees are operating in the parliament. A committee is identified by name and it has several PM numbers, whose number may change from term to term. A PM may be a member of several committees, and in each committee he/she may have a certain role, for example, chair, vice chair, secretary, or just member.

A government is identified by a number and it is sworn in at a certain date. The prime minister is head of the government for its entire term. This means that replacing the prime minister causes the establishment of a new government (but not necessarily elections for the parliament). Several governments may be established throughout a certain parliament's term, with a different or the same prime minister. Certain parties form coalitions. (A coalition consists of parties who take part in a government.) A party may join and leave a coalition several times throughout a term of a government, and the dates of joining and leaving are registered.

Figure 4.15. ERD of the parliament example

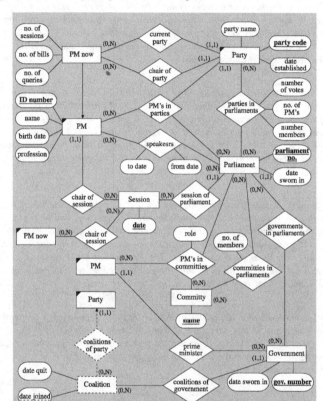

- **ERD:** The ERD is presented in Figure 4.15.[10]
- **OOD:** Since this example is relatively large, it is impossible to display a clear class diagram on one page. Therefore, the solution is presented in two complimentary forms:
  1. **A "Skeleton" class diagram:** The diagram presented in Figure 4.16 only shows the classes and relationships, but not the attributes. This

way it is possible to present a "compact" diagram for a nontrivial problem.

2. **An objects schema:** The objects schema that follows specifies the classes and their attributes. For brevity, we do not detail the data type definitions and the inverse of the reference attributes.

Objects Schema of Parliament

Class: PM   *(parliament member)*

    Attributes {

        <u>*ID number*</u>

        birth date

        profession

        set PM in parliaments [PM in Parliament]

        set speaker of parliaments {[Parliament], from date, to date}

        set prime minister of [Government]

        set member of committees [PM in Committee]

        set chair of parliament sessions [Session]

    }

Class: PM Now Inherits PM

    Attributes {

        number of sessions attended

        number of bills proposed

        number of queries asked

        member of party [Party]

        chairperson of party [Party]

        set sessions attended [Session]

    }

Class: Party

    Attributes {

        <u>*party code*</u>

        party name

        date established

        set current PM's of today [PM Now]

        set PMs in parliaments [PM in Parliament]

        chair of party [PM Now]

        set acted in parliaments [PM in Parliament]

        set party in coalitions [Coalition]

    }

Class: Parliament
    Attributes {

        parliament number
        date sworn in
        set parties in parliament [Party in Parliament]
        set members of parliament [PM in Parliament]
        set governments in parliament [Government]
        set speakers {[PM], from date, to date}
        set committees of parliament {[Committee], no. of members}
        set parliament sessions [Session]
    }

Class: Party in Parliament
    Attributes {

        party in parliament {[Party], [Parliament]}
        number of PMs
        number of votes
        number of members
    }

Class: PM in Parliament
    Attributes {

        PM in parliament {[PM], [Parliament]}
        in party [party]
    }

Class: Government
    Attributes {

        government number
        governed during parliament [Parliament]
        date sworn in
        prime minister [PM]
        set coalitions of government [Coalition]
    }

Class: Coalition
    Attributes {

        coalition {[Party], date joined}
        of government [Government]
        date quit coalition
    }
Class: Session

Figure 4.16. A skeletal class diagram of the parliament example

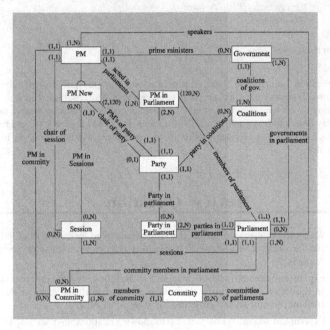

Attributes {

    session date

    held during parliament [Parliament]

    chair of session [PM Now]

    set PM's in Session [PM Now]

  }

Class: Committee

    Attributes {

        committee name

        set acted in parliaments {[Parliament], no. of members}

        set committee members [PM in Committee]

    }

Class: PM in Committee

Attributes {

    <u>*PM in committee*</u> *{[PM], [Parliament], [Committee]}*

    role in committee

}

End of Parliament schema.

As mention before, this form of presentation is appropriate for real-size schemas. If a computer aided software engineering (CASE) tool is used for the creation of the class diagram, it may be assumed that such tool enables us to display a skeleton diagram, similar to the one presented in Figure 4.16, and to "zoom" in on a class chosen by the user by opening a window detailing its attributes.

Review Questions

1. What can be the reasons for an analyst/designer to prefer creating an ERD and then map it to a class diagram rather than create a class diagram "directly?"

2. Explain and exemplify how to map each of the following attribute types to an equivalent construct in a class diagram: a simple attribute; a complex attribute; a multi-valued attribute; and a key of an entity.

3. Explain and exemplify how to map the following relationship types: one-to-one; one-to-many; and many-to-many with no relationship attributes.

4. Explain and exemplify two options for mapping a many-to-many relationship with relationship attributes.

5. Explain and exemplify the mapping of each of the following ternary relationships: N:N:N; N:N:1; and N:1:1.

6. Explain and exemplify the mapping of the following weak entity types: (1) the weak entity type has one strong entity type and no other relationships; (2) the weak entity type has two strong entity types and a partial key; and (3) the weak entity type has one strong entity type which is also a weak entity type.

7. Explain and exemplify the mapping of an inheritance relationship.

8. Explain and exemplify the mapping of an aggregation relationship.

References

Batini, C., Ceri, S., & Navathe, S. (1992). *Conceptual database design: An entity-relationship approach*. Redwood City, CA: Benjamin/Cummings.

Chen, P. (1976). The entity-relationship model—Toward a unified view of data. *Transactions on Database Systems, 1*(1), 9-36.

Dietrich, S., & Urban, S. (2005). *An advanced course in database systems—Beyond relational databases*. Upper Saddle River, NJ: Prentice Hall.

Elmasri, P., & Navathe, S. (2003). *Fundamentals of database systems* (4th ed.). Boston: Addison Wesley.

Garcia-Molina, H., Ullman, J., & Widom, J. (2002). *Database systems—The complete book*. Upper Saddle River, NJ: Prentice Hall.

Shoval, P. (1998). *Planning, analysis and design of information systems* (Vols. 1-3). Tel-Aviv, Israel: Open University Press.

Shoval, P., & Frumermann, I. (1994). OO and EER conceptual schemas: A comparison of use comprehension. *Journal of Database Management, 5*(4), 28-38.

Shoval, P., & Shiran, S. (1997). Entity-relationship and object oriented data modeling—An experimental comparison of design quality. *Data & Knowledge-Engineering, 21,* 297-315.

Thalheim, B. (2000). *Entity-relationship modeling: Foundations of database technology*. Berlin; New York: Springer.

Endnotes

[1]   The ER model was created by Chen (1976) and since then it was in widespread use and had many extensions and variations. The model is described in numerous books and papers in the areas of database design and systems analysis and design. A few sources are: Batini, Ceri, and Navathe (1992), Dietrich and Urban (2005), Elmasri and Navathe (2003), Garcial-Molina, Ullman, and Widom (2002), Shoval (1998), and Thalheim (2000).

[2]   More details on the findings of these researches can be found in the references listed in footnote one.

[3]   Because each object of the relationship-class must be connected to exactly one object of each of the classes it connects.

[4]   This constraint may not be realistic; it is given only to exemplify the mapping of a N:N:1 relationship.

[5]   By analogy to the relational model, this is a situation of two candidate keys, in which any of the two attributes may be defined as primary key.

[6]   Again it must be noted that these "strange" constraints have been invented only to be able to demonstrate the mapping rule. In reality N:1:1 and N:N:1 are vary rare.

[7]   Note that if we want to permit more than one assignment/shift per day, the partial key, in both the ERD and the OOD would be *day* and *from hour*.

[8]   The reader is encouraged to read the narrative descriptions and then create the respective ERDs by himself/herself before looking at the ERDs provided here.

[9]   The reader is welcome to propose an alternative solution, using a relationship-class.

[10]   The black triangle in an entity's left corner indicates that it appears more than once in the diagram. This enables us to shorten lines and avoid crossing lines.

Chapter V

Mapping Class Diagrams to Relational Schemas

This chapter first explains the need to map a class diagram to a relational schema. Then, most of the chapter is dedicated to presenting and demonstrating the mapping rules based on which a relational schema (made of normalized relations) is created. The mapping process is demonstrated with several comprehensive examples.

Why Map a Class Diagram to a Relational Schema?

The objects model can serve two purposes: (1) as a mean for planning, that is, to create a conceptual data model of the reality (this model, a class diagram, can be used to communicate between the users and the analysts/designers, similar to the role of an entity relationship diagram [ERD]), and (2) as a means for implementation, that is, the class diagram can be converted to an objects schema and then implemented in an object oriented database management system (OO-DBMS), as a substitute for a relational DBMS.

However, OO-DBMSs are not in widespread use. Although various OO-DBMSs have been developed and marketed (mainly during the 1990s, and mostly by small companies who tried to commercialize ideas created by researchers), they were not very successful. In fact, relational DBMSs continue to dominate the market. A reasonable explanation to this fact is that the big companies in the

DBMS market invested huge amounts on their relational systems and have many customers, and there seems to be little reason to abandon these investments and risk their customer base with the new technology. Another possible explanation is that for data processing systems (i.e., systems serving the business organizational world) there is no real need for a data model which is so different from the relational model. Despite claims regarding limitations of the relational model (see discussion in Chapter I) it seems that the model is adequate for most business-oriented data processing needs. Rather than seeing OO-DBMSs replacing the relational systems, we see that relational DBMSs are being enhanced with certain features of the objects model, thus enabling them to provide specific needs which they were unable to fulfill according to the "pure" relational model. The "new generation" relational systems are called object relational DBMS (OR-DBMS). Here are a few typical object oriented extensions to relational DBMSs[1]:

- **Array (or multi-valued attribute):** A field (attribute) does not need to be "atomic" (meaning, contain only one value), but it can contain several values. For example, in a **Students** relation, it is possible to define an attribute *array phone numbers (3)*, which allows us to save up to three phone numbers for each student (instead of having a separate relation for student phone numbers).

- **Structure (or nested relation):** It is possible to group several attributes in a relation and define them as a subrelation (subrecord, to be exact). This extension enables us to implement set attributes in a relation. For example, in the **Students** relation, it is possible to define an attribute *nested relation registration to courses (course code, grade)*. This enables each student's record to contain a subrecord of the student's course registrations (instead of having a separate relation for course registrations).

- **Methods (or procedures):** In addition to attributes and "simple" constraints (e.g., key, unique, not-null) this extension enables to define methods which perform more complex constraint-checking operations on attributes in one or more relations. (This is actually an extension of the "check" procedure in relational DBMSs.)

- **Internal ID for a structure:** By analogy to object identification (OID) in the objects model, an OR-DBMS enables us to assign an internal ID to a structure (i.e., a subrecord). This enables us to save the subrecord apart from the main record (e.g., for the sake of efficiency), and use the internal ID to refer to it (like a reference attribute in the objects model). For example, instead of saving the nested relation *registration to courses* along with all other attributes of a student, it is possible to save it separately and refer to it (thus enable locating it) using its ID.

Since on the one hand the objects model has become a commonly used conceptual data model (like the entity relationship [ER] model), and on the other the relational model remained dominant in the DBMS field, there is a need to map one model to the other. In the next section we provide rules for mapping a class diagram to a relational schema consisting of normalized relations.[2]

The Mapping Rules

First, we wish to point out that the main problem with objects-to-relational model mapping is that a class is not a "normalized" data structure; it may contain different kinds of attributes (simple, tuples, sets, reference attributes, and their combinations). Moreover, in the objects model there is a possibility of data duplicity (e.g., relationship attributes in the case of many-to-many relationships between classes). Another problem is with keys of classes: Sometimes a key consists of not just ordinary attributes but also or only reference attributes to other classes.

In contrast, a normalized database schema, according to the relational model, consists of "simple" and well-defined relations. A normalized relation has certain characteristics which adhere to certain rules called normal forms (NF in short). Here is a brief summary of these characteristics[3]:

1. A relation consists of attributes; each attribute is of a certain data type and has an atomic value. The key of a relation consisting of one or more attributes. (A relation which adheres to these definitions is considered 1NF—1st normal form.)

2. All no-key attributes of the relation are functionally dependent on the entire key—not just on part of the key (2NF); and not on any other non-key attribute (3NF). (A more precise definition, termed BC/NF, is: every determinant [i.e., an attribute which functionally determines another attribute] is a candidate key of the relation.)

3. There are no multi-valued dependencies between attributes within the key; each multi-valued dependency must be in a separate relation (4NF and 5NF).

In addition to normalized relations, a normalized relational schema defines referential integrity constraints between relations, using foreign-key to primary-key relationships. One or more (key or non-key) attributes of a relation may be defined as foreign-key if there exists another relation (termed "parent" or "base" relation), in which those attributes constitute its primary key.

The mapping rules presented next ensure the creation of a relational database schema consisting of normalized relations and foreign-key to primary-key relationships between them.

Generally, each class is mapped to one relation or more, depending on the types of its attributes and relationships. The mapping process includes going over the classes in the following order:

1. First, we deal with classes which have a key made of a simple attribute, or a tuple of simple attributes.

2. Then we deal with the rest of other classes according to the number of reference attributes included in their key.[4] This means that we first deal with classes whose key contains one reference attribute, then those with two, and so on.

3. When dealing with any class, we first map its key attributes and only then its other attributes—except for the reference attributes which will be mapped separately.

4. Afterwards, we go back and map the reference attributes. The reason for this is that every reference attribute has an inverse reference attribute (usually in a different class) so it is possible to efficiently deal with the mapping of the relationships after the initial mapping of the respective classes is completed.

5. Eventually, we deal with subclasses (i.e., classes which inherit from superclasses) and with classes which are "parts" of aggregations.

Mapping of the Class

A relation is created for the class. The name of the relation may be identical or similar to that of the class. (Usually, in our examples relation names are in plural, while class names are in singular.)

Mapping of the Key

The key of a class is mapped to the key of the respective relation, according to the following possibilities for the key of the class:

- **The key is a simple attribute:** It is mapped to a single-attribute key. For example, the key *student ID* of **Student** class is mapped to the key *student ID* of **Students** relation.

- **The key is a tuple made of several simple attributes:** It is mapped to the key which is made up of the components attributes. For example, the key *course offering {course code, year, semester}* of class **Course Offering** is mapped to key *{course code, year, semester}* of the **Course Offerings** relation.

- **The key is a tuple which includes one reference attribute and one or more simple attributes:**[5] It is mapped to a key which includes the simple attribute(s) and the key of the relation created from the referenced class (we term it "parent relation"). (Note that according to the order of mapping defined earlier, the parent relation has already been created and its key is known.) In addition, that part of the key is defined foreign-key, referring to the parent relation. For example, in Figure 8 (Chapter IV) there is class **Visit** whose key is *visit {[Patient], date of visit}*. It is mapped to the key *{patient ID, date of visit}* of the relation **Visits**. In addition, *patient ID* is defined as foreign-key referring to the relation **Patients**.

- **The key is a tuple containing two or three reference attributes, with or without simple attributes:**[6] It is mapped to a key which includes the simple attributes (if any exist) and the keys of the two or three parent relations created from the referenced classes. In addition, each of those parts of the key is defined foreign-key referring to the respective parent relation. Here are a few examples:

  o In Figure 4.2 (Chapter IV) there is a class **Job** whose key is *job {[Employee], [Project]}*. It is mapped to the key *{employee ID, project code}* of the relation **Jobs**. In addition, *employee ID* is defined foreign-key of **Employees** relation, and *project code* is defined foreign-key of **Projects** relation.

  o In Figure 4.3 (Chapter IV) there is a class **Sale** whose key is *sale {[Customer], [Agent], [Product]}*. It is mapped to the key of the *{customer ID, agent ID, product code}* of relation **Sales**. In addition, each of these attributes is defined foreign-key referring to **Customers, Agents,** and **Products** relations, respectively.

  o In Figure 4.7 (Chapter IV) there is a class **Prescription** whose key is *prescription {[Medicine], [Patient], date}*. It is mapped to the key *{medicine name, patient ID, date}* of relation **Prescriptions**. In addition, *medicine name* is defined foreign-key of **Medicines**, and patient ID—foreign-key of **Patients**.

Mapping of Other Class Attributes

The other attributes of a class are mapped as follows:

- **A simple (ordinary) attribute** is mapped to a simple attribute of the respective relation. For example, *student name* in the class **Student** is mapped to an attribute of relation **Students**.

- **A tuple made up of simple attributes** is mapped to simple attributes of the respective relation. For example, the tuple *address {street, number, city, zip code}* is mapped to four simple attributes in the relation **Students**.

- **Every set attribute which is made up of a simple attribute** is mapped to a new relation whose key consists of two parts: one is the key of the relation already created from that class, and the other is the name of the set attribute. The name of the new relation is based on the names of the set and its class. In addition, the first part of the key is defined foreign-key referring to the parent relation. For example, In Figure 4.1 (Chapter IV) the class **Employee** includes the attribute *set phone numbers*. It is mapped to a new relation named **Employees' Phones** whose key is *{employee ID, phone number}*. In addition, *employee ID* is defined as a foreign-key of **Employees** relation.

Note that **every set of a class is mapped to a different new relation**; hence, a certain class has several set attributes, there will be a new relation for each of them.

- **Every set attribute which is made up of a tuple of simple attributes** is mapped to a new relation whose key consists of two parts, similar to the previous case. However, in this case the second part of the key may include all or only parts of tuple's attributes, depending if tuple includes a partial-key.[7] For example, in Figure 10 (Chapter IV) there is a class **Doctor** with the attribute *set assignments {day, from hour, to hour}* which dictates no more than one shift per day. It is mapped to a new relation **Doctors' Assignments** whose key is *{doctor license number, day}*. The rest of the tuple's attributes, *from hour* and *to hour,* are mapped to simple (non-key) attributes of the new relation. In addition, *doctor license number* is defined foreign-key of the relation **Doctors**. (By the way, had we assumed that more than one shift per day is possible for a doctor, the partial key of the tuple would have included both *day* and *from hour*, and therefore the key of the new relation would have been *{doctor license number, day,* *from hour*} while only *to hour* would have been added as an ordinary attribute.

Mapping of reference attributes are dealt with in the next section.

Mapping of Relationships and Reference Attributes

In the class diagram there are both relationships, signified by labeled lines and multiplicities, and reference attributes in the respective classes; every reference attribute of a class has an inverse reference attribute in the other class (unless it is a unary relationship in which case the reference attributes refer to the same class). A reference attribute can appear in different forms: as a single reference attribute, as a set of reference attributes, or as part of a tuple containing both reference and ordinary attributes—in accordance with the possible types of relationships between classes. The mapping of relationships is as follows.

- **One-to-One Relationship:** This type of relationship is also represented by a single reference attribute in each of the involved classes. The mapping is as follows: the key of one of the created relations is added as an ordinary attribute of the other relation, where it is defined as foreign-key of the first relation. We may randomly choose the relation to which to add the attribute, but it is better to choose the relation which we think there will be fewer records or fewer null values in the added attribute.

  For example, in Figure 4.1(b) (Chapter IV) there is a 1:1 relationship *management* between the classes **Employee** and **Department**, and two respective reference attributes: *manager of [Department]* and *dept. manager [Employee]*. Each of the two classes have already been mapped to a relation. Therefore, it is possible to add an attribute *manager ID* (based on the attribute *Employee ID* which is the key of **Employees**) to the relation **Departments**, or to add an attribute *manager of department* (based on the attribute name *department name* which is the key of **Departments**) to **Employees**. Since there are fewer departments than employees, and only a few employees are department managers (note that the min multiplicity of the relationship in the **Department** side is 0), it is better to add *manager ID* to **Departments**. Hence, this attribute will also be defined as foreign-key, referring to **Employees** relation.

- **One-to-Many Relationship:** This type of relationship is also represented by a single reference attribute of the class at the 'N' side of the relationship and a set of reference attributes in the class at the '1' side of the relationship. The mapping is as follows: the key of the relation created from the class at the '1' side is added as an ordinary attribute of the relation created from the class at the 'N' side of the relationship. This field is also defined as foreign-key, referring to the other relation. (Note that no attribute is added to the relation created from the class at the '1' side of the relationship.)

For example, in Figure 4.1 (Chapter IV) there is a one-to-many relationship *belonging* between the classes **Employee** and **Department**, where 'N' is on the **Employee** side. Therefore, the attribute *department name* is added to the relation Employees and defined foreign-key referring to **Departments**. (A better name for this attribute might be *department of employee.*)

- **Many-to-Many Relationship:** This type of relationship is also represented by a set reference attribute in each side of the involved classes. If the relationship also has attributes, these are included within the two sets (which are actually tuples containing both the reference and the relationship attributes). The N:N relationship is mapped to a new relation (a "relationship relation") whose key is made of the keys of the two relations created from the classes involved in the relationship. Each of these parts of the key is defined as a foreign-key referring to the respective parent relation. If the relationship has attributes (either simple attributes or tuples), they are mapped to respective attributes of the new relation. If the relationship has a set attribute—a new (additional) relation is created for each set, and its key will consist of the key of the aforementioned relationship relation (which will also be defined foreign-key) plus the set attribute.

Note that if the is more than one N:N relationship between two classes, every such relationship is mapped to a different relationship relation.

For example, in Figure 4.1 (Chapter IV) there is a N:N relationship *buildings of departments* between the classes **Department** and **Building**. The relationship is also represented by two respective set reference attributes. In this example there are no relationship attributes. The relationship is mapped to a new relation named **Buildings of Departments** whose key is *{department name, building number}*. Each of the components of the key is defined foreign-key referring to the respective relation.

Another example, in Figure 4.2 (Chapter IV) there is a N:N relationship *customers of projects* between the classes **Project** and **Customer**. There is also a relationship attribute *% of ownership* which is included in each of the respective set reference attributes. The relationship is mapped to a new class named **Customers of Projects** whose key is *{project code, customer ID}*, while *% of ownership* is added as an ordinary attribute.

- **Ternary Relationships:** It should be pointed out that a ternary relationship in reality is expressed in the objects model by a relationship class whose key contains references to the related classes. This means that such classes have already been mapped to relations, and there is nothing else to be mapped. It should be pointed out that every class which is related to the relationship class has a set reference attribute to that class, standing for the 1:N relationship between them (where the 'N' is at the side of the relationship class). According to the mapping rule of 1:N relationships, there is no need to add anything to any of the relations. This applies to all kinds of ternary relationships, whatever their multiplicities.

  For example, in Figure 4.3 (Chapter IV) there is a class named **Sale** representing the ternary relationship between **Customer**, **Agent,** and **Product**. A relation has already been created for each of the four classes involved, including the relation **Sales** whose key is {*customer ID, agent ID, product code*}; each of the three components of the key is defined foreign-key, referring to the respective relation. Note that the relation has two other, non-key attributes: *date* and *price*.

Mapping of Subclasses (Inheritance Relationships)

First of all, it should be pointed out that by now the superclasses have already been mapped to relations. All that remains now is to map the subclasses. There are several alternative mappings. Here are three of them:

- **Alternative 1:** Create a new relation for every subclass (in addition to the relation already created for the superclass). The key of each new "subrelation" is identical to that of the relation created from the superclass (namely "super relation"). The mapping of the attributes and the relationships (of each subclass) is done exactly like in any other class (but the attributes of the superclass are not copied to the new relations). In addition, the key of every subrelation is defined as foreign-key, referring to the super relation. If a subclass has a key attribute of its own (in addition to the key of its superclass), it may be mapped to an ordinary and not-null attribute, or be defined key of the subrelation, while the key of the super relation is defined as an ordinary and not-null attribute, and foreign-key of the super relation.

  It is important to point out that according to this solution; the super relation contains all the common attributes, while each subrelation only contains its specific attributes, plus the key of the super relation. Therefore, it should be clear that the data of each object of a subclass are "spread" (stored) in two different relations: It has a data record in the super relation including the "common" attributes, and a record in the subrelation including the specific attributes. This also means that an inquiry about such an object may involve the two relations (and hence require performing a joint operation).

It must be noted that the relational model provides no means (at the schema definition level) to constraint the population of records across the subrelations, that is, there are no equivalents to the **total** (T) and exclusion (X) participation constraints. Hence, these constraints, if defined in the class diagram, are not mapped and their enforcement is up to the application programmers.

For example, in Figure 2.9 (Chapter II) there are two subclasses, **Undergraduate Students** and **Research Students** which inherit from **Students**. The subclasses are mapped to the following relations (note that the attributes of the superclass are not copied into the subrelations, except for the key):

o   **Undergraduate Students** (*student ID, average grade, sports club*)

o   **Research Students** (*student ID, supervisor ID, subject of thesis, completion date*)

- **Alternative 2:** Add the common attributes (which are in the super relation) to each of the subrelations. This way each subrelation contains all the attributes of the subobjects, and therefore the super relation does not contain records of the subclasses' objects. Hence, the super relation contains only records of objects of the superclass only. In case there is a "total" participation constraint on the subclasses (meaning that there are no additional subtypes of objects besides those in the defined subclasses), the super relation is redundant and should be dropped, because all data about the objects are kept in the respective subrelations.

  Example: In the previous example, the following relations will be created:

  o   **Undergraduate Students** (*student ID, name, address, department name, average grade, sports club*)

  o   **Research Students** (*student ID, name, address, department name, supervisor ID, subject of thesis, completion date*)

- **Alternative 3:** Map the specific attributes of the subclasses to attributes of the super relation. This means that no new relations are created because of the subclasses; only the relation created for the superclass gets more attributes. Obviously, the specific attributes of this multi-attributed relation may have many null values, because it includes all types of records, and for many of them some of the attributes may not be applicable. This is why this solution is not desirable if there are many different subclasses which have many specific attributes.

For example, had this solution been chosen for the previous example, we would have obtained the following single relation:

o   **Students** (*student ID, name, address, department name, average grade, sports club, supervisor ID, subject of thesis, completion date*)

As said, more mapping alternatives for inheritance relationships are possible. As far as normalization is concerned, the alternative mappings provide normalized relations, but each may have some advantages and disadvantages—depending on the specific application and its users' needs (e.g., which queries are typical of the users). More details on this are beyond the scope of this book.

Mapping Aggregations

As we already know, aggregation relationships are considered like ordinary relationship classes. Therefore, the mapping of the classes involved in aggregations is done the same way. For example, Figure 7 (Chapter II) shows a "whole-parts" relationship between **Airplanes** (the "whole") and **Engines** and **Gears** (the "parts"). The mapping of these classes provides the following relations:

*   **Airplanes** *(airplane ID, ...)*
*   **Engines** *(engine ID, installed in airplane ID, ...)*
*   **Gears** *(gear ID, installed in airplane ID, ...)*

Examples and Exercises of Mapping Class Diagrams to Relational Schemas

In this section, we present examples for the mapping of class diagrams to relational schemas consisting of normalized relations and foreign-keys to primary-key constraints. We use examples already shown in previous chapters (such as Chapter I). For the sake of convenience, the class diagrams are brought here once again. The reader is asked to treat the examples as self-practice exercises This means that before looking at the relational schema created from each class diagram, the reader is expected to create his/her own solution by applying the mapping rules; and only then compare his/her solution with the one presented in the book.

Example A: University Workers

- **Class diagram:** The class diagram of this example was presented in Figure 2.10 (Chapter II).

- **Relational schema:** Figure 5.1 presents the relational schema created as a result of the mapping. Here are several clarifications:

  o   The **University Workers** class was mapped to a relation whose key (*ID number*) and other attributes are derived from the class' simple attributes and the tuple *address*. The set attribute *phone numbers* was mapped to a separate relation **Employees' Telephones** whose key consists of *ID number* and *phone number*.

  o   The three subclasses were mapped to three subrelations (according to Alternative 1 of the mapping rules). The key of each of the three relations is based on *ID number*, but we changed the names slightly so as to better define the population of objects in each relation. The **Teachers** relation also has a candidate key *teacher number* (marked by a dashed line above it). Note the foreign-key of each of the subrelations which is also the (primary) key of its relation. This means that the relationship between each of the subrelations and the super

Figure 5.1. Relational schema of the University Workers example

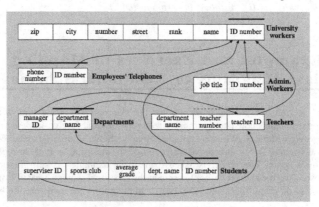

relation is one-to-one, that is, for each record in a subrelation there is only one record in the super relation, and for each record in the super relation there may be no more than one record in each of the subrelations.

o   On the other hand, we chose not to create separate relations for the subclasses **Undergraduate Students** and **Research Students** but rather to map them according to Alternative 3 by adding their attributes to the relation **Students**. Therefore, this relation will have records with null values for undergraduate students (who are not research students) and for research students (who are not undergraduates).

o   The relation **Teachers** has a *department name* attribute because of the N:1 *belonging* relationship with **Departments**; the relation also has this attribute for the same reason.

o   The **Departments** relation has a *manager ID* attribute as a result of mapping the 1:1 *management* relationship between the **Teachers** and **Departments** classes. We preferred this mapping rather than mapping the relationship to an attribute *manages department* in the relation **Teachers** because only a few teachers manage departments, while every department has a manager.

o   Note the lines connecting the relations, denoting a foreign-key to primary-key relationships. The arrow heads point to the primary keys of the parent relations.

o   Needless to say that all the relations in the relational schema are fully normalized.

Example B: Research Proposals

•   **Class diagram:** This class diagram of this example was presented Figure 3.1 (Chapter III).

•   **Relational schema:** Figure 5.4 presents the relational schema created as a result of the mapping. Here are a few clarifications:

o   Like in the class diagram in the relational schema, we too use the acronym PI for principal investigator (i.e., researcher) and CI for co-investigator.

o   The **PIs of Researches** relation is the result of the many-to-many relationship between **Researcher** and **Research** classes. Its key (*research code, researcher ID*) is made of the keys of the related relations.

Figure 5.2. Relational schema of the Research Proposals example

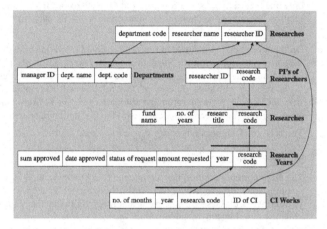

- ○ The key of **Research Years** relations is made of *research code* and *year*—like the key of the class from which it was created.

- ○ The **CI Works** relation is the result of the many-to-many relationship between the classes **Researcher** and **Research Year**. Its key is made of three attributes which are a combination of the keys of the two relations involved: (*CI ID, research code, year*).

- ○ The same relational schema would have been created had we applied the mapping rules on the alternative class diagram of this example, which has been presented in Figure 3.3 (Chapter III). In that class diagram, there is already a relationship class **CI Works**, which would be mapped directly to the **CI Works** relation.

- ○ Had we chosen to refer to the class diagram presented in Figure 3.2 (Chapter III), we could have allegedly gotten a slightly different mapping as a result of the distinction between the **Researcher**, superclass, and the subclasses **PI** and **CI**. We could have mapped each subclass into a relation, but then we would have discovered that each of these relations does not have any attributes other than *researcher ID*, so we would have chosen a different mapping alternative anyway, that is—to group all the researchers into one relation, as presented in Figure 5.4.

Example C: Parts, Orders, and Suppliers

- **Class diagram:** This class diagram of this example was presented in Figure 3.4 (Chapter III).

- **Relational schema:** Figure 5.3 presents the relational schema created as a result of the mapping. Here are several clarifications:

  o The **Parts in Orders** relation was created as a result of the many-to-many relationship between the **Part** and **Order** classes; its key (*order number, part code*) consists of the two key keys of the relations that were created from those classes.

  o The relation **Ordered Parts in Deliveries** is created from three mappings: because of the attribute *set in deliveries {[Delivery], [Order], qty. in delivery}* of class **Parts**, because of the attribute *set where delivered {[Delivery], [Part], qty. in delivery}* of class **Order**, and because of the attribute *set parts per orders {[Order], [Part], qty. in delivery}* of class **Delivery**. It is clear that we obtain only one relation dealing with the details of deliveries, and not three: Because of the symmetry of the reference attributes the same relation is created from the three mappings.

  o The same relational schema would be created had the mapping rules been applied on the alternative class diagram presented in Figure 3.5

Figure 5.3. Relational schema of the Parts, Orders, and Suppliers example

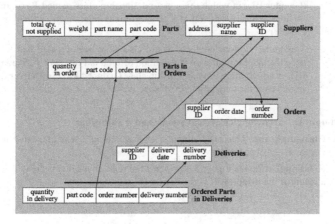

Figure 5.4. Relational schema of the Archeological Excavations and Exhibitions example

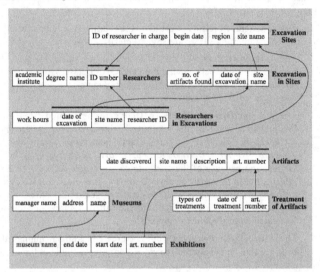

(Chapter III), in which there is a relationship class named **Parts in Orders**, which is in itself in a many-to-many relationship with class **Delivery**.

o   The same relational schema would also have been created had we used the mapping rules on the solution offered in Figure 3.6 (Chapter III), in which there is a relationship class **Ordered Part in Delivery**. In this case the mapping to the respective relation is straightforward.

Example D: Archeological Excavations and Exhibitions

•   **Class diagram:** This class diagram of this example was presented in Figure 4.12 (Chapter IV).

•   **Relational schema:** Figure 5.4 presents the relational schema created as a result of the mapping.[8]

Figure 5.5. Relational schema of the Travel Agency example

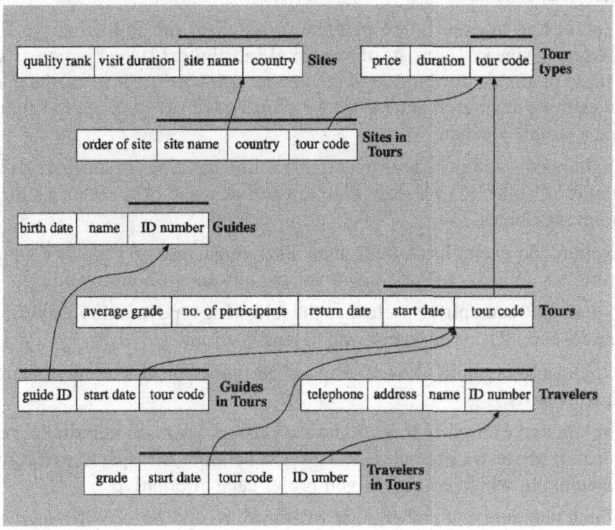

Example E: Travel Agency

- **Class diagram:** This class diagram of this example was presented in Figure 4.14 (Chapter IV).
- **Relational schema:** Figure 5.5 presents the relational schema created as a result of the mapping.

Review Questions

1. What are the main uses of the objects model?
2. Why is there a need to map a class diagram into a relational schema?
3. Which additions from the objects model are included on OR-DBMSs?
4. What are the two alternative approaches to create a relational schema?

5. What is the order of activities when mapping a class diagram into a relational schema?

6. Explain and exemplify the mapping of each of the following types of classes: (1) the key consists of one simple attribute; (2) the key consists of a tuple of simple attributes; (3) the key includes a reference attribute and two simple attributes; and (4) the key consists of two reference attributes and a simple attribute.

7. Explain and exemplify how to map the following types of attributes: (1) a simple attribute; (2) a tuple of simple attributes; and (3) a set consisting of simple attributes.

8. Explain and exemplify how to map a set consisting of a tuple of simple attributes. Which problem may arise and how can it be resolved?

9. Explain and exemplify how to map the following types of relationships: (1) one-to-one; (2) one-to-many; and (3) many-to-many.

10. Explain and exemplify how to map a class representing a ternary relationship in reality.

11. Explain and exemplify three alternative mappings of an inheritance relationship between a superclass and three subclasses to respective relational schemas. In which cases will you prefer each alternative?

12. Which mapping of an inheritance relationship is preferred when there is a "total" constraint among the subclasses? Explain why.

13. Explain and exemplify the mapping of a whole-parts relationship.

References

Dietrich, S., & Urban, S. (2005). *An advanced course in database systems—Beyond relational databases.* Upper Saddle River, NJ: Prentice Hall.

Elmasri, P., & Navathe, S. (2003). *Fundamentals of database systems* (4th ed.). Boston: Addison Wesley.

Endnotes

[1]   The examples brought here are typical extensions to relational DBMSs, but they do not represent any particular OR-DBMS; different systems have

different extensions. For more details see, for example, Elmasri and Navathe (2003) and Dietrich and Urban (2005).

2   By presenting the mapping rules we ignore OO extensions to relational DBMSs. However, if an OR-DBMS implements a certain feature of the objects model, its mapping should be "one-to-one" (meaning, the mapping is straightforward).

3   Here we only briefly summarize the theory of normalization and normal forms. More details can be found in various textbooks on databases.

4   At this stage the key of each class consists of one or more reference attributes.

5   This situation is typical of a class created for a weak entity type (in the ER terminology) which has one strong entity type and one or more partial-key attributes.

6   This situation is typical of the following cases: a class which was created for a weak entity type which has more than one strong entity type, a result of a many-to-many binary relationship, or a ternary relationship.

7   Note the discussion on partial-key of a tuple within a set attribute in Chapter II.

8   No clarifications are provided on this and the next example.

Section II:
Functional and
Object Oriented Analysis

This unit provides a background on the development of the unified modeling language (UML) for modeling systems in the object oriented approach, and also with the reasons for the development of the functional and object oriented methodology (FOOM) which combines the objects and the functional approaches. Most of the unit is devoted to FOOM's analysis phase, which includes creating a data model in the form of an initial class diagram and a functional model in the form of object oriented data flow diagrams (OO-DFDs).

Chapter VI (Object Oriented Methodologies and the UML) reviews the evolution of OO methodologies and UML. Most of the chapter is dedicated to presenting and demonstrating the various techniques and diagrams which make up UML, and then it provides a detailed example of information system modeling using a UML-based methodology.

Chapter VII (Combining the Functional and Object Oriented Approaches: Introduction to FOOM) starts by introducing the motivation for the development of a combined methodology. Then it presents the stages, sub-stages and products of FOOM.

Chapter VIII (Information Systems Analysis with FOOM) elaborates on the activities and products of the analysis stage. The products of the analysis stage include a data/objects model in the form of an initial class diagram, and a functional model in the form of hierarchical OO-DFDs (which are similar to traditional DFD but have data classes instead of data stores). The two diagram types are synchronized in order to guarantee the correctness and completeness of the two models. The chapter presents various examples of diagrams from both kinds.

Chapter IX (Data Dictionary) explains the roles of a data dictionary in the development of the information system and describes its components. The chapter presents a possible implementation of the data dictionary both with the relational and the OO models.

Chapter VI

Object Oriented Methodologies and the UML

This chapter reviews the evolution of object oriented (OO) methodologies and unified modeling language (UML). Most of the chapter is dedicated to presenting and demonstrating the various techniques and diagrams which make up UML, and then it provides a detailed example of information system (IS) modeling using a UML-based methodology.

A Review of OO Methodologies

OO methodologies had begun to evolve in the early 1990s. Some of the famous early methodologies are: object modeling technique (OMT) developed by Rumbaugh, Blaha, Premerlani, Eddy, and Lorensen (1992); Booch Method developed by Booch (1994); object oriented analysis/design (OOA/OOD) developed by Coad and Yourdon (1990; 1991); object oriented software engineering (OOSE) developed by Jacobson (1992); object oriented analysis and design method developed by Martin and Odell (1993); object life cycles developed by Shlaer and Mellor (1992); and object oriented software developed by Wirfs-Brock, Wilkerson, and Wiener (1990). The major thing all OO methodologies have in common is the use of class diagrams for data modeling. In addition to the class diagrams, different methodologies include other techniques and diagram types which enable modeling other aspects of the system. The OMT methodology, for example, includes data flow diagrams (DFD) and state charts,[1] and the OOSE methodology included use cases. Over the years, new OO methodologies (with new techniques) were created, and some have been combined (e.g., the combination of Booch and Rambaugh et al.'s methodologies, and later on the combination of that methodology with Jacobson's methodology).[2]

Many of the OO methodologies were aimed mainly for the development of real time or reactive systems. From a modeling point of view the main concern in such systems is to model events which occur in the external environment of the system, and the required system's response to the events, which also means modeling the possible states of objects in response to events affecting them. Only some of the OO methodologies were aimed mainly for the development of business-oriented (i.e., organizational-managerial) IS. One of the popular early OO methodologies for the development of such systems was OOA/OOD (Coad & Yourdon, 1991, 1991). We use it to demonstrate this type of OO methodology. It deals with two phases of development: OOA deals with system analysis and OOD—with system design.

OOA involves five main activities:

1. **Identifying classes and objects:**[3] This is the main activity at the analysis phase, and from it the other activities are derived. During this activity, all the object classes that exist in reality and need to be included in the system are discovered and defined.

2. **Identifying structures:** In this activity a distinction between two kinds of structures is made: generalization-specification (also termed is-a, or inheritance relationship), and aggregation (also termed whole-parts relationship).

3. **Identification of subjects:** In this activity, which is relevant when dealing with large-scale systems, the main subjects of the sought system are identified, and the various classes are assigned to those subjects. Every subject includes classes which have relatively many structural relationships among themselves and relatively few structural relationships with classes outside the subject.

4. **Defining attributes:** In this activity, the attributes of the various classes and the (ordinary) relationships between classes are defined (besides the structures identified earlier).[4]

5. **Defining services:**[5] In this activity, the functions of every class are identified, and their logic is described. Sometimes, a certain service needs the assistance of another service (in the same class or in another one); therefore, message connections are defined between the calling classes (the sender) and the receiving classes.

These are the main activities of OOA at the analysis phase. OOA does not prescribe that they must be performed exactly in the aforementioned order, and it is even possible to work on some of them concurrently. Moreover, since system analysis is an iterative process, the same activity may be repeated until a "good" model is obtained. At the end of this phase, an OO schema consisting of the five following layers is created: (1) a subject layer; (2) an object and classe layer; (3) a structure layer; (4) an attribute layer; and (5) a function (service) layer. The five layers are described using an objects diagram.[6] In addition to it, it is possible to create a messages diagram which includes only the classes (without their attributes and relationships) in which the names of their services are written, and lines which represent the messages that can be passed between the classes.

OO methodologies usually do not make a clear distinction between the analysis and design phases. The design phase sometimes involves mainly refinements of the analysis products, and addition of implementation-related aspects; sometimes analysis and design are considered as a major phase. Let us look, for example, at the design phase according to OOD (Coad & Yourdon, 1991). It adds the following four activities (or components, as termed by Coad & Yourdon) to the analysis layers:

1. **Problem domain component:** this activity consists of reviewing the products of the analysis phase in order to improve them. Improvements may include changes and additions to the definitions of classes, attributes, services and relationships.

2. **Database management component:** this activity is concerned with the way the database will be implementation. The methodology takes into account the possibility of using a files system, a relational DBMS or an OO-DBMS. Every possibility requires different objects and services in order to deal with data retrievals and updates.

3. **Human interface component:** this activity creates the interface model according to the users' needs. It includes the classification of users, creation of task scenarios and organization of the tasks in a hierarchy. All this is done in order to create a hierarchy of menus that will enable the various users to use the various services offered by the system. Following that, windows objects (containing menus) are added to the OO schema.

4. **Task management component:** this activity involves defining the components of the operating system which are needed in order to implement the information system.

This brief review of the OOA/OOD methodology was brought as an example for an early OO methodology for IS development. Another popular early OO methodology worth mentioning is OMT (Rumbaugh et al., 1992; Rumbaugh, 1995). This methodology provides three models: an objects model, a dynamic model, and a functional model. The objects model deals with the data structure of the system and is expressed by an objects diagram which is actually a variant of an entity relationship diagram (ERD). The dynamic model deals with the various states in which each object can be throughout its lifetime and with defining the transition between those states; this model is expressed by state charts.[7] The functional model defines the various functions carried out by the objects, and is expressed by "traditional" DFDs. Although the methodology enables us to define a system from three different perspectives, each using a different type of diagram, the integration of these models is not well-defined, and the method of integrating the dynamic and functional model with the static model is unclear.[8]

Throughout the 1990s, many other OO methodologies were developed. Some were developed in the academic world; they were described in journal articles and textbooks and used in classrooms and student projects. Other methodologies were developed in the industry (e.g., consulting companies and software houses); such methodologies were actually used in real-life development of systems. The huge number of methodologies, techniques, and types of diagrams caused a lot of difficulties and confusion, including difficulties to learn the different methodologies; incompatibility between the different techniques and diagrams; ill communication between developers and users; and more. These problems encountered by OO developers and developing organizations motivated the desire to create a "standard language" for OO modeling—the UML.

Unified Modeling Language

Object management group (OMG) is a consortium of companies and organizations operating in the fields of computers, software, and related areas whose goal is to standardize methodologies and techniques for the development of software in the OO approach. In the middle 1990s, OMG initiated a request for proposals of a standard language for the modeling of software systems. By "language" they meant visual techniques and notations that will enable OO developers to describe and define the components of the system being developed from various viewpoints and in various stages of development. The standard was meant to tear down the "Tower of Babylon" of techniques and notations that dominated until then, and to be used as a standard by OMG members. As a result of the request, OMG received several proposals from researchers and developers in the academia and the industry. Among them were Booch (the creator of Booch

Method) and Rumbaugh (one of the creators of OMT), who joined forces and proposed (in 1995) a series of techniques that were based on their methodologies. They named their techniques unified method (UM). Later on, they were joined by Jacobson (the creator of OOSE methodology), and together they proposed a series of techniques which they named unified modeling language (UML). UML was chosen by OMG in 1997 as a standard modeling language for OO development. Since then UML has become widely accepted as the "industry standard" for modeling software systems. New versions of the language, including additional techniques, are published from time to time. In addition, computer aided software engineering (CASE) tools which implement various UML techniques have been developed, and many books which offer OO methodologies that implement UML techniques have been written.[9]

It is important to clarify that UML is not a development methodology. It provides various techniques with graphic notations (diagrams) enabling developers to present software system models in different forms and from different viewpoints, but UML in itself does not dictate which techniques to use in the development of an application or the order in which they should be used. Although UML consists of 12 techniques,[10] not all of them need to be applied in a specific development project; actually only a few of them are in widespread use.[11] In spite of its popularity, heuristics, design guidelines, and lessons learned from experiences are extremely important for the effective use of UML.

The 12 diagrammatic techniques included in UML can be classified in three categories:

- **Structure diagrams:** diagrams which deal with the static structure of the system. They describe the system's components and the relationships between them. There are four types of structure diagrams: class diagram, objects diagram, components diagram, and deployment diagram.

- **Behavior diagrams:** diagrams which deal with the dynamic, that is, functional aspects of the system. They describe the system's behavior over time. There are five types of behavior diagrams: use case diagram, sequence diagram, collaboration diagram, state chart, and activity diagram.

- **Model management diagrams:** diagrams which deal with the management and organization of the system's components. There are three types of model management diagrams: package, subsystem diagram, and model diagram.

In the next sections we elaborate on the four structure diagrams and the five behavior diagrams. The three model management diagrams will be reviewed only briefly.[12]

Structure Diagrams

Class Diagram

A class diagram is, as we know, the most commonly used diagram for the description of a system's static structure. It displays the object classes, their attributes, methods, and various relationship types. This diagram is used in all OO development methodologies. Since the class diagram was studied in depth in Unit I of this book, we will deal here mainly with the specific characteristics and notations of the UML class diagram.

A class is signified by a rectangle divided into three parts: The upper contains the class name, the middle—its attributes, and the lower—its functions. Relationships between classes are marked by connecting lines. The multiplicities of a relationship are signified a bit differently from the way presented in Unit I of this book. Tables 6.1 and 6.2 present the UML notations.

Table 6.1. Components of a class diagram

Notation	Meaning
Class Name -attribute : String +doOperation(in Parameter :1 Double: (Integer	**Class:** A class rectangle is divided into three parts: (1) class name; (2) attributes: Each attribute has a name and data type. It is possible to write "+", "-" or "#" in front of an attribute's name indicating its visibility, that is, who may access the attribute;[1] and (3) functions: Each function has a name, parameters, and a data type of the return value. It is possible to write the visibility indicators here as well.
+Role1 -Role2 *..1 5..2	**Ordinary relationship:** A relationship is represented by a labeled line; the multiplicities are indicated at the ends of the line. Table 6.2 details the symbols for the different multiplicities. At each end of the line it is also possible to write the object's role in the relationship.
△	**Inheritance:** This symbol indicates superclass and subclass relationship. The arrow pointed to the superclass.
♦	**Composite Aggregation:** The symbol indicates "whole-parts" relationship. The diamond shaped arrow head points to the "whole" class. The black diamond means that the whole and its parts are one unit and cannot be separated (e.g., a human body and its various organs).
◇	**Shared Aggregation:** This symbol too indicates a "whole-parts" relationship. The difference is that in a shared aggregation the parts may belong to different "wholes" (at different times); that is, it is possible to remove a part from its "whole" and connect it to another "whole" (e.g., a car and its engine and other components).

[1] *These notations are relevant in the programming stage*

Table 6.2. Multiplicity constraints in UML

Type	Notation	Example			Meaning
Exactly 1	1 or nothing	Teacher	teaches	Course — 1	A teacher may teach exactly one course—no more, no less.
0 or 1	0..1	Teacher	teaches	Course — 0..1	A teacher may teach one course at most, or none.
0 or more	0..* or *	Teacher	teaches	Course — 0..*	A teacher may teach many courses (indefinitely) or none.
		Teacher	teaches	Course — *	
1 or more	1..*	Teacher	teaches	Course — 1..*	A teacher may teach many courses, but at least one.
A defined range of numbers	3..5	Teacher	teaches	Course — 3..5	A teacher may teach between 3 to 5 courses.

There are some differences between the UML class diagrams and the class diagram introduced in Unit I of this book; here are some of them: A minor difference is in the min/max notations of the relationship multiplicities. Another difference is that in UML a class may not have a key (because the diagram is meant to model not only data objects, but also temporal objects which reside only in memory; such objects are identifiable by system assigned object identification number (OID) and not necessarily by values of attribute). Nonetheless, UML enables defining key attributes for persistent objects (objects which are saved in the database). As for attributes, reference attributes are not defined in UML; hence, it is assumed that the relationship lines between classes will be mapped to reference attributes at the system implementation stage.

Figure 6.1 presents a UML class diagram of the music programs system for a radio station.[14] Several classes are displayed in this diagram, including: musical piece, listener request, musical program, and actual program (meaning a certain musical program broadcast on a certain date). In addition, there are classes representing the radio station's workers, including technicians and program editors.[15]

Figure 6.1. UML class diagram of the music programs example

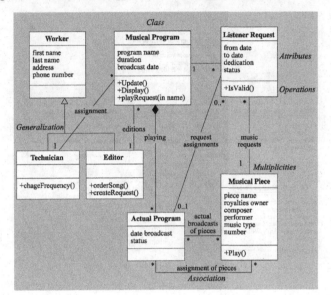

Objects Diagram

An object diagram is similar to a class diagram, but it displays instantiations of classes, that is, certain objects. The objects diagram provides a snapshot of the system's state. The diagram is meant to help the user understand the class diagram by demonstrating states (attribute values) of several specific objects and their relationships. It can also be used by system analysts to test the compatibility of the static model (defined in the class diagram) with the user requirements and the reality it describes. In general, the use of this type of diagram is limited because the class diagram can be verified without it and it might be useful for only a short period of time. In this diagram every object is notated by a rectangle which is divided into two parts: the upper part (headline) contains the name of the object and the name of the class it belongs to; the lower part contains the names of the attributes and their value.

Figure 6.2. Objects diagram for the music programs example

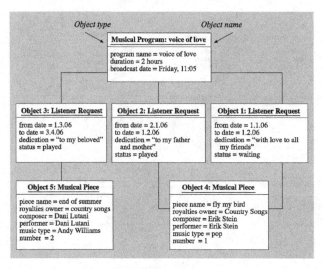

Figure 6.2 presents a possible objects diagram for the music programs example. It shows three listener requests for songs in the program named "voice of love"; two requests are for the same song ("fly my bird"), and the third is for another song ("end of the summer").

Components Diagram

A components diagram describes the physical architecture of the system. It enables us to show how the software components of the system are distributed among independent units, each dealing with a different aspect of the system. The diagram also describes the relationships among the units and with external units. This diagram is useful at the phases of programming and maintenance, but not of analysis and design.

Table 6.3 presents the notations of the components diagram, and Figure 6.3 displays a possible components diagram of the Music Programs example.

Table 6.3. Components of the components diagram

Notation	Meaning
Component	**Component:** Represents one software component in the system which deals with one aspect of the system.
○ Interface	**Interface:** Represents a software component's interface with other components or with the external environment. Every component may have several interfaces, which will be represented by attaching several of these notations to it.
←-------	**Client:** Represents the use of an interface or a software component by a client. Several of these notations can be attached to each component and interface of the system.
☖	**Actor**: Represents every element which interacts with the system's components. Such an element can be a user of the system or an external system which interacts with the system.

Figure 6.3. Components diagram for the music programs example

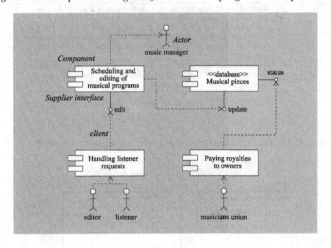

According to this diagram, the Music Programs system is divided into four units: one unit is the database which stores the musical pieces, and the other three units provide services to each other and to external units (using interfaces). A line with a small circle at its end signifies a service/interface that a software component can provide, and a dashed line signifies the use of a software component or an interface by a client.

Deployment Diagram

A deployment diagram also displays the physical architecture of the system's hardware and software, that is, the software, processes, and devices that make up the system. The physical resources (computers, terminals, and various devices) are described as nodes (junctions) connected by communication lines. Clearly, this diagram too is not relevant at the analysis and design phases, but it is especially useful in building a distributed system, where it is possible to divide the run units of the application among several interconnected servers. Table 6.4 displays the notations of the diagram.

Table 6.4. Components of the deployment diagram

Notation	Meaning
Node Name	**Hardware node**: Represents a hardware device. In each box we draw the software components installed in it, similar to the way the software components are drawn in the components diagram. The name of the hardware is written at the upper left corner of the box, and at the lower right corner we write how many hardware units of this type may be used when the system is implemented.
Association Name	**Communication association**: Represents a possible communication between two hardware nodes. Here too, it is possible to specify how many hardware units may take part in an association.

Figure 6.4. Deployment diagram for the music programs example

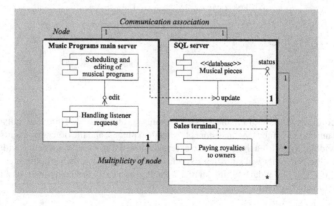

Figure 6.5. An occurrence of the deployment diagram

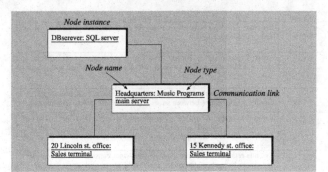

Figure 6.4 displays a deployment diagram for the Music Programs example. The diagram presents a possible division of the system into three types of hardware units: the music programs main server which uses two software components, a database (structured query language [SQL]) server which contains the system's database, and a Sales terminal server which manages the payments to royalty owners. Just as it is possible to create an objects diagram for a class diagram, it is also possible to create an occurrences diagram for a deployment diagram, as shown in Figure 6.5. It is possible to see that there is one main server and one database server, while there are two terminal servers located in two different locations.

Behavior Diagrams

Use Case Diagram

A use case diagram presents interactions between the system and other systems or with the system's users, who are called actors. It describes who will use the system and the ways in which a user will interact with the system to achieve a certain goal. Usually, the diagram is accompanied by a narrative description, which details, in a structured manner, the steps of each interaction. The use case technique enables creating an initial description of the users' needs, so that later on the system's behavior can be defined by using other means, for example,

Table 6.5. Components of a use case diagram

Notation	Meaning
UseCase	**Use case:** An ellipse represents a single use case. The name of the use case is written inside the ellipse.[16]
Actor	**Actor:** Represents every element which interacts with the system. It may be a user or another system which interacts with the system described in the use case.
——	**Ordinary relationship:** Represents a connection, that is, a channel for the transfer of information between an actor and a use case or between use cases.
«uses» ←	**Uses relationship:** Represents a dependency among use cases, that is, one use case uses another one. The use case being used (to which the arrow points) is usually a general or multi-purpose process that can be used by many other use cases.
«extends» ◁	**Extends relationship:** A complex use case, which consists of many activities that cannot be easily understood, it can be split into several simple use cases. In that case, a dependency is created among them. **Extends relationship** specifies the dependency among those use cases: The use case to which the arrow points can only be used by the use case on the other side of the line.
System	**System boundary:** A square represents the borders of the system. Inside the square are the use cases, and outside are the actors who interact with the system. The system may also be divided into subunits by using squares inside squares.

sequence or collaboration diagrams. Table 6.5 presents the components of a use case diagram.

Figure 6.6 displays a use case diagram for the music programs example. The diagram consists of six use cases, divided into two subsystems, each in a separate square: **Assignments and Production** and **External Relations**. This division makes it possible for two teams to develop the system. As can be seen, the **Assignments and Production** subsystem consists of four use cases, including **Edit musical programs**. This use case extends the **Edit radio programs** use case, and it also uses **Handle listener requests**. The **External Relations** subsystem consists of two use cases. The system has a total of six actors.

As said, a narrative description can be added to each use case diagram. Such a description elaborates on the way the process is carried out and provides additional information, such as preconditions, post conditions, and reference to a user requirements document. The use case description is usually presented in a tabular format, as shown in Table 6.6. Table 6.7 demonstrates a description for the **Payments of royalties** use case, which is included in Figure 6.6.

Figure 6.6. Use case diagram for the music programs example

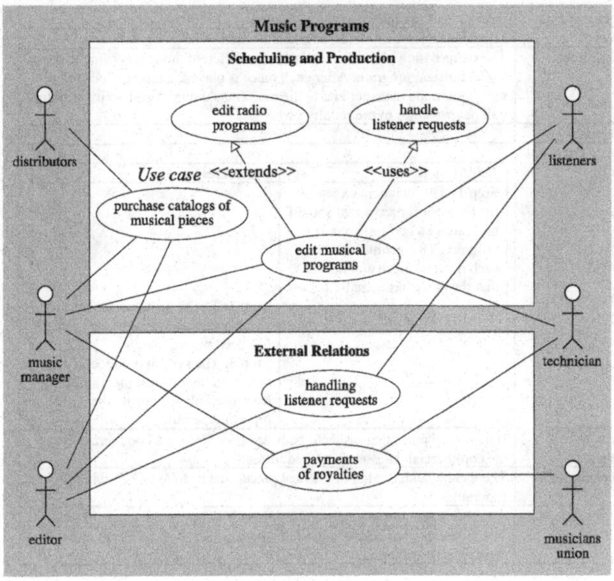

Table 6.6. Format of a use case description

Use case name	In this field we write the name of the use case
Actor(s)	List of the actors who take part in the use case
Description	A short verbal description of the use case and its goals
References	Links to a requirements document and other related use cases
Typical course of event	This is the main part of the use case description. Its purpose is to describe the sequence of the use case's activities. This part is divided into two columns: Actor Action and System Response. The actions performed by external elements are written in the left column, and the actions performed by the system are written in the right. This part may also be described by a sequence diagram. <table><tr><td>Actor Action</td><td>System Response</td></tr><tr><td>Step 1: … Step 4: …</td><td>Step 2: … Step 3: …</td></tr></table>
Alternate course	This part describes special courses of action, for example, dealing with error conditions, which are not described in the general (typical) course of events.
Preconditions	Lists preconditions that must be fulfilled before the use case can take place.
Post conditions	Lists events that have to occur after the use case is completed.
Assumptions	Basic assumptions and other remarks.

Table 6.7. Example for a verbal description of a use case

Use case Name:	Payments of royalties	
Actors:	Music manager, technician, musicians union	
Description:	The radio station plays musical pieces at different times according to the actual musical program. After each piece is played, a report needs to be sent both to the manager and to the musicians union; based on it the station will pay royalties to the royalty owners.	
References:		
Typical course of event		
	Actor action	System response
	Step 1: The technician keeps a list of musical pieces that should be heard in a certain (actual) program. The technician plays each musical piece and marks that the piece has actually been aired.	**Step 2:** The system updates the number of times the musical piece has been played. **Step 3:** The system produces a report on the musical pieces that have been played during the reporting period.
Alternate courses:	If a musical piece that needs to be heard is not found, a commercial from the commercial database is played instead.	
Preconditions:	The technician has a list of musical pieces that need to be heard in the program.	
Post conditions:	A report is sent to the musicians union with a copy to the music manager.	
Assumptions:	The technician has access to both the database of musical pieces and the commercials databases.	

Sequence Diagrams

A sequence diagram describes a scenario of the interactions among the objects participating in a use case. The interaction is described by messages which are sent from one object to another. Sequence diagrams can be used as a means to find out which methods need to be attached to which object classes.

A sequence diagram can be used to describe the interaction between the system and external elements. In such case it is called "black box diagram," and it complements the use case diagram. This diagram describes, for each use case, the subevents it is made of, the order of these events, and the possible reactions of the system to each of them. The only components of such a diagram are the external element and the system.

A more common use of sequence diagrams is to describe the interaction among the system's objects and the messages they exchange. The messages are ordered chronologically. Each participating object has a "life line" (shown as a

Figure 6.7. Sequence diagram of handling a listener request

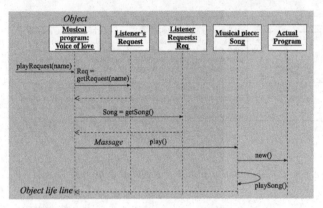

dashed line drawn under the square which signifies the object) indicating that the object is active (alive) during the event. The passed messages are shown by arrows, which connect the different objects' life lines. If a message is sent, it means that the receiving object has the necessary function to perform the required service.

Table 6.8 presents the notations of a sequence diagram. Figure 6.7 presents a sequence diagram for handling a listener's request to hear a musical piece in the music programs example.

Collaboration Diagram

A collaboration diagram has the same purpose as a sequence diagram. However, it emphasizes the interaction between objects in a different way: Each of the participating objects appears as a node, and each message from one object node to another is numbered according the order of its activation in the course of execution. It is possible to pass a message from one object to another only if the two have a relationship in the class diagram. The advantage in presenting the interaction this way is the possibility of arranging the participating objects similarly to the way they appear in the class diagram. This makes it easy to find inconsistencies between the class and collaboration diagrams, unlike in the case

Table 6.8. Components of a sequence diagram

Notation	Meaning
Object Name : Class Name ✕	**Object:** Represents an object in the system. The object can respond to messages that are being sent to it, and it can also send messages to other objects. Inside the square are the object's name and the class it belongs to. The dashed line signifies the object's "life line". It is possible to draw an "X" at the end of the line in order to signify the object's "destruction point".
Message ⟶	**Message:** An arrow represents the sending of a message from one object to another. Usually, a message triggers a function of the target object, and therefore it is possible to write the name of that function (at the destination object), including parameters.

Figure 6.8. Collaboration diagram of handling a listener request

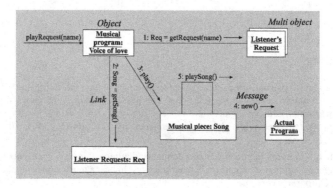

of sequence diagrams. On the other hand, the sequence diagram's advantage is in its ability to express more clearly the times in which messages are passed; therefore it is considered as more suitable for the modeling of real-time systems.[17]

Table 6.9 presents the notations of a collaboration diagram. Figure 6.8 exemplifies a collaboration diagram for handling a listener's request to hear a musical piece—equivalent to the one described in a sequence diagram.

Table 6.9. Components of the collaboration diagram

Notation	Meaning
Object Name : Class Name	**Object:** Represents an object that can receive and send messages. The name of the object and its class are written inside the square.
Object Name :Class Name	**Collection of objects:** A double square represents a collection of objects that belong to the same class.
Message ➡	**Message:** A message is signified by an arrow above a link. Every message has a number indicating its order of activation. As in a sequence diagram, the message name may be identical to that of the function that will be triggered in the target object.

Figure 6.9. State chart of musical piece object

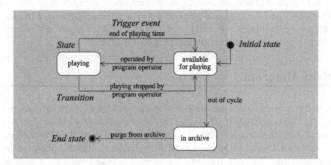

State Chart

A state chart describes the dynamic behavior of an object during its lifetime in the system. An object may be in different states during its life, depending on various events that may occur and change its current state. A state chart presents all of the object's possible states, connected by transition links which indicate the possible events that may occur and hence change the object's state. State charts can also be used to model interfaces, controls, and reactive systems. They are mainly used to model the behavior of objects in real-time systems in which there are real-time events which affect the states of objects. However, they are hardly used in the modeling of IS.

Table 6.10. Components of the state chart

Notation	Meaning
State Name	**State:** Represents a possible state of an object. A name representing the state is written inside the square. Hierarchy can be created among the states by drawing squares inside squares.
when: Event [condition] / Action	**Transition:** Represents transition between states. For every transition it is possible to specify: • The triggering event that starts the transition. • Conditions which define the constraints that must be met to enable the transition. • Actions that will be carried out when the transition takes place.
●	**Initial state:** Represents the initial state of the object.
◉	**Final state:** Represents the object's final state.

Table 6.10 presents the notations of a state chart, and Figure 6.9 exemplifies a possible state chart for a musical piece object in the music programs example.[18] The diagram presents three possible states of the object. The arrows describe the object's possible state transitions throughout its life.

Activity Diagram

An activity diagram can be seen as a combination of a state chart and a program flowchart. Like a state chart, it too describes transitions between states, but here instead of states there are activities. Like a program flowchart, it shows the order of the activities. Unlike a flowchart, an activity diagram is capable of presenting parallel activities. Activity diagrams can be used to model business processes, use cases, or computer programs.

Table 6.11 presents the notations of an activity diagram. Figure 6.10 exemplifies an activity diagram for the preparation of a new musical program.

Model Management Diagrams

Package

A package is a group of well-connected elements belonging to a model. It is usually used to group elements of a class diagram. It enables drawing partial class diagrams containing only those elements which are well connected. This

Figure 6.10. Activity diagram of preparing a musical program

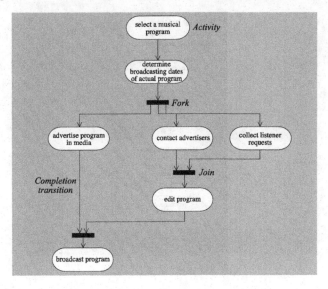

Table 6.11. Components of the activity diagram

Notation	Meaning
Activity	**Activity:** An ellipse represents one activity. An activity can represent a business process, a use case, or a software component. The transition between activities is described by arrows.
↓↓	**Fork:** Signifies the splitting of an activity to several parallel activities.
↓↓↓	**Join:** Signifies the unification of several activities into one.

Figure 6.11. Use cases model

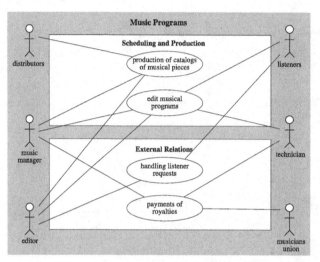

is necessary when the whole class diagram is very large and it is impossible to display all of it in one diagram. Every element in the model can be assigned to one package, so the packages can be displayed in a hierarchical fashion.

Subsystem Diagram

A subsystem diagram enables grouping elements which model the behavior of a certain part of the system. The elements in a subsystem are of two types: (1) specification elements, which define the subsystem's behavior, and (2) realization elements, which specify how the aforementioned specifications elements can be implemented.

Model Diagram

A model diagram provides a certain point of view of the system, for example, a description of the dynamic/behavioral aspects of the system. The diagram includes all the model elements needed in order to represent the system perfectly. The model's elements are presented in the diagram in a hierarchical of packages, where the top level represents the entire system.

UML-Based Methodology: An Example

As we have seen, UML is made up of a variety of modeling techniques, dealing with various aspects of the system. Following UML's popularity and widespread adoption as the "industry standard," many OO development methodologies which utilize its techniques have been developed in recent years and published in numerous books. In this section we present one of these methodologies: The one described in Whitten, Bentley, and Dittman (2000).[19] The methodology deals with the system's analysis and design phases. We elaborate and demonstrate the activities in each of these phases, using the Music Programs example.

The Analysis Phase

As in other methodologies, the analysis phase deals mainly with defining the users' requirements. In this phase the objects and their attributes, behavior, and relationships are being discovered. This is done in four subphases:

1. Creating the system's functional model.
2. Discovering and defining the business objects.
3. Organizing the objects in classes and identifying relationships among them.
4. Modeling the objects' behavior.

Creating the System's Functional Model

The functional model is created with use cases. The use case model describes the system's functions from the users' point of view. The model created in this subphase is termed "requirement use case model." Its creation involves four steps:

1. **Identifying users and use cases:** Using popular techniques for eliciting user requirements (such as interviews, observations, and documents analysis), the various types of users and their business processes are identified.

Based on the findings, a use case list is made. For every use case the following details are written: the use case name, its users' names, and a short narrative description of what it involves. Table 6.12 exemplifies several use cases identified in the Music Programs example.

2. **Creating a use case model:** Every use case is presented in a diagram. It is possible to group several use cases which deal with the same business function into a subsystem. This can ease comprehensibility of the system (especially if the system has many use cases), and provides for several development teams to work concurrently on different subsystems. Figure 6.11 exemplifies the use case model including the four use cases shown in Table 6.12.[20] As can be seen, they are grouped in two subsystems: Program Assignments and Production, and External Relations.

3. **Description of the use cases:** A narrative description is created for each use case, according to the format and example shown in Tables 6 and 7, respectively. At this point the description is general and not necessarily accurate; it will be extended and refined throughout the development process. This first version of the functional model is called "requirement use case model," and it should be approved by the users or their representatives. Table 6.13 provides an example of a use case description, for the use case **handling listener requests**.

4. **Analysis of the use cases:** In this step the aforementioned use case descriptions are refined and detailed. During the refinement it is possible

Table 6.12. Use cases identified in the music programs example

Use case name	Users	Description
Production of musical pieces catalogs	Music manager, Distributors, Editor	Music catalogs are being produced and distributed based on various criteria such as types of music, composers, signers, and so forth.
Editing musical programs	Music manager, Editor, Listener, Technician	Program editors and technicians are assigned to each musical program; the musical programs that will be broadcast during the planned period are planned by the music manager, while the editor assigned to each program will determine which musical pieces will be heard in each program actually broadcasted, depending also on listeners' requests.
Handling listener requests	Editor, Listener	Requests sent by mail from listeners are processed by the editor of the respective musical program.
Payments of royalties	Music manager, Musicians union, Technician	Various reports on musical pieces actually heard in programs are produced (according to different parameters). These are sent to the music manager and the musicians union and will be used to prepare payment orders to the royalty owners.

Table 6.13. Description of a use case

Use case name:	Handling listener requests	
Actor(s):	Editor, Listener	
Description:	The listeners send postcards with requests to hear certain musical pieces. A request includes, among other things, the name of the program, the name of the requested musical piece, a range of requested dates to hear it, and a dedication. The editor feeds the users' requests into the system, assuming that both the musical program and the musical piece exist in the database.	
References:	See the use case model in Figure 11	
Typical course of events	Actor action	System response
	Step 1: The editor obtains the postcards sent by listeners and feeds them into the system.	
		Step 2: For every request, the system checks if the musical piece exists in the database, and if requested musical program exists and will actually be broadcast during the required period.
	Step 3: The editor determines whether or not the requested musical piece will indeed be heard and records his/her decision.	
		Step 4: (a) If the editor decided to approve the request—the system adds the details of the requests to the list of approved requests for that program. (b) At any rate, the system sends an approval or disapproval message to the listener.
Alternate courses:	If the requested program does not exist or the requested musical piece does not exist, the system sends a proper message to the listener.	
Preconditions:	A program of musical programs that will be broadcast during the planning period must exist as well as a database (catalog) of the musical pieces.	
Post conditions:	An appropriate object is created for each listener's request and connected to the actual program in which it is planned to be heard.	
Assumptions:	The editor of the musical program is connected to the system.	

that additional use cases will be defined. Two typical refinements are: (1) a certain use case may be too complex and difficult to comprehend because of the number of activities and conditions involved. In such case it is possible to define some parts of it as a separate use case, that is, to "extend" the use case. The new use case can only be activated by the use case from which it was extracted. This situation is signified in the use case model by an "extends" link. (2) There are cases in which several use cases need to perform the same activity. Instead of repeating that activity in every use case, it is possible to extract and present it as a stand alone use case. This use case may be activated by any of the use cases from which it was extracted. This situation is signified in the use case model by a "uses" link. Figure 6.6, which extends Figure 6.11, demonstrates the two cases: The use case *edit musical programs* seems to be complex; therefore two additional use cases are created: *edit radio programs*, which is assumed to be a more general use case; and *handle listeners' requests*, which represents an activity that may be used by other use cases in the system. Obviously, these changes require not only changing the use case diagrams but also their descriptions.

Discovering and Defining the Business Objects

The modeling of the system's static structure begins by discovering its objects. At this stage, this means discovering the business objects (also termed entity objects or data objects). During the design phase, other types of objects will be added. The discovery of the objects may rely on the use cases and also the user requirements which were used to create the functional model. This subphase includes two steps:

1. **Locating potential objects:** In this step, all use case descriptions are reviewed in search of nouns that refer to business entities or events. This way, a list of potential objects is obtained. In the Music Programs example, in light of the use cases described earlier, the following potential objects can be located:

    *   **Potential objects due to business entities:** radio station, music manager, musical editor, musical programs editor, technician, distributor, listener, musicians union, copyright owners, composer, singer, and performing artist.

    *   **Potential objects due to events:** musical pieces catalog, musical programs catalog, musical piece, listener request, seasonal music program, report on played musical pieces, and financial settlement with the musicians union.

2. **Choosing the right objects:** Not all of the potential objects are "good" business objects; some of them will be deleted or merged. For example, there may be duplicate objects, that is, the same objects have more than one name (e.g., "performing artist" is considered synonym of "singer"); or objects which are not within the scope of the system, or names of objects which should be considered attributes of other objects. This way, for example, it is possible to remove "composer" and "singer" from the list of objects and make them attributes of the "musical piece" object. In addition,

Figure 6.12. Initial class diagram of the music programs example

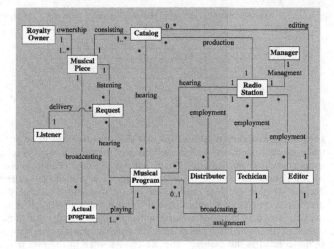

it is possible to consider the "musicians union" and the "copyright owners" as the same object.

It is important to understand that the process of discovering the objects is not well structured and done in an iterative manner. The process usually begins by focusing on the primary objects; then, during the creation of the static model, other objects may be discovered. For example, it is possible to add a new object "actual hearing" (of a musical piece) which has not been identified initially.

Organizing the Object in Classes and Identifying Relationships Among Them

In this subphase the objects are organized in classes, and various types of relationships among them are defined. This results with a class diagram. Here are four steps of this subphase:

Table 6.14. Relationship matrix of the music programs example

Source / Destination	Editor	Catalog	Musical piece	Request	Listener
Editor	-	one	-	-	-
Catalog	many	-	many	-	-
Musical piece	-	many	-	-	-
Request	-	-	-	-	many
Listener	-	-		one	-

1. **Identifying ordinary relationships and their cardinality:** In order to make the identification of the relationships easy, the methodology suggests using a two dimensional matrix with the names of the object classes in both its rows and columns. The analyst examines each pair of classes and decides whether the two need to have a relationship; if so, he/she determines the type of relationship and writes it in the proper cell in the matrix. Table 6.14 exemplifies possible relationships among some of the classes of the Music Programs system. It is assumed that the class written in the column is the "source" and the class written in the row is the "destination." For example, the 'one' in the cell intersecting the column of "request" and row of "listener" means that a request comes from a single listener, while the 'many" in the cell intersecting column "listener" and row "request" means that a listener may send many (different) requests. Note that there the 'one' and 'many' only indicate the max multiplicities.

    After the relationships are identified and defined, an initial class diagram is drawn. In this diagram, the types of the relationships are defined more precisely, that is, they include min and max multiplicities. Note that attributes of classes are not included yet. Figure 6.12 exemplifies the initial class diagram of the Music Program example.[21]

2. **Identifying inheritance relationships:** In this step the class diagram is reviewed in search for classes which have inheritance relationships. As a result, it is possible that a new class is defined as superclass of one or more existing classes. In our example, we can see that "editor," "technician," and "distributor" have the same relationship type with "radio station," so it may be assumed that these classes have some common attributes (e.g., a name, a phone number, and an address). Therefore, it is deduced that they are subclasses of a new class named "worker."

3. **Identifying aggregations and compositions:** This step complements the previous one. Here we identify and define aggregations of classes, that is, "whole-parts" relationships. Recall the distinction between compositions

Figure 6.13. Class diagram of the music programs example including structural relationships

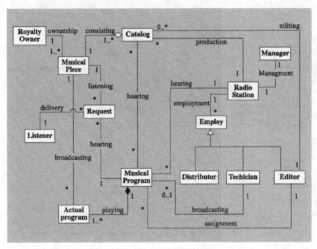

(signified by a black diamond) in which the whole and the parts are always together, and aggregation relationships (signified by an empty diamond) in which the part can be separated from the whole. In our example we can see an aggregation consisting of "catalog" as the whole and "musical piece" as its part (because a musical piece may appear in several catalogs), and a composition consisting of "musical program" as the whole and "actual program" as its part (because an actual program is always apart of its program type).

Figure 6.13 displays the updated class diagram that includes the structural relationships added in last two steps.

4.   **Completion of the class diagram:** Finally, the class diagram is completed by adding the attributes of the classes. In order to find the attributes we must return to the use cases and their descriptions. Figure 6.14 exemplifies the class diagram after having added the attributes. (Note that the attributes of "editor," "technician," and "distributor" are written at their superclass "worker.")

Figure 6.14. Class diagram of the music programs example including attributes

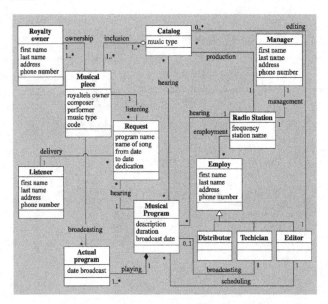

Modeling the Objects' Behavior

The state of an object is the collection of the object's attribute values and its relationships with other objects at a given moment. An object changes its state when an event that affects one or more of its attributes or relationships occurs. UML's technique for defining states and the transitions among them is a state chart. It has already been said that this technique is useful mainly in real-time systems but is hardly used in IS; therefore we opt not to elaborate on it. Note that Figure 6.9 already exemplified a state chart for the musical piece object.

This completes the analysis phase according to the demonstrated methodology. The modeling of the system's behavior and other aspects belong to the design phase.

The Design Phase

In the analysis phase we dealt with the modeling of the data (or entity) objects. In the design phase we add new types of objects concerned with the implementation of the system. One type is **interface objects**, which enable the users to communicate with the system, that is, to make menu selections, feed input, or obtain output. Another type is **control objects**, which contain the process logic of the use cases. Some behavior is neither related with interface objects (i.e., not dealing with the way the users communicates with the system) nor with data objects (i.e., not dealing with the way the data are updated or retrieved), but rather deal with managing the interactions among objects involved in a use case. The process logic of the use case is, therefore, placed in its control object.

During the design phase, the use case model and the objects model need to be improved so that they can take into account the system's implementation environment. This phase consists of three subphases:

1. refining the use case model,
2. modeling the interactions among objects and altering their behavior, and
3. updating the objects model.

Refining the Use Case Model

In this subphase the use cases are modified so that they contain details concerning how the users actually communicate with the system, and how the system reacts and carries out the business function. The way the user accesses the system needs to be explained in detail, for example, by menus, windows, buttons, barcode readers, magnetic card readers, and so forth. Based on these detailed definitions the users will be able to verify that their requirements are being fulfilled, and the programs will be able to code the applications programs. This subphase consists of two steps:

1. **Turning the use case analysis model into a use case design model:** In this step we go over the description of each use case and extend it by referring to the physical aspects of the application. For example, who will activate the use case, what device will be used, what exactly will be the data input and output, what will the error message be, what will every window contain, and so forth. Table 6.15 demonstrates design details for the use case "handling listener requests" that was initially presented in Table 6.13.

Table 6.15. Physical aspects of the "handling listener requests" use case

Name of use case	Handling listener requests
Operator	A program editor who has clearance to feed data into the system
Input device	Keyboard and mouse
The manner of accessing the system	The system will support three access methods: • a graphic client installed in the station's computer and linked to the server who runs the application, • a browser allowing Internet access, and • a terminal presenting textual information.
Input data	See details in Figure 6.15
Error messages	Each of the input fields are to be verified according to its data type, and a proper message is to be displayed in case of an error.

2. **Updating the use case diagrams and their descriptions:** Many changes in the use cases may have occurred during the previous step; it is even possible that new use cases have been created (such as the "uses" and "extends" use cases). It is important to keep all the diagrams and their descriptions updated.

Modeling the Interactions Among Objects and Altering Their Behavior

In this subphase it is important to identify and classify the objects required according to the functionality defined in the use cases and to define the interaction among the objects. This is done according to the following steps:

1. **Identifying and classifying the objects in each use case:** Recall that we have distinguished between data, interface, and control objects. In this step we go over the description of each use case in order to identify and classify the required objects according to the use case's logic/functionality. For every use case we create three lists of objects, according to the aforementioned types. The interface objects will include windows to enable the users to feed in input data and receive messages and reports. The control objects will contain the use case's process logic, and the data objects will include the real-world (domain) objects. For example, here are the three types of objects required in order to implement the "handling listener requests" use case:

    • **Data objects:** listener, request, musical program, musical piece, catalog, editor, and radio station. (Other classes which appear in the class diagram of this example are not relevant to this use case.)

Figure 6.15. Example of an input screen for accepting a user request

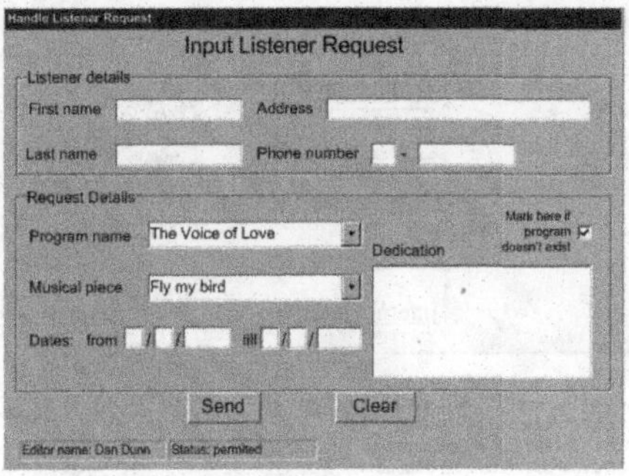

- **Interface objects:** graphic interface, textual interface, and Internet interface.
- **Control objects:** a controller that handles listener requests.

2. **Identifying object attributes:** The object's attributes can be identified and detailed both at the analysis phase (as we did already) and the design phase. In any case, in this step we once more go over all the use case descriptions in order to make sure that all the attributes appearing in them also appear in the class diagram.

3. **Creating an objects interaction model for each use case:** After having prepared the lists of objects (of the three types) for each use case, an objects-interaction model is created, using an objects-interaction diagram. This diagram is similar to a collaboration diagram, but it includes, besides the use case's objects, also its users.[22] Clearly, a user can only be connected to an interface object. The connections between the various objects and their order of execution (as indicated by their numbers) are derived from the process logic description of the use case. Based on these diagrams it will be possible to create a more detailed behavior model later on.

Figure 6.16 demonstrates an objects interaction diagram of the "handling listener requests" use case. As can be seen, at first the user chooses an interface he/she wishes to connect to the system through. Using any of the interfaces, the user can feed in the required input. After being fed in, the data is passed from the interface object to the controller object which

Figure 6.16. Example of an objects interaction diagram

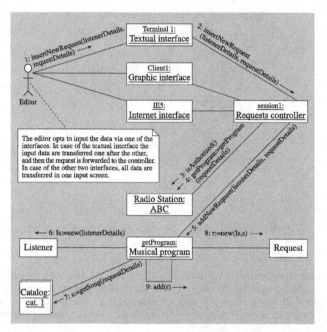

manages the process logic. It first verifies the user's identity and the existence of the requested musical program (by sending messages to the radio station object); then it passes a request to the musical program object to add a new listener's request. The musical program object asks the catalog object to verify that the requested musical piece exists, and then it creates a new request objects.

4. **Identifying the behavior of each object:** After having created an objects-interaction model for each use case, it is possible to define the overall behavior of each of the class objects in the system. This is done according to the following steps:

    1. **Analyzing every use case in order to identify its behavior:** The verbal description of a use case includes verbs and expressions whose

meaning are behaviors or functions that need to be carried out. According to these a list of behaviors is made for the use case; each behavior is given a brief name.

Here is an example of the behaviors/functions needed for the execution of the "handling listener requests" use case:

- add a new user request—insertNewRequest,
- find the musical program which the request needs to be added—getProgram,
- find the requested musical piece—getSong, and
- verify that the user is authorized to perform the operation—isAuthorized.

2. **Assigning behaviors to the appropriate objects:** Based on the objects interaction model it is possible to determine to which objects each behavior should be assigned. Actually, the behavior is assigned to the object's class. Once this step is completed, we obtain a list of functions assigned to each class.

The functions that were added to the classes according to Figure 6.16 are:

- Each of the interface classes was added to the "insertNewRequest" function.
- The controller was added the "insertNewRequest" function.
- The "radio station" class was added the "getProgram" and "isAutorized" functions.
- The "musical program" class was added the "addNewRequest" function.
- The "catalog" class was added the "getSong" function.

3. **Examining the class diagram in order to identify more behaviors:** The analysis of behavior, which is based on the use case description as previously described, will not necessarily find all the needed functions. In addition, the class diagram has to be reviewed in order to look for more functions. For example, a relationship between two classes requires the creation of a function in one of the classes that will be in charge of connecting or disconnecting objects belonging to the two classes.

For example, due to the interactions previously shown we need to add the following functions (that were not identified in the use case description):

- A function named "add" is added to the class "musical program"; it connects a new listener request to the program.

- A function named "new" is added to the class "listener"; it creates a new listener object based on details received from the interface.

- A function named "new" is added to the class "request"; it creates a new listener request object and connects it to the listener's object and to the musical piece object.

Based on the previous steps, Figure 6.17 displays the class diagram that was created during the system analysis phase, along with the functions that were added to the classes due to behavior identified in the "handling listener requests" use case.

4. **Verification:** Many diagrams have been created by the analyst so far. It is important to verify that they are complete and consistent, and that the classes include all the necessary functions. This can be

Figure 6.17. Class diagram of the musical programs example including functions due to one use case

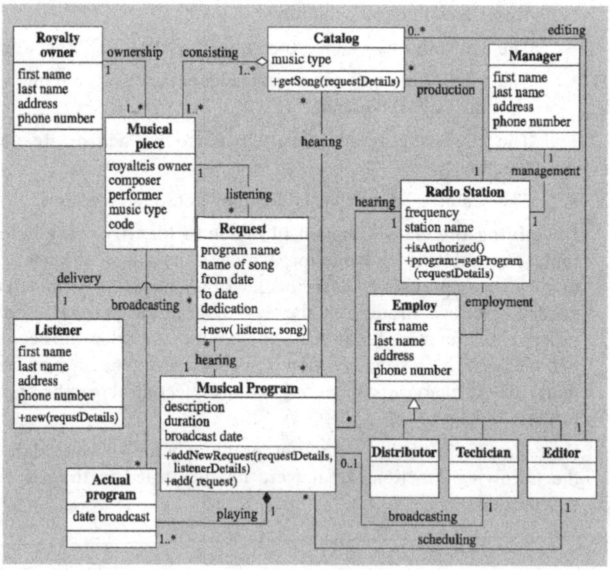

achieved by going over every use case, preferably along with a user, and performing a "role playing": the description of the use case is traced while making sure that every relevant class has the functions which are needed to perform the requirements.

5. **Creating an accurate interaction model for each use case:** Now it is possible to create an accurate model that will show how the objects are going to carry out their interactions in order to fulfill the functionality of every use case. In order to achieve that it is possible to use sequence diagrams or a collaboration diagram.[23] (Examples of each of these diagrams can be seen in Figure 6.7 and 6.8.)

Updating the Object Model in Order to Reflect the Development Environment

At the end of the design phase, the objects model is completed by writing in every class rectangle of the class diagram the names of its functions. The methodology does not require the creation of one complete class diagram for the entire system (presumably because it might be very big), but rather it suggests to create partial class diagrams, one for each use case.

This concludes the example of a UML-based methodology.

Review Questions

1. What is the major component that all OO methodologies have in common?
2. According to OOA methodology, what are the five main activities of the analysis phase?
3. What are the layers of the OO schema?
4. According to OOD methodology, what are the main activities of the design phase?
5. Which models are included in OMT methodology?
6. Explain the background and motivation for the adoption of UML as a "de facto" standard for OO notations.
7. What are the three main categories of modeling methods included in UML?
8. Which techniques are included among the structure charts of UML?
9. Explain the difference between UMLs class diagram and objects diagram.

10. What are the objectives of components diagrams and deployment diagrams?

11. Which techniques are included among the behavior diagrams of UML?

12. Which techniques are included among the model management diagrams of UML?

13. What is the difference between composite aggregation and shared aggregation? Show examples.

14. What are the differences in the notations of multiplicity constraints between a UML class diagram and the class diagram learned in Section I of this book?

15. Explain the different components of the components diagram.

16. What are hardware nodes and communication associations in deployment diagrams?

17. What are "uses" relationships and "extends" relationships in use cases? Show examples.

18. Describe the structure of a use case narrative description. Show an example.

19. What is the objective of sequence diagrams? Explain the relationship between sequence diagram, use case, and class diagram.

20. What are the commonalities and differences between sequence diagram and collaboration diagram?

21. What is the objective of state charts? Explain the relationship between state chart and class diagram?

22. What is a "state" and what is a "transition"? What can be specified for every transition?

23. What is the similarity between activity diagram and state chart? What is the similarity between activity diagram and program flowchart?

The following questions relate to the OO methodology of Whitten et al. (2001).

24. What are the four substages of the analysis stage?

25. What are the four steps in creating a requirement use case model?

26. What is done in the step of use cases analysis? What may be the results?

27. What steps are involved in the definition of relationship types among classes?

28. What are interface objects? Control objects?

29. What are the three steps of the design phase?

30. What is involved in turning a use case analysis model into a use case design model?

31. What is an objects interaction diagram and how is it used to create the objects interaction model?

32. What steps are involved in the definition of the overall behavior of the class objects in the system?

33. Which functions which do not evolve from the use cases can be added to the class diagram?

34. How can it be verified that the various diagrams created in the analysis and design phases are complete and consistent?

References

Booch, G. (1994). *Object-oriented analysis and design with applications* (2nd ed.). Redwood City, CA: Benjamin/Cummings.

Booch, G., Rumbaugh, J., & Jacobson, I. (2004). *UML reference manual* (2nd ed.). Reading, MA: Addison Wesley.

Champeaux, D., Lea, D., & Faure, P. (1993). *Object-oriented system development*. Reading, MA: Addison Wesley.

Coad, P., & Yourdon, E. (1990). *Object oriented analysis*. Englewood Cliffs, NJ: Prentice Hall.

Coad, P., & Yourdon, E. (1991). *Object oriented design*. Englewood Cliffs, NJ: Prentice Hall.

Embley, D., Kurtz, B., & Woodfield, S. (1992). *Object-oriented systems analysis: A model driven approach*. Englewood Cliffs, NJ: Prentice Hall.

Firesmith, D. (1993). *Object-oriented requirements analysis and logical design*. New York: Wiley & Sons.

Fowler, M. (2003). *UML distilled—A brief guide to the standard object modeling language* (3rd ed.). Reading, MA: Addison Wesley.

Harel, D. (1988). On visual formalisms. *Communications of the ACM, 31*(5), 514-530.

Henderson-Sellers, B. (1992). *A book of object-oriented knowledge*. New York: Prentice Hall.

Jacobson, I. (1992). *Object-oriented software engineering: A use case driven approach*. New York: Addison Wesley.

Jacobson, I., Booch, G., & Rumbaugh, J. (1999). *The unified software development process*. Reading, MA: Addison Wesley.

Khoshafian, S., & Abnous, R. (1990). *Object-orientation: Concepts, languages, databases, user interfaces*. New York: Wiley & Sons.

Larman, C. (2002). *Applying UML and patterns—An introduction to object oriented analysis and design* (2nd ed.). Prentice Hall.

Larman, C. (2004). *Agile and iterative development: A manager's guide*. Addison Wesley.

Maciaszek, L. A. (2001). *Requirements analysis and system design—Developing information systems with UML*. Essex, UK: Addison Wesley.

Martin, J., & Odell, J. (1993). *Object-oriented analysis and design*. Englewood Cliffs, NJ: Prentice Hall.

Norman, R. (1996). *Object-oriented systems analysis and design*. Upper Saddle River, NJ: Prentice Hall.

OMG - Object Management Group. Home Web site. http://www.omg.org.

Otero, C., & Dolado, J. (2004). Evaluation of the comprehension of the dynamic modeling in UML. *Information and Software Technology, 46,* 35-53.

Page-Jones, M. (2000). *Fundamentals of object-oriented design in UML*. Reading, MA: Addison Wesley.

Rumbaugh, J. (1995). OMT: The dynamic model, the functional model, the object model. *Journal of Object-Oriented Programming, 7*(9), 6-12; *8*(1), 10-14; *7*(8), 21-27.

Rumbaugh, J., Blaha, M., Premerlani, W., Eddy, F., & Lorensen, W. (1992). *Object-oriented modeling and design*. Englewood Cliffs, NJ: Prentice Hall.

Rumbaugh, J., Jacobson, I., & Booch, G. (1999). *The unified modeling language reference manual*. Reading, MA: Addison Wesley.

Shlaer, S., & Mellor, S. (1992a). *Object lifecycles—Modeling the world in states*. Englewood Cliffs, NJ: Yourdon Press, Prentice Hall.

Shlaer, S., & Mellor, S. (1992b). *Object-oriented systems analysis: Modeling the world in data*. Englewood Cliffs, NJ: Yourdon Press, Prentice Hall.

Siau, K., & Qing, C. (2001). Unified modeling language (UML)—A complexity analysis. *Journal of Database Management, 12*(1), 26-34.

UML - Unified Modeling Language. http://www.uml.org/

UML 2.0 - The Current Official Version. http://www.uml.org/#UML2.0

Whitten, J., Bentley, L., & Dittman, K. (2000). *Systems analysis and design methods* (5th ed.). Berkeley, CA: McGraw Hill.

Wieringa, R. (1998). A survey of structured and object-oriented software specification methods and techniques. *ACM Computing Surveys, 30*(4), 459-527.

Wirfs-Brock, R., Wilkerson, B., & Wiener, L. (1990). *Designing object-oriented software*. Englewood Cliffs, NJ: Prentice Hall.

Yourdon, E. (1994). *Object-oriented systems design: An integrated approach*. Englewood Cliffs, NJ: Prentice Hall.

Endnotes

[1]   At this point we only mention the names of the techniques; explanations will be given later on.

[2]   More on early OO methodologies can be found, among others, in Champeaux, Lea, and Faure (1993), Embley, Kurtz, and Woodfield (1992), Firesmith (1993), Henderson-Sellers (1992), Khoshafian and Abnous (1990), Martin and Odell (1993), Norman (1996), Wieringa (1998), and Yourdon (1994).

[3]   Coad and Yourdon use the term Class-&-Object, indicating that that a class contains objects.

[4]   This is according to OOA; usually ordinary relationships are dealt with together or even before structural relationships.

[5]   More common terms for services are, as we already know, functions or methods.

[6]   The differences between an OOD objects diagram and a class diagram (as learned in the previous chapters) will not be specified here.

[7]   Based on Harel's (1988) State charts.

[8]   More details on the OMT and its limitation are beyond the scope of this book.

[9]   There are plenty of books on UML; here are a few references: Booch, Rumbaugh, and Jacobson (2004), Fowel (2003), Jacobson, Booch, and Rumbaugh (1999), Larman (2002, 2004), Maciaszek (2001), Page-Jones (2000), and Rumbaugh, Jacobson, and Booch (1999). In addition, there are Web sites: UML - Unified Modeling Language. http://www.uml.org/ and UML 2.0 - The Current Official Version. http://www.uml.org/#UML2.0.

[10]   The number of techniques may increase over time.

[11]   For an analysis of the complexity of UML see Siau and Qing (2001).

[12]   The review provided here does not cover, of course, all the notations and rules of UML. More details and can be found in various books and on UML Web sites—see references.

[13]   These notations are relevant in the programming stage.

[14]   In this diagram, as in other diagrams in this chapter, we demonstrate the UML techniques using the Music Programs example without fully describing the user requirements of this system. A full description of the requirements will be presented in Chapter VIII, where the FOOM analysis methodology will be presented.

[15]   This is only a partial and simplified class diagram of the Music Programs example. More detailed diagrams of this example will be displayed later on in this chapter.

[16]   Note that a use case is not equivalent to an elementary function in a DFD; a more precise comparison will be provided in the next chapter of this book.

[17]   An experimental comparison of sequence diagrams and collaboration diagrams is provided in Otero and Dolado (2004).

[18]   The problem description of the Music Programs example does not deal with the possible states of the "musical piece" object; the model presented in the diagram is merely an example.

[19]   This is just one of many UML-based development methodologies. A few more have already been cited earlier in this chapter.

[20]   This diagram is somewhat different from the one presented in Figure 6.6, which includes components which we had not yet dealt with in this example.

[21]   This class diagram is more elaborate than the one presented in Figure 6.1, which merely gave a "first taste" of a UML class diagram.

[22]   It must be noted that this diagram is not part of UML; it was introduced by the creators of the described methodology.

[23]   The demonstrated methodology does not recommend any of the two techniques.

Chapter VII

Combining the Functional and Object Oriented Approaches: Introduction to FOOM

This chapter starts with a brief discussion on approaches to system development methodologies and the motivation for the development of the integrated methodology FOOM. Then it presents the stages and products of FOOM.

Approaches to System Development Methodologies

Many paradigms for information systems (IS) development, particularly for their analysis and design, have been proposed over the years. The functional approach (also known as "process-oriented" or "traditional" approach) was very popular during the 1980s and the 1990s of the 20th century. The life cycle for developing an IS according to this approach is based on the "water fall" model (or variations of it), which distinguishes between certain stages of development which are carried out in a serial manner, with the possibility of iterations between the stages. According to this approach the IS is built from functions (or processes) that are connected in a complex manner, and there are constant flows of data between functions. IS analysis focuses on the identification and definition of the functions and the dataflows.

Common methodologies that support the functional approach are system structure analysis (SSA) for analysis and system structure design (SSD) for design. SSA (DeMarco, 1978; Gane & Sarson, 1979) is based on the use of data flow diagrams (DFDs), which define the functions of the system; the data stores within the system; the external entities, which are the sources of inputs and the destinations of outputs of the system; and the dataflows among the aforementioned components.

Early development methodologies such as SSA emphasized the functional aspects of system analysis, that is, functional modeling, but neglected the somewhat structural aspects, that is, data modeling. This was remedied by enhancing those methodologies with conceptual data modeling methods, usually the entity relationship (ER) model (Chen, 1976), that is used to create a diagram of the data model, which is later mapped to a relational database schema. The role of entity relationship diagrams (ERD) in data modeling can be viewed as equivalent to the role of DFD in the functional modeling. For years, DFDs and ERDs have complemented each other in the traditional development methodologies (see, for example, Hoffer, George, & Valacich, 1999; Yourdon, 1989).

SSD methodology for systems design (Yourdon & Constantine, 1979) is based on the use of structure charts (SC), which describe the division of the system to program modules as well as the hierarchy of the different modules and their interfaces. Certain techniques have been proposed to create SCs from DFDs. But the transition from DFDs to SCs is problematic because DFDs are basically a network structure, while SCs are hierarchical. Despite various guidelines and rules for conversion from one structure to the other, the problem has not been resolved by those methodologies (Coad & Yourdon, 1990).

Architectural design of information systems based on structural analysis (ADISSA)[1] methodology (Shoval, 1988, 1991, 1998) resolved this problem. It uses hierarchical DFDs during the analysis stage (similar to other functional analysis methodologies), but the design is based on *transactions*. A transaction in ADISSA is defined as a process that supports a user who performs a business function and is triggered as a result of an event.[2] Transactions will eventually become the application programs. At the beginning of the design stage the transactions are derived from DFDs (according to certain rules) and the process logic of each transaction is defined by means of structured programming techniques, for example, pseudo code. Based on the DFDs and the transactions, ADISSA provides structured techniques to design the user interface—a menus tree (Shoval, 1990), the inputs and outputs (forms and reports), the relational database schema, and detailed descriptions of the transactions, which will eventually become the application programs.

The **Objects Approach** for the development of IS became very popular during the 1990s.[3] As we already know, in the object oriented (OO) approach the world is composed of objects with attributes (defining its state) and behavior (methods), which constitute the only way by which the data included in the object can be accessed.

While there may be no doubts about the advantages of the OO approach in programming, as it supports information hiding (encapsulation), software reuse, and maintenance, there may be doubts with respect to the effectiveness of the approach for analyzing business-oriented IS (as opposed to real-time systems). Early OO methodologies tended to neglect the functionality aspect of system analysis, and did not show clearly how to integrate the application's functions with the class diagram. Another difficulty with those methodologies was that they involved many types of nonstandard diagrams and notations. The multiplicity of diagram types in the OO approach has been a major motivation for the adoption of the unified modeling language (UML) as a standard modeling language. But UML in itself is not a development methodology; it is a collection of notations (visual techniques), but it does not guide the developer, step by step, to which of its repertoire of techniques to use. Some of these techniques are primarily intended for modeling real-time systems or computer-embedded systems (e.g., state charts) and not business-organization IS. As we saw, the techniques are not integrative; there is some redundancy or overlap between techniques (e.g., sequence diagrams and collaboration diagrams) and it is not always clear which technique to use in a certain situation. The text books about UML methodologies usually present the various techniques and only recommend how to use them for different activities at the developing process. But they do not specify exactly, step by step, in which technique to use when developing a certain type of IS; how exactly does the output of one technique serve as input for another, and so on. It is obvious that the numerous techniques, terms, and notations, and the need to switch from one to another and maintain consistency between them, makes it difficult to learn, understand, and utilize the various techniques.[4]

In conclusion, in spite of the popularity of OO and UML-based development methodologies, there are still doubts regarding the efficiency and effectiveness of such methodologies for analyzing and designing business-oriented (i.e., organizational, managerial) IS. Generally, one might say that the efficacy of OO development methodologies for such systems has not been proven yet. However, OO methodologies continue to grow and change.

Motivation for the Development of a Combined Functional and Object Oriented Methodology

In system analysis we try to model the reality or parts of it from certain points of view. We do so in an attempt to understand, explain, and improve existing systems, or to design new ones. Visual modeling of the reality and its systems is essential in order to establish good communication between the system's developers and the users, and is an important factor in the system's successful development and implementation.

Since the late 1970s, system developers encountered two major problems: one is the gap between analysis and design, and the other, the gap between processes and data.

The **gap between analysis and design** is manifested in an unnatural and unclear transition from the analysis stage to the design stage. In general, at the analysis stage we deal with **what** will the system do for its users, while at the design stage we deal with **how** the system will do it. Although it is obvious that the design should be a natural continuation of the analysis, and the outputs of the former should serve as inputs to the latter, development methodologies often do not follow that properly. Some methodologies do not clarify what "belongs" to the analysis stage and what to the design stage; when does one stage end and the other begin; and more importantly, what exactly to do with the outputs of the analysis stage at the design stage. For example, in the functional approach, SSA did not deal at all with the question of what to do with the DFDs that are its main product; SSD, on the other hand, which primarily dealt with the modular design of programs, tried—with little success—to use DFDs as a starting point for designing SCs. A good solution to the gap between analysis and design in the functional approach was introduced in ADISSA methodology which uses the DFDs produced in the analysis stage and smoothly derives from them the transactions of the system (which later on become programs), the user interface, the inputs and outputs, and the database schema.

OO methodologies have tried to bridge the analysis-design gap by blurring the distinction between them. Some OO methodologies do not determine what belongs to the analysis stage and what to the design; some methodologies consider the design stage as a refinement of the analysis stage. There are techniques that we cannot tell whether they belong to analysis or design and hence different methodologies use them in different stages (e.g., sequence diagrams and collaboration diagrams).

The **gap between processes and data** (or between behavior and structure) could be seen in the traditional development methodologies, which used mainly

DFDs that emphasize process (functional) analysis but somewhat neglect data analysis. A remedy was found when those methodologies adopted ER as a data modeling method, but the two techniques have not been fully integrated. In early OO methodologies the process-data gap has not narrowed—it has grown, mainly because of referring to objects as the primary building blocks of the system, while the processes are "encapsulated" within them. To compensate for this gap, additional techniques that dealt with the functional aspects have emerged, notably use cases. As a result, we have now multiple techniques of all kinds for all purposes, without well-defined connections between them.

It seams that the transition from emphasizing the processes in the functional approach to emphasizing the objects in the OO approach was a step in the right direction, but it went too far; the transition to objects was made at the account of processes. Instead of emphasizing and preferring one approach over the other, the two must be balanced; objects (data) and processes (functions) must be treated "equally" and compliment each other in both the analysis and design stages. There is a need for a methodology that combines the two approaches evenly and closes both the analysis-design gap and the process-data gap.

Review of the Stages of FOOM and Its Products

FOOM for analyzing and designing IS, combines the functional approach and the OO approach.[5]

At the **analysis** stage, the users' requirements are specified in two modeling activities: (1) data modeling, producing an **initial class diagram**, which is a class diagram consisting of data classes, their attributes and relationships—but not methods; and (2) functional modeling, producing **object oriented data flow diagrams (OO-DFDs)**, which are hierarchical DFDs that resemble traditional DFDs, but instead of data stores they include data classes. A by-product of the analysis stage is a **data dictionary**.

At the **design** stage the aforementioned analysis products are used to design the system. The products in this stage include: (1) a **complete class diagram**, which includes additional classes and all classes include their method; (2) **descriptions of methods**; each method is described in pseudo code or message chart; (3) a **user interface** (a menus tree); and (4) **input/output screens and reports**. As said, all these products are derived systematically from the products of the analysis stage. The transition from the analysis stage to the design stage is based on techniques adopted from the ADISSA methodology. The design products enable building (programming) the system in an OO environment.

Table 7.1. Summary of the stages and substages of FOOM

1. Analysis phase	
a) Data modeling	Initial class diagram
b) Functional modeling	Hierarchical OO-DFDs
c) Data dictionary	
2. Design phase	
d) Discovering transactions	Top-level descriptions of transactions
e) Designing the user interface	Menus class and objects
f) Designing the inputs and outputs	- Forms class and objects - Reports classes and objects
g) Creating detailed descriptions of transactions and their decomposing into methods	- Transactions class - Transaction methods and class methods—in pseudo code or message charts

Here are more details about the stages, substages, and products of the methodology. They are also summarized in Table 7.1.

The Analysis Stage

The analysis stage consists of two primary activities: data modeling, providing an initial class diagram, and functional modeling, providing hierarchical OO-DFDs.

The **initial class diagram** consists of data (entity) classes, namely classes that are derived from the users' requirements and contain "real-world" data.[6] Each class includes attributes of various types (e.g., atomic, multi-valued, sets, and reference attributes). Association types between classes include ordinary relationships, generalizations (inheritance relationships), and aggregations (whole-parts relationships). Relationships are signified by links between respective classes and by reference attributes to those classes. The initial class diagram does not include methods; these will be defined in functional modeling and added at the design phase.

The OO-DFDs consist of general and elementary functions, classes (that appear in the initial class diagram), external-entities (providing the inputs and receiving the outputs of the system), and dataflows among them.

The two modeling activities of the analysis stage can be performed in any order. For instance, the analyst may start the process by creating the OO-DFDs (as based on the users' requirements). Then the analyst may continue by creating an initial class diagram—using the classes already appearing in the OO-DFDs. This means mainly defining proper class associations and attributes. Alternatively, the analyst may start the analysis process by first creating an initial class diagram, and then continue by creating the OO-DFDs, using the already defined classes. The initial class diagram can be created "directly" based on the users' requirements or "indirectly" by first creating an ERD (based on the users' requirement) and then mapping it, using the mapping algorithm, to a class diagram.[7] This order of activities may be more appropriate since the data structure elements of a certain reality seem to be more tangible/concrete and easy to define than functions, which are intangible and less well-defined. Yet another possibility is to perform the two modeling activities simultaneously and incrementally. The pros and cons of the two opposing orders of analysis activities have been investigated in controlled experiments, and it was found that an analysis process which starts with data modeling provides better class diagrams and is preferred by analysts (Kabeli & Shoval, 2003; Shoval & Kabeli, in press). Therefore, the methodology follows this order of activities, that is, first—data modeling; second—functional modeling.

At any rate, the two products of the analysis stage are synchronized. This means that it is verified that every class appearing in the class diagram appears also in the OO-DFDs, and vise versa; and that each attribute of a class is updated by at least one function and retrieved by at least one function. This is done with the help of a data dictionary which is also created at the analysis stage. The data dictionary stores various details regarding the components of the OO-DFDs. In particular, it includes details about the data elements of the dataflows connecting the various components of the diagrams. This dictionary will continue to evolve and be used in further stages of development.

The Design Stage

The design stage includes the following substages: (1) discovering transactions and creating top-level descriptions; (2) designing the user interface and adding a 'menus' class; (3) designing the inputs and outputs and adding 'forms' and 'reports' classes; and (4) creating detailed descriptions of transactions and their decomposing into methods.

Discovering Transactions and Creating Top-Level Descriptions

From the user's point of view, a transaction is a process performed by the IS to support a business process he/she has to perform, and it is executed in response to an event that occurs in the real world. From a designer's point of view, the transactions of the system are derived from the OO-DFDs. A transaction consists of one or more elementary functions in the OO-DFDs which are chained through dataflows. The transaction also includes the external entities and classes (rather than data stores in traditional DFDs) that are connected to these functions. A transaction is triggered by a user who interacts with the system, or automatically, on a predefined (timely) basis. The transactions will eventually be transformed and decomposed into class methods.

This substage involves discovering the transactions in the OO-DFDs and creating a top-level description for each of them, using pseudo code. This description specifies the process logic for the transaction, according to its user's needs. (The process logic of a transaction cannot be determined automatically from a diagram, since a diagram can be interoperated in different ways, and only the user, assisted by the analyst, can determine the desired flow of control (process logic).

Designing the User Interface and Adding a Menus Class

A menus tree interface is derived from the hierarchical OO-DFDs in a semialgorithmic process. This process consists of two main steps. In the first step, which is an algorithmic one, an initial menus tree is derived from the OO-DFDs following certain rules concerning general and elementary functions that are connected to user entities. In the second step, the analyst and the user interact and apply heuristic rules and "behavioral" considerations (e.g., aesthetics) in order to improve in the initial menus tree, until the designed menus please the users. Following that, a Menus class is added to the class diagram, whose objects are the various menus designed. The Menus class also includes certain methods enabling the analyst to present the menus and follow the users' selections. Imagine that at run time a certain user operates the system by making selections from menus; the user actually sends messages to certain menu objects. He/she may select a menu item/option which might cause the invocation and presentation of another menu object (submenu), or he might cause the activation of a transaction, meaning an application-specific method which will then perform the desired task (as will be detailed later on).

Designing the Inputs and Outputs and Adding Forms and Reports Classes

The design of the input and output screens and reports is based on the "input" and "output" commands appearing in top-level transactions' descriptions. (An "input" command is created because of a dataflow from a user entity to a function; an "output" command is created because of a dataflow from a function to a user-entity.) For each "input" command an input/form screen is designed, and for each "output" command an output screen or report is designed. Sometimes input and output screens are combined. Eventually, two new classes are added to the class diagram: a forms (or inputs) class whose objects are the input screens/forms, and a reports (or outputs) class whose objects are the outputs screens and reports. The two classes also include certain methods which enable their presentation and accepting the input (for input objects).

Creating Detailed Descriptions of Transactions and Their Decomposing into Methods

This is a primary substage of design in which the top-level description of each transaction is converted into a detailed description, and then the detailed description is decomposed into methods which are attached to proper classes. In the course of that decomposition we distinguish between three types of methods: (1) **basic methods** exist in every data class, enabling the basic operations (i.e., create, read, update, and delete of objects); (2) **application-specific methods** are identified in the transaction descriptions and attached to respective data classes; and (3) the remaining parts of each transaction become a **transaction method**, which is attached to a new class named "transactions." A transaction method can be viewed as the "main" part of the transaction's program. In addition to its internal procedures, it includes messages to basic and application-specific methods of certain classes, methods which have been extracted from the original transaction and associated with the respective classes.

Hence, the designed system consists of transaction methods and class methods which can be activated by messages from transaction methods. Imagine again a user at run time, who wishes to activate (run) a certain application program; at a certain point in time the user selects a menu item which actually sends a message to a specific transaction method (the program's main) and activates it; that method performs, and depending on its process logic, it might send messages to other class methods, who in turn may include messages to other methods of related classes. Eventually, the chain effect terminates and control returns to the menus interface, waiting for further activations by users.

A detailed description of each transaction method and application-specific method can be expressed in two complementary techniques: **pseudo code** and **message chart**. A message chart is similar to a collaboration diagram but in addition to classes and messages involved in the method, it also includes symbols expressing the process logic, that is, selection (branching) and repetition (loop) operations. A message chart is entirely equivalent (from the aspect of the information it bears) to a pseudo-code description presents. Hence, either of the two techniques can be used to describe a method.

FOOM and CASE Tools

One of the advantages of FOOM is that no specific computer aided software engineering (CASE) tools are needed for its utilization. Any software tools which have drawing capabilities can be used to create FOOM's products. In particular, the only diagrams which need to be created are a class diagram and OO-DFDs in the analysis stage and message charts in the design stage. Such diagrams can be created by many software tools.[8]

This concludes the survey of FOOM's analysis and design stages, substages, and products. FOOM does not deal with the stage of construction/programming. However, the products of the design stage are sufficient to enable programming teams to construct the system using an OO programming environment.

Review Questions

1.   What characterizes development methodologies that are based on the functional approach?

2.   How do ERDs combine in traditional development methodologies?

3.   How does ADISSA methodology provide a smooth transition from the analysis phase to the design phase?

4.   In what way did the objects approach change the "balance" between treatment of processes and structures? Discuss the advantages and disadvantages of this change.

5.   Explain the process-data gap. How is the gap handled by the different development approaches?

6.   Explain the analysis-design gap. How is the gap handled by the different development approaches?

7.   What are the three products of the analysis phase of FOOM?

8.   What is the advantage in creating an initial class diagram before the OO-DFDs?

9.   How can ERDs be integrated in the analysis phase?

10. What are the five substages of the design?

11. What is a top-level transaction description and what is it based on?

12. Describe the method for designing the menus tree user interface.

13. What is the basis for the design of the inputs and the outputs?

14. What is the difference between a transaction's top-level description and its detailed description?

15. What is the difference between a basic function, an application-specific function, and a "main" function of a transaction?

16. What is included in the message chart? How does it differ from a pseudo-code description?

References

Chen, P. (1976). The entity-relationship model—Toward a unified view of data. *Transactions on Database Systems, 1*(1), 9-36.

Coad, P., & Yourdon, E. (1990). *Object oriented analysis.* Englewood Cliffs, NJ: Prentice Hall.

DeMarco, T. (1978). *Structure analysis and system specification.* Englewood Cliffs, NJ: Prentice Hall.

Dori, D. (2002). *Object-process methodology—A holistic systems paradigm.* Berlin: Springer Verlag.

Gane, C., & Sarson, T. (1979). *Structured systems analysis, tools and techniques.* Englewood Cliffs, NJ: Prentice Hall.

Hoffer, J., George, J., & Valacich, J. (1999). *Modern systems analysis and design* (2nd ed.). Reading, MA: Addison Wesley.

Kabeli, J., & Shoval, P. (2003). Data modeling and functional analysis: What comes next? An experimental comparison using FOOM methodology. Proceedings of the Eight CAISE/ IFIP8.1 International Workshop on Evaluation of Modeling Methods in Systems Analysis and Design (pp. 48-57). Velden, Austria.

Shoval, P. (1988). ADISSA: Architectural design of information systems based on structured analysis. *Information System, 13*(2), 193-210.

Shoval, P. (1990). Functional design of a menu-tree interface within structured system development. *International Journal of Man-Machine Studies, 33*, 537-556.

Shoval, P. (1991). An integrated methodology for functional analysis, process design and database design. *Information Systems, 16*(1), 49-64.

Shoval, P. (1998). *Planning, analysis and design of information systems* (Vols. 1-3). Tel-Aviv, Israel: Open University Press.

Shoval, P., & Frumermann, I. (1994). OO and EER conceptual schemas: A comparison of use comprehension. *Journal of Database Management, 5*(4), 28-38.

Shoval, P., & Kabeli, J. (2001). FOOM: Functional- and object-oriented analysis and design of information systems—An integrated methodology. *Journal of Database Management, 12*(1), 15-25.

Shoval, P., & Kabeli, J. (2005). Essentials of functional and object-oriented methodology. In M. Khosrow-Pour (Ed.), *Encyclopedia of information science and technology* (pp. 1108-1115). Hershey, PA: Idea Group.

Shoval, P., & Kabeli, J. (in press). Data modeling or functional modeling—What comes first? An experimental comparison. *Communications of the AIS.*

Shoval, P., & Shiran, S. (1997). Entity-relationship and object-oriented data modeling—An experimental comparison of design quality. *Data & Knowledge-Engineering, 21,* 297-315.

Yourdon, E. (1989). *Modern structured analysis.* Englewood Cliffs, NJ: Prentice Hall.

Yourdon, E., & Constantine, L. (1979). *Structured design.* Englewood Cliffs, NJ: Prentice Hall.

Endnotes

[1] ADISSA stands for: Architectural Design of Information Systems based on Structured Analysis.

[2] One can see some similarity between a transaction in ADISSA and a use case in UML. More details on this point will be provided in further chapters.

[3] Some of the early OO methodologies have been mentioned in Chapter VI.

[4] The various UML techniques include approximately 150 different terms and symbols. There are studies on complexity of techniques which showed that UML is much more complex than other system modeling techniques.

[5] FOOM was developed by Peretz Shoval, the author of this book, in cooperation with his doctoral student, Judith Kabeli, while working on her PhD under his supervision. It was originally published in Shoval and Kabeli (2001). Additional publications describing the methodology include Kabeli

and Shoval (2003) and Shoval and Kabeli (2005). The paper Kabeli and Shoval (2005) describes experimental evaluations and comparisons of FOOM with another methodology OPM (Dori, 2002) which combines the functional and OO approaches.

⁶ Additional classes will be added at the design stage.

⁷ As already discussed in Chapter IV, previous research (Shoval & Frumermann, 1994; Shoval & Shiran, 1987) has shown that in some cases, especially when dealing with ternary relationships, an ERD is more comprehensible by users, and analysts can create more correct data models when using the ER model. In addition, an ERD can be mapped easily to an initial class diagram.

⁸ Of course, specific tools which utilize and enforce the specific notations and rules of the aforementioned types of diagrams could be an advantage, but they have not been developed yet.

Chapter VIII

Information Systems Analysis with FOOM

This chapter elaborates on the activities and products of the analysis stage with functional and object oriented methodology (FOOM). The products of this stage include a data/objects model in the form of an initial class diagram, and a functional model in the form of hierarchical object oriented Data flow diagram (OO-DFDs). The two diagram types are synchronized in order to guarantee the correctness and completeness of the two models. The chapter presents various examples of diagrams of both types.

Data Modeling: Creating an Initial Class Diagram

An initial class diagram includes, as we already know, data/entity classes. These classes are derived from the users' requirement and are made up of objects which keep real-world data.[1] For each class in the initial class diagram we only define its attributes and relationships (but not its functions). At this stage we already know how to create an initial class diagram. Recall that there are two alternative ways to create it: (1) "directly"—based on the users' requirements; and (2) "indirectly"—first to create an entity relationship diagram (ERD) and then to map it to an initial class diagram using the mapping algorithm.[2]

In Chapter VII we dealt with the possible orders of activities in the analysis stage and came to the conclusion that it is preferred to start by creating a data model and continue by creating a functional model. Since we have already studied how to create an initial class diagram, here we will only show another example of such a diagram. The example is more detailed than previous examples and involves both data (structural) and functional requirements, because we will use it also to demonstrate functional modeling.

Example: The Apartments Building Information System[3]

An information system (IS) needs to be developed for a company which manages an apartment building. The system will provide information on the tenants, their monthly payments to the company (for maintenance of the building), and maintenance works requested by the tenants and conducted by contractors. Here is a description of the requirements from the system:

Tenant Fees

The IS will be able to store, update, and retrieve information on the tenants of the building and their payments to the company. For each apartment it will store the apartment number, its size (in square meters), the family name living in the apartment,[4] their phone numbers, and the number of persons. Based on these details (and other considerations), the managing company will determine, for each apartment/family the monthly fees for maintenance of the building. The fee may be updated from time to time by the company. The tenants may pay their dues in cash or by check. The system will store the payment details (including the amount, date, and form of payment), and produce a receipt for the tenant. The system will enable the company to retrieve and report on the payments and debts of certain apartments (families) in certain periods (months). At the end of each month the system will produce a report on all tenants detailing the amounts paid and debt (as based on the monthly fees on one hand and the actual payments on the other hand). The total debt of all tenants will be stored to enable easy retrieval. In addition, the system will issue a notification (reminder) on the debt to each tenant whose debt is bigger than a three months fee, or whose debt is bigger than a two months fee but who already received a notification in the previous month.

Maintenance Works

The maintenance works for the building will be dealt with as follows: A tenant or several tenants together may request a maintenance work to be commenced in any of the common (public) parts of the building. For every request the following details will be saved: the tenants who requested the work, the date of request, the description of the needed work, and its type (e.g., plumbing, electricity, and gardening). The system will be able to update the work requests, if needed.

The system will maintain data on contractors who may be asked to perform maintenance works for the building. The data on each contractor will include, among other things, its fields of expertise (e.g., plumber, gardener, etc.) in order to assist in choosing the right contractor for any requested work.

A company officer will be authorized to decide on the commencement of a requested work. He will be assisted by the IS, which will present him the requested works which were not yet dealt with (those that are still in a "proposal" status). The officer will choose one of those requests, and the system will retrieve and present details of contractors who are suitable for the required work. The officer will contact the potential contractors, describe the desired work and ask them to submit proposals. Contractors will submit their proposals, and the company officer will review them, perhaps negotiate with some of them, and eventually will select one of the proposals. It was decided that the IS will not deal with addressing the contractors, accepting their proposals, and the negotiation and selection process. The system will only store the details of the agreement with the selected contractor, including a description of the work that will be done; the beginning and ending dates; and of course, the agreed upon payments. The system will produce printed versions of the agreement: one will be sent to the contractor and one will be saved in the company's files. At this stage, the status of the requested work will be changed from to "in progress," and the building's financial status (i.e., obligation to pay) will be updated.

The contractor will carry out the work and will be paid from time to time, according to the agreement. The date and sum of each payment will be saved, and the remainder of the total debts of the building will also be updated. The system will enable to retrieve and present details of the works in progress. Once a certain work is completed (as agreed upon by the company and the contractor) a completion report will be produced and sent to the tenants who requested the work. The status of that work will be changed to "completed."

Initial Class Diagram

Figure 8.1 displays the initial class diagram of the apartments building IS. Several clarifications follow:

- Based on the users' requirements, it is quite easy to discover and define the classes **Apartment, Work**, and **Contractor** (which include objects of apartments, requested works, and contractors, respectively). Since tenants of apartments may move in and out over time, we opted to refer to objects of apartments, and include relevant details on tenants within the apartment objects. Hence, an apartment as well as a family living in an apartment is

Figure 8.1. Initial class diagram of the apartments building system

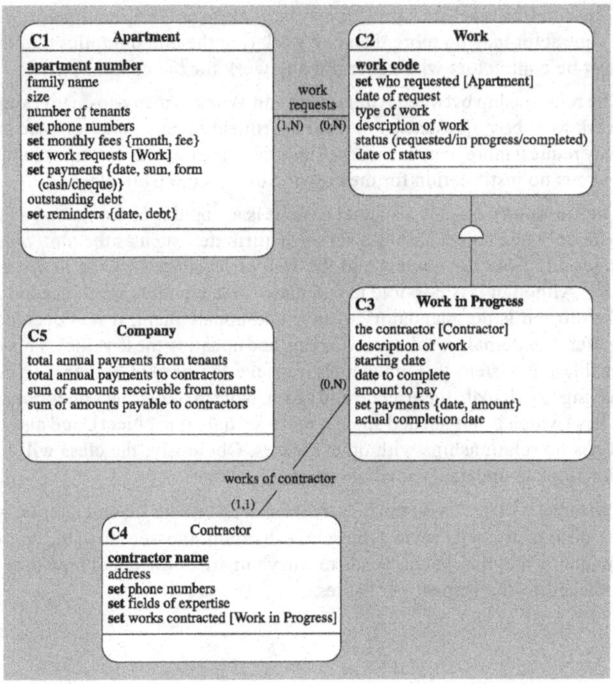

identified by its *apartment number* (and not an ID number or the family name of the tenants).

- Every class is identified (in addition to its name) by a code consisting of the letter "C" and a serial number. This code will also be used later on in the OO-DFDs and in the data dictionary (DD).

- Each requested work is identified by *work code*. This code will be used throughout the lifetime of the. Note the *status* attribute of a work and its possible values.

- The **Work in Progress** class is not as trivial as the former classes. A system analyst may not see the need for this subclass right away, and perhaps only define the Work class, in which he might include all possible attributes of a work, including those related to its actual conduct by a contractor. However, a more thorough examination should reveal that there are enough specific attributes regarding works that are underway to justify the creation of a subclass that we term **Work in Progress**, which will contain those attributes. **Work in Progress** has a many-to-one relationship with **Contractor**: A project may be given to only one contractor, while a contractor may do more than one work (but the min 0 implies that there may be contractors who never did any work for the company).

- The relationship between **Apartment** and **Work** is many-to-many, since a work may be requested by several apartment tenants, and an apartment may request more than one work. Since there are no relationship attributes, there is no justification for the creation of a relationship class.

- The **Company** class is a special case: It is a singular class, that is, a class with only one object having a series of attributes, such as the *total annual payments from the tenants* and the *sum of amounts payable to contractors*. Although it is possible to calculate these amounts when needed and therefore it is not mandatory to save and update them, it was decided to prefer the alternative solution of saving and updating these values. This will enable the system to immediately retrieve the needed amounts without having to calculate them again and again. Note that this class does not have a key (which is not needed since it includes only one object), and also that it has no relationships with other classes. Obviously, the class will have functions to update its attribute values.

- When we will deal with the functional analysis of the IS, and later on with its design, we will review the class diagram and see how the various functions that the system needs to carry out are defined and how they are attached to the respective classes.

Figure 8.2. ERD of the apartments building system

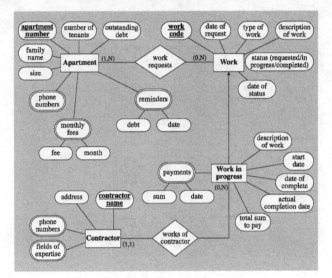

Figure 8.1 displayed the initial class diagram as created directly from the users' requirements. For the sake of completeness, we also demonstrate the "indirect" way to create the data model, using an ERD. Figure 8.2 displays the respective ERD. Obviously, this diagram can be mapped to the respective class diagram, based on the mapping rules learned in Chapter IV.

Functional Analysis-Creating OO-DFDs

OO-DFDs are a graphic mean for the definition of the functions of the IS and the flows of data among them. They are similar to traditional hierarchical DFDs (as, for example, in DeMarco, 1978), but instead of data stores they include data classes. This section reviews the components of an OO-DFD and the rules for the construction of hierarchical OO-DFDs.

Figure 8.3. A schematic OO-DFD

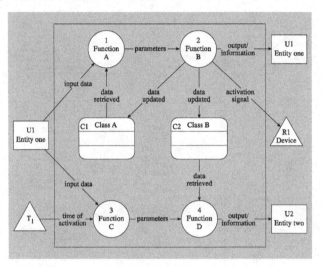

Components of an OO-DFD

The components of an OO-DFD are: (1) function—we distinguish between elementary (basic) functions and general (complex) functions; (2) external entities—we distinguish between user entities, time entities, and real-time entities; (3) data classes; and (4) data flows among those components. Figure 8.3 demonstrates a schematic OO-DFD. In the following sections we elaborate on each of the components.

Functions

A function represents an action that the system will carry out. A function may receive data from various sources, internal or external to the system; it carries out actions which may affect/change the data, and it may produce output to various internal or external destinations. Hence, a function must have at least one source for its input and at least one destination for its output. Data move from a source to a function and from a function to a destination via data flow, which can be viewed as a channel for transition of data. It is reasonable to compare a function to a small computer program or parts of a program which carries out a certain task. As a matter of fact, the functions defined in the OO-DFDs will eventually become programs of the implemented system: A function may become a whole program or part of a program (i.e., a procedure consisting of a set of commands performing a certain task). In other words, a certain function in an OO-DFD may represent a very simple task which the system ought to perform or a very complex one, or anything in between.

The discovery and definition of the functions of an IS are carried out in a hierarchical decomposition process, which starts with the discovery of the general functions and ends with the most elementary (basic) ones. For example, the most general functions of an IS for a marketing chain may be **order products from suppliers**, **sell products to costumers**, and **inventory reports**. Each of these general functions may actually consist of many subfunctions. For example, the **order products from supplier** function may consist of subfunctions such as **determine products to order, choose a supplier, issue an order to a supplier, update inventory in order**, and more. Each of these subfunctions is somewhat smaller/simpler than its parent function. Each subfunction may also be decomposed into even smaller/simpler subfunctions. For example, the function **determine products to order** may be decomposed into the subfunctions **find a product with low quantity, check quantity in order, check rate of sales**, and **calculate quantity to order**. Hence, hierarchical decomposition involves the discovery of the most general functions of the sought system and then an iterative process in which each such function may be decomposed into subfunctions, until all functions are elementary.

There is no exact, formal mechanism to determine if a certain function is general (complex) and hence decomposable, or it is elementary and need not be decomposed into more elementary functions. It sometimes depends on the eyes of the analyst and user who cooperate in the process of functional-hierarchical decomposition. Hence, it is possible to see different diagrams, each with different functions and subfunctions for the same requirements, and it is not always possible to tell which diagram is more "correct." A diagram is correct if it represents correctly and completely the users' requirements; but more than one such diagram may be such.[5]

Despite the possible distinction between different levels of "generality" and "simplicity" of functions, in OO-DFDs we distinguish only between two kinds of functions: general and elementary:

- **General function:** notated by a double circle. A general function is determined by the analysts as complex to some degree, so that he/she can identify its subfunctions. The components of a general function will be described in a separate diagram.

- **Elementary function:** notated by a circle. An elementary function (also termed basic or primitive) is simple enough, according to the system analyst's view, that it needs no decomposition into subfunctions. Rather, it can be described easily in a few words or sentences (as will be elaborated later on).

From the previous definitions it is obvious that any function which is not defined as elementary is general, no matter if it also a subfunction of a super function, at any level.

Figure 8.3 demonstrated four elementary functions only.[6] As we can see, every function has a unique number and a name consisting of one or a few words, written inside the circle. (It is also possible to write "F," for function, before the number.)

As said, whether a certain function is elementary or general is not always clear and determined from the beginning, and it might even change during the hierarchical decomposition process. In other words, it is possible that at a certain point in the process a function is defined as elementary and later on is defined general (and thus needs to be described in a separate diagram). Yet, it is also possible that a function that is defined as general is changed to one or more elementary functions (with appropriate dataflows between them).

An OO-DFD includes several functions, whether general or elementary. If an OO-DFD includes less than three functions, it is reasonable to eliminate it and include its details (i.e., its functions and other components) in its parent OO-DFD. This means that the parent function which was defined as general will be converted to one or two elementary functions. This will avoid too many, too small/ simple OO-DFDs in a system. On the other hand, too many functions in an OO-DFD may make it too complex to read and comprehend. Note that in addition to functions, a diagram includes also classes, external entities, and dataflows, so the number of elements in a diagram increases with the number of functions. An OO-DFD which includes more than 10-12 functions is considered complex and should be avoided. This can be done by grouping certain tightly related functions into a general function, which will be described in a separate diagram. Anyhow, there is no mandatory rule concerning how many functions or elements a diagram must include. Note also that the size of the OO-DFD elements, the distances between them, their names, and fonts may be changed (if the diagrams are created with any software), so there is a certain degree of freedom when determining the number of functions and other elements in a diagram.

External Entities

An external entity is an element (person, organization, or device) which provides input (data) to the system or receives output (information) from the system. An **external** entity provides input to a function via a dataflow, or receives output from a function via a dataflow. The term external entity means that it is not a part of the software system that will be created; it is only a source of input to the system or destination of output from the system. This is why external entities are drawn outside of the diagram's frame. It may appear on the left, right, or both sides of the frame, in accordance with the role it plays: An entity that provides input to the system is drawn on the left while an entity that receives output is drawn on the right. Obviously, the same may appear on both sides of the diagram. For the sake of simplicity of the diagram, the same entity may appear more than once on the same side (to avoid crossing of the dataflow lines, if the same entity provides input or receives output from more than one function).

We distinguish between three types of external entities: **user entity**, **time entity**, and **real-time entity**.

- **User entity:** A user entity is a person or an organization that uses the IS, whether as a source of input or as a destination of output. For example, a supplier who gets an order from the company is an *output* user entity, while the supplier who delivers the supplies is an *input* user entity; a customer who buys certain products and receives a receipt is an *output* user entity; an employee of the company may be both an *input* and *output* user entity because he/she provides various personal and other data and receives various reports (e.g., a salary paycheck) from the system.

  A user entity is notated by a rectangle. The entity name is written inside the rectangle, along with a unique code made up of the letter "U" (for user) and a number. A user entity provides input to a function via an input dataflow, and gets output from a function via an output dataflow. From the point of view of the involved function, it means that the function must be activated by some user in order to perform the input or output operation.

- It is important to point out that the user is not necessarily one who actually operates the system (i.e., activate the involved function) in order to feed the system with the input or produce the output, nor does the user have to be in direct contact with the system. The actual operator will be determined at a later stage (as part of the system design phase); the diagram does not specify who operates the system and its various functions. The user is, as said, the person or organization from where the input data arrives and who receives the information produced by the system, no matter how these will be done. Let us take, for example, an educational system (e.g., of a university) which includes a function to store grades of students in a course. The external entity in this case would be the teacher who provides the grades, no matter how the grades will be fed into the system. This can be done in different ways that will be determined separately; for example, by the teacher, by a secretary, or by a scanner.

- **Time entity:** An IS may include functions that are not activated by users, but rather in certain predefined points of time or time intervals. For example, assume that an IS of a marketing chain has to produce, every morning, a list of cashiers and their shifts; at the end of every week it has to produce a report on the quantities and values of all items in stock, and at the end of every month it has to produce paychecks to all employees. In such cases, we must specify which of the respective functions of the system will be activated (fired) at what times; this is done by the time entities. A time entity can actually be viewed as a clock of the system which initiates the respective function in predefined time intervals.

A time entity is notated by a triangle and identified by the letter "T" (for time) and a number. A time entity may only appear on the left side of the diagram (because it is viewed as a kind of *input*).[7]

- **Real-time entity:** A system may include functions that activated "automatically" by devices which are connected to the system and provide/ transmit real-time data. Here are a few examples: radar sends signals on objects it identifies to an aircraft or a ground station; a humidity meter sends signals if the humidity of the soil drops below or goes above certain points to a computerized irrigation system; a system sends a signal which fires a certain weapon. The commonality of these examples is that they are all devices which are connected to the system, and they either activate or are activated by a function of the system; not by a user and not in a predefined time.

A real-time entity is notated by a triangle. It has a name (usually of the device) and a unique code made up of the letter "R" (for real time) and a number. A real-time entity may appear on both the left and right sides of the diagram.[8]

Generally, real-time entities are very rare in organizational/business IS. Note that when a device which is connected to the IS is operated by a user, the entity is considered user entity, not real-time entity. For example, an automated teller machine (ATM) is not a real-time entity, it is simply an input/output device which enables a user (customer of a bank) to perform monetary transactions.

Classes

In "traditional" DFDs, a data store is a repository of data of a certain type—data which is added, updated, and retrieved by functions. In OO-DFDs, we have data classes instead of data stores. A class, as we know, is a collection of objects of a certain type. Just like a data store which is an abstract repository of data of the same type but not necessarily a file or a (relational) relation, so it can be viewed a class in an OO-DFD. However, the advantage of using classes is that the classes which we need to include in the OO-DFDs **are already defined in the initial class diagram**; they only need to be "used" in the right places in the OO-DFDs.

In the OO-DFD, a class is notated like in a class diagram—by a rectangle divided in three. The class name is written in the upper part, along with its unique code which is made up of the letter "C" and a number. Attributes and functions are not specified in the rectangle. Relationships between classes too, are not shown in OO-DFDs.

Every class in an OO-DFD must be connected to at least one function that updates it (meaning, there must be at lest one dataflow from a function to the class) and at least one function that retrieves data from it (meaning, there must be at least one dataflow from the class to a function). Note that *update* may mean any of the following three operations: (1) adding a new object to the class; (2) changing the values (of attributes) of an existing object; or (3) deleting an object. Each of these possible operations is expressed by a dataflow from a function to the updated class. It is well known that every update must be preceded by a retrieval (search) operation. For example, before a new object is added to a class, the object must be searched in order to make sure that it does not already exist. The same is true if we wish to change an object or delete it. Hence, in an OO-DFD, it seems that wherever there is an update dataflow (from a function to a class) there should also be a retrieval dataflow in the opposite direction. However, the rule is that such retrieval dataflows are not specified in the diagram; the retrieval (search) is implied by the updating dataflow. This simplifies the diagram. But it should be emphasized that if a function not only needs to update a class but also to retrieve data from it for other purposes (e.g., if it has to perform some computations on data retrieved from the class, or to transfer data to another function, or output it to a user), then a dataflow from the class to the function needs to be specified too.

A class is drawn inside the frame of the diagram, close to the functions it is connected to. If the same class serves more than one function in a diagram, it may not be close to all of them, and therefore there may be intersecting lines (dataflows) which would make the diagram incomprehensible. Therefore, it is allowed to draw the same class more than once in the same diagram, next to the involved functions. In order to make it clear this is the same class; it is possible to draw a diagonal line at the upper left corner of the class.

A class can only be connected (by dataflows) to functions. There is no meaning for a direct connection between an external entity and a class or between classes.[9]

- **External class:** An IS sometimes needs to use (retrieve) data which already exist in databases of other systems. We refer to data used/retrieved from other databases as an "external class," which appears outside of the diagram's frame, on its left side—similar to an external entity. For example, assume that a certain IS includes a function **issue order to supplier** where the order has to include information about the buyer (an employee of the company who is in charge of the order). Assuming that the company already has a human resource IS which includes a database of its employees; the personnel database will be treated as an "external class."[10] It is also possible (although in very rare cases) for an external class to appear on the right side of the frame, like an external entity that receives information from the system. This situation is only good for saving information needed only by other systems, or for saving information for some future use.

Dataflows

Dataflows represent channels which transfer data to functions or from functions. A dataflow to a function may carry data from an external entity, a class, or another function. Similarly, a dataflow from a function may carry data to another function, a class, or an external entity (excluding a time entity). This means that there must be a function at least on end of any dataflow. The data carried by a dataflow consist of data elements which will be defined and described in a DD.

In the OO-DFD, a dataflow is represented by an arrow. The dataflow name is written above or below the arrow. The name may consist of a few words characterizing the carried data. A dataflow name is not necessarily unique (i.e., many dataflows may have the same name); it is identifiable by its two ends (each of which has a unique code). A dataflow from a time entity actually does not carry data but signifies a trigger; instead of a name it has a time interval.

Similar to the distinction we made between elementary and general functions, we make a distinction between two types of dataflows, based on the types of functions at their either ends.

- An **elementary dataflow** is a dataflow on whose end or two ends (if it connects two functions) are elementary functions. This dataflow carries specific data elements which will be specified in a DD. (In Figure 8.3 all dataflows are elementary because all the functions are elementary.)

- A **general dataflow** is a dataflow on whose ends there is at least one general function. Recall that every general function will be decomposed into subfunctions and described in a separate diagram. Similarly, every dataflow which is connected to a general function may be "decomposed" to subdataflows, each connected to a certain subfunction and carrying some specific data elements. Therefore, the data elements of a general function need not be specified. Obviously, the data carried by a general function is the union of data carried by its subelementary dataflows.

While an elementary dataflow must be unidirectional (one way), because it carries specific data elements from a source to a destination (which is indicated by the arrow head), a general dataflow may be bidirectional (two-way), that is, with an arrow head at each of its two ends, because (as we will see) it may be decomposed into subdataflows, each of which may carry data in opposite directions. Two separate unidirectional dataflows in the opposing directions are allowed too, but one bidirectional dataflow instead saves space on the diagram.

It is obvious that a dataflow from an external entity to any function must be unidirectional, and so must be a dataflow from any function to an external entity. Hence, only dataflows between general functions and classes may be bidirectional.

Dataflows connecting between different components of an OO-DFD may have different meanings, as explained herein:

- **A dataflow from a class to a function** carries data retrieved from a class. The data retrieved depends on selection criteria which are part of the function's process logic; generally, it may include data elements (i.e., values of attributes) of one or more objects of the class.

- **A dataflow from a function to a class** carries data which updates the class. Recall that update may mean adding one or more new objects, changing the values of attributes of existing objects, or the deletion of objects—depending on the function's process logic.

- **A dataflow from a user entity to a function** carries data (i.e., data element) originating from the user entity that has to be fed into the system and used by the target function. It also signifies a need to create an interface between the user and the system that will enable to input the data.[11]

- **A dataflow from a function to a user entity** carries information generated by the system (actually the source function) and transmitted to the user. It too signifies a need to create an interface between the user and the system that will enable to produce the output.

- **A dataflow from a time entity to a function** does not carry data; it only represents the activation of the target function at a certain time interval. If the dataflow is elementary (i.e., pointed at an elementary function) the time of activation is written on it; but if it is pointed at a general function, no time is written on it because of the (unlikely) possibility that it will be decomposed into several dataflows, each sent to a different function at a different time. Therefore, instead of a specific time interval, this dataflow is labeled *time of activation*. Note also that a dataflow from a time entity to a function does not signify a need to create a user interface because the target function will not be activated by a user but rather by an "automatic" process that will utilize the internal clock of the system.

- **A dataflow from a real-time entity to a function** carries signals from the real-time device. The target function examines the signals and reacts as needed. Like a dataflow that originates from a time entity, this dataflow too does not signify a need to create a user interface.

- **A dataflow from a function to a real-time entity** carries signals from the source function to the real-time device which causes its activation.

- **A dataflow between two functions** carries data from the source function that is needed by the target function. In addition, it means that the source function activates the target function. This implies that the source and target functions are part of the same process and execute in that order.[12] Actually, the source function activates the target function and passes to it parameters which are the data carried by the dataflow.

When a dataflow connects two general functions or a basic and a general function, it is not true to assume that the whole general function activates or is activated by the connecting dataflow, because the general function will be decomposed into subfunctions, and similarly, the above general dataflow will be decomposed into subdataflows; it is reasonable that only one or some of those subfunctions will activate or be activated. It will become clear exactly which functions activate or are activated only after the functional decomposition process is completed and all functions dealt with are elementary.

Hierarchical OO-DFDs

A functional model of a real-world IS may consist of many dozens, even hundreds of functions—much more than can be included in a single OO-DFD. There are two approaches for modeling such systems with OO-DFDs: flat diagram (as in Gane & Sarson, 1979) and hierarchical diagrams (as in DeMarco, 1978). In the flat diagram approach all functions are elementary; there is no functional decomposition process and no hierarchies of diagrams. The modeling process may start by choosing a certain part of the system (actually of the user requirements) and creating a diagram for it, including the required (elementary functions) and the other OO-DFD components. Afterwards, another part is chosen and the first diagram is extended with the new functions and other related components. The process continues until the entire system is described and one "big" diagram is obtained. Of course, the diagram created this way must be very big and cannot fit into a reasonable size of page (or screen, if a software tool is used). But it can be "cut" somehow into ordinary pages (or screens), where each page contains some part of the entire diagram and points to the neighboring parts—similar to the way it is done in road maps or atlases. Since our methodology does not follow this approach, we do not elaborate on it any further.

The hierarchical diagrams approach creates a hierarchy (tree) of OO-DFDs: At the top (actually root) of the hierarchy there is the most general diagram, including the main and most general functions of the system. Below it there are additional diagrams, each describing in more detail one of the general functions included in the root diagram. Below each of those diagrams there may be more diagrams, each describing a function defined as "general" in the diagram above. The resulting tree of diagrams enables us to see the system in different degrees of detail, depending on our needs: When we wish to see a most general model of the system we will look at the root diagram; when we wish to see details we will look at a lower level diagram.

In addition to being able to see the system in different levels of detail, the hierarchical diagrams approach has the advantage of enabling a top-down analysis process: First the analyst identifies and defines the main functions of the system; next the analyst may perform a decomposition of a certain main function and create its "child" diagrams, and so on, until all functions in all diagrams are elementary. This also facilitates working in parallel by several teams of analysts, each working on a certain main function of the system.

Hence, the work order is as follows: Based on the input documents and additional information provided by the users or their representatives, the analyst creates the root OO-DFD. In order to do that the analyst first identifies the primary, most general functions of the sought system. In a large-scale system, the most general functions may be viewed as subsystems. Here are several examples for such functions: In a financial system of an organization, the primary functions may be: accounting, budgets, management, sales to customers, orders from suppliers, inventory management; in a students management system of a university the primary functions may be: students admission, tuition fees, registration to courses, grades management, graduation management; in a human resources management system the primary functions may be: hiring employees, personal information management, salaries, job assignments and promotion, retirement.

Along with identifying the primary functions of the IS, the analyst also identifies the external entities which are sources of data needed by the functions or destination of information produced by the functions. Similarly, the analyst identifies the data classes from which those functions need to retrieve data or update. Given that at this stage we already have an initial class diagram, this task is relatively easy because the analyst has to use classes which exist in that diagram. The next step is to create the root diagram, including the dataflows among those components. The root diagram only includes classes that serve more than function (each). This means that every class that appears in the root diagram must be "shared" by at least two functions so that at least one function is updating it and at least one is retrieving information from it. (Of course, it is possible that a certain function will both update and retrieve data from the same class.) This means that some of the classes appearing in the initial class diagram may not be included in the root OO-DFD; they will be included in lower level diagrams, where they will serve (be used for update and retrieval) subfunctions of the primary ones.

Every OO-DFD has a name (label) and identification code. The code of the root diagram is OO-DFD-0 (because its function numbers are 1, 2, etc.). The code of any "child" diagram is OO-DFD-x where x stands for the number of the general function which it describes, and its name is identical to the name of that function. Every function in a child diagram has a unique number consisting of the number of its parent function, a decimal point and a serial number (starting with 1 in).

Figure 8.4 demonstrates the OO-DFD-0 of a (small and rather "trivial") system named **Customers and Suppliers**. The system has two general functions:[13] **Management of customers** and **Management of suppliers**, several user entities, a time entity, and a class Customers that serves both functions. Function 1 both updates the class and retrieves information from it, while function 2 only retrieves from it. We assume that the initial class scheme, including the class **Customers**, had been created. Beside **Customers**, the initial class diagram includes also a class **Suppliers** which does not appear in OO-DFD-0. The reason is that it only serves the subfunctions of the general function **Management of suppliers**, but not the function **Management of customers**.

Figure 8.4. OO-DFD-0 of customers and suppliers system

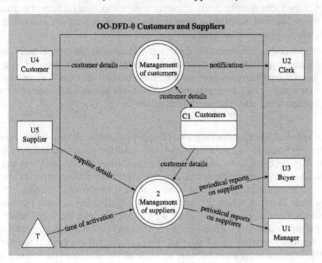

After the creation of OO-DFD-0, each of its general functions is decomposed into subfunctions and a "child" OO-DFD is created. A subfunction in a child diagram may be defined as either general or elementary. Whether it is general or elementary depends on the analyst's judgment. It is possible for an analyst to first define a function as elementary, assuming it is simple and need not be further decomposed; but later on the analyst may change his/her mind and define it as general. The opposite may also happen, that is, that a function defined as general is later defined as one or more elementary functions. There are no precise rules and measures for deciding whether a function is elementary or general. There are several rules of thumb which may guide the analyst, as follows:

- If it is possible to describe the process logic of a function in a few sentences or a simple structured description or flowchart, there is probably no need to define it as general and create for it a child diagram.

- If a function cannot be decomposed into more than two or three subfunctions, there is probably no need to define it as general and create a child diagram for it; those two or three (elementary) functions may be included in the same diagram.

- If an OO-DFD consists of relatively many functions (say more than about 12) and looks complex and difficult to understand, it might be best to group several related functions, define them as a general function, and create a child diagram for that function.

- If a function is connected (by dataflows) to relatively many other functions, classes, and external entities (say more than about eight), it seems to be a function which involves many activities, that is, consists of many subfunctions. In that case it may be reasonable to define it as general, decompose it into subfunctions, and create a child diagram.

When a general function in a diagram is directly connected (by a dataflow) to an elementary function, and a child diagram is created for the general function, the elementary function is not included in the child diagram (because it is not a subfunction of the general function). However, in the child diagram there should be a dataflow emanating from one or more of the subfunctions, pointing to the above basic function, which appears outside of the diagram's frame. The basic function is represented as a small circle with its function number in it. The small circle signifies a connector between the function(s) within the diagram and the basic function. Similarly, if a basic function is connected to a general function, it will be represented as a small connector circle on the left side of the frame, with at least one dataflow coming from it to one or more of the subfunctions within the diagram. If two general functions are connected in a certain diagram, in each of their child diagrams there will be respective connector circles, in the left or right side of the diagram.

Along with subfunctions of a general, which will be included in its child diagram, it will also include data classes which need to be used by those subfunctions and external entities from which data will be input or to which information will be provided. As a rule, every class and external entity connected to a general function must also appear in the child diagram of that function—they have to be connected (via dataflows) to the appropriate subfunctions within the child diagrams. In addition, it is possible that new classes, which did not appear in the parent diagram (the diagram where the general function appears), will appear in the child diagram. A "new" class in an OO-DFD is not really new, because it already appears in the initial class diagram; but it did not appear in the parent diagram because it did not serve more than one of its functions. A new class appears in a child diagram because there it serves at least two of its functions, where at least one function updates it and at least one function retrieves data from it. Hence, such a "new" class is actually "internal" to the above general function, as it is used only by its subfunctions.

Figure 8.5 shows OO-DFD-1 of the general function **Management of customers**. It includes two subfunctions, each of which obtains input from the user entity

Figure 8.5. OO-DFD-1 of customers and suppliers system

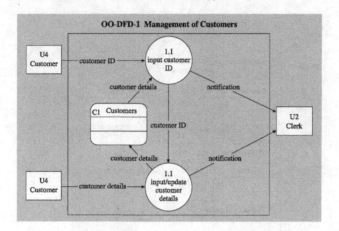

Customer and provides output (information) to the user entity **Clerk**. The class **Customers**, which appeared in the root diagram with a two-way dataflow connecting it to the general function, appears again here, where we can see exactly which of the subfunctions updates it and which of them retrieves data from it. Figure 8.6 shows OO-DFD-2 of the general function **Management of suppliers**. Here we see first time the class **Suppliers** which is updated by function 2.1 and from which functions 2.2 and 2.3 retrieve.[14] In addition, we see that the time entity (T) in the root diagram has been decomposed into two specific time entities: One will trigger function 2.2 which will produce a daily end-of-day report, and the other will trigger function 2.3 which will produce a monthly end-of-month report. Note that in the parent diagram the dataflow from the time entity to the general function is labeled *time of activation*, while in the child diagram the respective dataflows to the elementary functions are labeled with the specific time intervals.

When presenting the tree of OO-DFDs of an entire system, it is customary to add on top of an OO-DFD a "content diagram," which includes one big circle of a general function representing the whole system. Inside the circle is written the name of the system. This diagram shows no classes, while on the two sides of the frame it shows some primary external entities of the system. The content diagram has only a descriptive purpose—it may be considered as a "cover page" of the document which includes the tree of OO-DFDs.

198 Shoval

Figure 8.6. OO-DFD-2 of customers and suppliers system

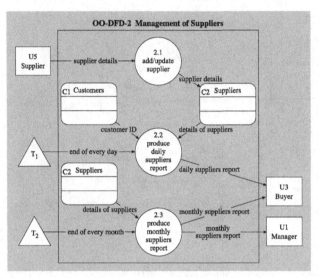

One of the main problems with functional-hierarchical decomposition is how "deep" to go and at what level of details. On the one hand, the more diagrams we create and the more details we provide, the easier might be the work at the later phases of development. On the other hand, too many details may make the diagrams too complex and uneasy to read and comprehend. We must remember that OO-DFDs are only meant to define diagrammatically "what" the system needs to do—"not how"! The diagrams are not meant to prescribe and describe the process logic of each of the system's functions. Details concerning how the functions will work do not belong in the analysis phase and are not included in the OO-DFDs. Since system analysis, including functional-hierarchical decomposition, is not an exact science, the analysts have a lot of "freedom degrees" with respect to how deep to go and how much to detail. Hence, it is possible that for a given description of user requirements, a certain analyst will create a deep hierarchy of diagrams, going into much detail, while another analyst might create a more "shallow" hierarchy of diagrams, with less detail. Again, there are no exact rules on the level of detail, but as said—the more we detail at the analysis stage, the more precise is the functional definition of the required system, but this may take more time. At any rate, there are several rules to remember regarding the need to avoid excessive detail of the diagrams:

- **Avoid describing the process logic of functions:** OO-DFDs are meant to define the flow of data/information to and from functions, but not the process logic of the functions. The process logic of functions is considered part of "how" and not of "what," and therefore it will be dealt with in the design phase, using other techniques suitable for this purpose. So, for example, if a certain function needs to check various conditions or perform certain things repeatedly (in a loop), there is no way and no need to describe the conditions and loops by using different functions and dataflows—an OO-DFD does not even have the proper tools for that (i.e., it provides no simple means to express conditions and loops).

- **Avoid describing data integrity checks and error messages:** As said, OO-DFDs model the functionality of the system from the point of view of the users, and it should not detail how the system performs the functions. Therefore, there is no need to deal with checking the integrity of input data and error messages sent to users if certain data are not entered properly, for example, a user feeding input data using an input screen and a keyboard. Obviously, we expect the system to check the correctness and completeness of the input data, according to the defined data types, and to present proper error messages to the user if anything is violated—but these things need not be dealt with at the analysis stage and not specified in the OO-DFDs; they will be dealt with at the programming phase.[15]

- **Avoid dealing with file administration:** There is no need to define functions which perform back up of data, reorganization of files/databases, or any similar "physical" activities with data. These will be dealt with by the database administrator of the system and are not part of the functional requirements which are of the users' concern.

- **Avoid dealing with functions outside the system:** The OO-DFDs should only specify the functions that will become part of the computerized system (i.e., functions that will eventually be performed by computer programs), not "manual" functions (that will be performed by humans). For example, if the system has to produce a certain report for a user, this function is of course part of the system, but if the user has to perform certain things with that report which are out of scope of the system, then those functions should not be included in the OO-DFDs.

- **Avoid over detail of user (external) entities:** User entities are not part of the software system and therefore their level of description in the OO-DFDs is not of major importance. Over detail of user entities may result in having too many rectangles of user entities on the two sides of the diagrams' frames. If there are too many user entities, it is possible to group "similar" entities (i.e., which have common characteristics) and represent them as a "general" entity in an upper-level diagram (somewhat similar to general function which is a grouping of its subfunctions). This enables reducing the amount of user entities in high-level diagrams, while showing the specific user entities in lower level diagrams. For example, in a large-scale system with many user entities, including may types of customers, the root diagram may include a "general" user entity named "customer," while in lower level diagrams this entity may be "decomposed" into subentities such as "retailer," "wholesaler," "private customer," and so forth. In such

Table 8.1. Summary of the correctness rules of OO-DFDs

• Every function must have at least one dataflow entering it and one dataflow emanating from it.
• A dataflow may connect two functions or a function and a class or external entity (hence, a class or external entity must be connected to a function).
• A function cannot be connected (with a dataflow) to itself.
• External entities on the left side of the frame are sources of input, while those on the right side are a destination for the output.
• A time entity can only appear on the left side of the frame.
• An elementary dataflow (a dataflow which is not connected to a general function) must be one-way, while a general dataflow may be two-way.
• Every class appearing in the OO-DFDs must also appear in the initial class diagram and vise versa.
• When a class appears **first time** in an OO-DFD, there has to be at least one function that updates it and one function that retrieves data from it. In the child diagram of a general function that used a certain class, that class will have **the same role**(s) as in the parent diagram. For example, if a class is used by a certain general function for retrieval only (or for update only) then it will appear in its child diagram and be used by at least one of its subfunctions for retrieval only (or for update only).
• An "external class" (that belongs to another IS) is drawn outside of the frame (hence the former rule does not apply).
• Every external entity connected to a general function must also appear on the child diagram of that function and in the same role. In addition, an external entity may not appear in a child diagram if it was not connected to the general function in the parent diagram. (However, it is possible to group similar user entities into a general user entity and show only it in a parent diagram.)
• If a general function is connected to another function (either elementary or general), in its child diagram there will be at least one connector (a little circle) on one of the frame's sides.
• The number within a connector must be that of an elementary function to which it refers.

case, the subuser entities will have to be numbered similar to the way subfunctions are numbered. For example, if the code of a general user entity is U1, then its subuser entities will be U1.1, U1.2, and so on.

Table 8.1 summarizes the correctness rules of OO-DFDs.

Keeping the Initial Class Diagram and the OO-DFDs Compatible

Verifying Identical Classes in the Two Diagram Types

The initial class diagram and the OO-DFDs must be compatible. This means that every class defined in the initial class diagram must appear at least once in an OO-DFD and vise versa. During the hierarchical decomposition process, when the analyst finds out that a certain function needs to retrieve or update data, he/she has to choose the proper class (from the initial class diagram) and draw it in the right place in the diagram next to the respective function. Naturally, in reality (and especially when the user requirements are not well described) there may be a situation in which there is a need to update or retrieve data which is not defined in the initial class diagram. If this is the case, the class diagram must be altered. This can be done by adding a new class to the diagram, or adding attributes to an existing class, or even dropping a class. Such changes may also cause changes in the relationships between classes (both ordinary and structural, e.g., the creation of is-a hierarchies between a superclass and its subclasses). Such changes are likely to occur because although we advocated creating the data model (an initial class diagram) prior to creating the functional model (OO-DFDs), actually the two modeling activities cannot be done entirely in sequence. Once again we emphasize that the process is iterative, and during the iterations both the initial class diagram and the OO-DFDs may change and improve.

Using Classes Which Have Inheritance Relationships

This issue is related to the way in which the functions in the OO-DFDs "use" classes which have inheritance relationships. The rule is simple: An OO-DFD should include only the specific class which the function uses (whether to update or retrieve from), not the whole hierarch of classes. Hence, if a function needs to update or retrieve data from a superclass, that superclass will only appear in the diagram; if it needs to update or retrieve from a subclass—only the subclass will appear. For example, in Figure 8.1 there is a class **Work** and a subclass **Work in progress**. Assuming that there is a certain function in a certain OO-DFD whose task is to handle work requests from tenants (apartments); this function needs to update the class **Work**, but it has nothing to do with the subclass **Work in progress**. On the other hand, assuming that there is a function whose task is to handle payments to contractors; this function needs to update only the class Work in progress. It is possible, of course, for a function to access both a superclass and its subclasses. For example, assume a function whose task is to save the details of a new contract with contractor; this function needs to access both the superclass (to update the attribute *status of request*) and the subclass (to add a new object of Work in progress).

Dealing with Attribute Duplicity and Relationship Attributes

As we know, in a class diagram every reference attribute has an inverse attribute in the referenced class. Moreover, if there are relationship attributes, they are saved twice, along with two (inverse) reference attributes. This "symmetry" of reference attributes and duplicity of relationship attributes is maintained in the class diagram because when this diagram is created we have not yet examined the users' functional needs and we are not sure whether or not all of this is needed. Now that we already created a functional model we can systematically review their attributes in order to verify if they are all needed, or perhaps some reference attributes or relationship attributes may be dropped. In order to clarify the problem let us look again at the class diagram in Figure 8.1, which includes a many-to-many relationship between **Apartment** and **Work**, that is, a tenant of an apartment may submit many work requests and a work request may be submitted by more than one apartment. The two set reference attributes are *set work requests [Work]* and *set who requested [Apartment]*. If this relationship also had attributes (e.g., each tenant's share in the request), they would have been included in both sets. The meaning is that every time a new work request is submitted a new **Work** object needs to be added, including references to the Apartment objects who submitted it, and each of the Apartment objects needs to be updated by adding a reference to the new **Work** object (the reference is added to the *set work requests*); and if there are relationship attributes they too need to be added in all those places. But now let us assume that during functional analysis we found out that no one ever needs to know the share of each apartment in each requested work. This means that this relationship attribute needs not be included in the class **Apartment**—only in class **Work**. Moreover, assume that we found out that no one needs to know which works have been requested by an apartment, only which apartments requested a work; if this is the case then there is no need for the *set work requests [Work]* at all. This is expressed in the OO-DFD by the fact that the function **Insert/update work request** only updates the class **Work** (although it needs to retrieve the objects of **Apartment** who requested the work in order to verify their existence).

Let us look at a different example. Assume that in a management IS on students, the initial class diagram includes a many-to-many relationship between the classes **Student** and **Course offering** which enables finding references from a student to each of the courses he/she registered to and reference from a course offering to each of the students who registered to it. Assume also that the initial class diagram includes a relationship attribute *grade*. The two respective sets are defined as: *set registered to courses {[Course offering], grade}* and *set registered students {[Student], grade}*. In the functional analysis stage we find out "who needs to know what," and according to that we decide whether these attributes with the redundant information are indeed needed. If indeed there is a need to know which courses a student took and what his/her grades were in each of them, as well as to know who registered to a course and what their grades were—then there is no choice but to maintain those two sets despite the data duplicity. On the other hand, if we find out that there is no need to know the grades of students who registered to a certain course (but only who are the students) then in the class **Course offering** we need only the *set registered students [Student]*' without the grade attribute (while we may need to add a separate attribute *average grade* instead, if it has not been defined already). In summary, as a result of the functional analysis process, various changes may occur in the initial class diagram, including deletion of reference attributes and relationship attributes.

How Can We Verify Compatibility?

At the end of the analysis phase it is important to verify that the data model and the functional model are fully compatible or synchronized. This involves checking compatibility at two levels: classes and attributes.

- Class level compatibility has already been dealt with in the section "**Verifying Identical Classes in the Two Diagram Types**."

- Attribute level compatibility means verifying, for each and every class, that every attribute is updated by at least one function and retrieved by at least one function. This can be checked once a DD for the system is created, because it specifies (among other things) the data elements of the dataflows in the OO-DFDs. This certainly includes the elements of dataflows from functions to classes (which mean attributes that will be updated by the functions) and the data elements of dataflows from classes to functions (which mean attributes that will be retrieved). More details about the DD and the data elements of dataflows will be provided later on (in chapter IX); at this stage let us assume that a DD already exists. So that the following procedure can be applied for each class:

1. Make a list of all data elements (i.e., attributes) of the class.

2. For each dataflow from an elementary function to the class (i.e., for all "update" elementary dataflows, in all diagrams including that class)—review its data elements and mark the respective attribute in that class. All attributes of the class should be marked at least once; otherwise it means that there is an attribute which is never updated.

3. Repeat the same process for each dataflow from the class to elementary functions (i.e., for all "retrieve" elementary dataflows). All attributes of the class should be marked at least one, otherwise it means that there is an attribute which is never retrieved.

All erroneous cases must be rechecked: There is a possibility that a certain data element of a certain dataflow was not defined by mistake in the DD, or that a certain dataflow from a function to a class or from a class to a function was not defined by mistake in an OO-DFD, or that a certain attribute was not included by mistake in the class diagram, and so forth. At the end of these checks (which as said requires the existence of a DD) it is guaranteed that each of the attributes of each of the classes is updated at least once and retrieved at least once. Examples for tests of compatibility will be provided later on.

Example of Functional Analysis: OO-DFDs of the Apartments Building System

This section presents a complete example of functional analysis with OO-DFDs. We use the Apartments Building system. The user requirements for this system have already been presented in the opening section of this chapter, and Figure 8.1 presented its initial class diagram. The OO-DFDs resulting from the functional analysis process are presented in Figures 8.7-8.10. Figure 8.7 presents the root diagram, comprising two general functions and one elementary function.[16] The general function **Payments of fees** is detailed in OO-DFD-1 (Figure 8.8) and the general function **Maintenance works** in OO-DFD-2

Figure 8.7. OO-DFD-0 of apartments building system

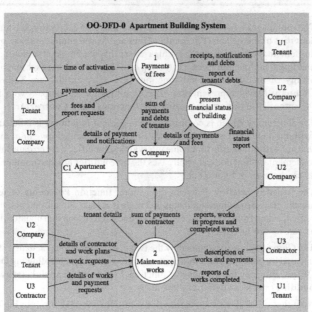

(Figure 8.9). This diagram includes a general function **Performance of works** which is detailed in OO-DFD-2.2 (Figure 8.10).

Before providing some clarifications of the diagrams, we wish to point out that the diagrams present the **result** of the analysis process; we cannot see the drafts of diagrams and the changes and refinements made during the functional analysis process. Naturally, it may be assumed that the process had begun with the creation of a root OO-DFD, but it is possible that initially it did not include exactly the functions, classes, and external entities which are shown in Figure 8.7. When the analyst went on and created an OO-DFD for any of the general functions in the root diagram, it is likely that he/she had discovered things (subfunctions and interactions between functions, classes, and external entities) that had an impact on the root diagram, which was updated accordingly. Such things are true for every diagram, no matter its level.

Clarifications to OO-DFD-0 (Figure 8.7)

- The root diagram includes two general functions that encompass the main activities of the system (**Payments of fees** and **Maintenance works**), and an elementary function which enables presenting the financial status of the building. This function appears at this top-level because it is not a subfunction of any of the above general functions. The user entities are **Tenant**, **Company** (which represents any officer working for the company who has the authority to perform the respective functions), and **Contractor**.

- The time entity which is connected to the general function 1 is labeled **T** (without a number) and the respective dataflow is named *time of activation* but with no specific time; time intervals are specified only on dataflows to elementary functions; in such cases the time entities are also numbered, as can be seen in Figure 8.8.

- The two-way dataflow between the general function **Payments of fees** and the class **Apartment** indicates that there is at least one subfunction that retrieves data from this class, and at least one subfunction that updates it— as can be see in OO-DFD-1.

- The **Company** class is updated by the two general functions (actually, it is updated by their specific subfunctions, as can be seen in the following OO-DFDs). But only the elementary function 3 (**present financial status of building**) retrieves data from this class.

- Note that other classes appearing in the initial class diagram (see Figure 8.1) do not appear in this diagram because they arc used only by the subfunctions of the general function **Maintenance works**. We will see it only in OO-DFD-2 and OO-DFD-2.2.

Clarifications to OO-DFD-1 (Figure 8.8)

- The diagram is consistent with the root diagram. The external entities (**Tenant** and **Company**), the time entity, and the classes (**Apartment** and **Company**) all appeared in the root diagram "surrounding" function 1.

- Function 1.1 deals with adding and updating of tenants' details. Although the external entity is **Tenant**, it is possible that the data on tenants/apartments are added or updated by an officer of the company or by the tenants themselves (say via the Internet site of the system)—depending on how the system will be designed and implemented. Anyhow, in the analysis stage we do not deal with such matters; the point is that the data on tenants originate from the tenants, so they are the external entities/users.

Figure 8.8. OO-DFD-1 of apartments building system

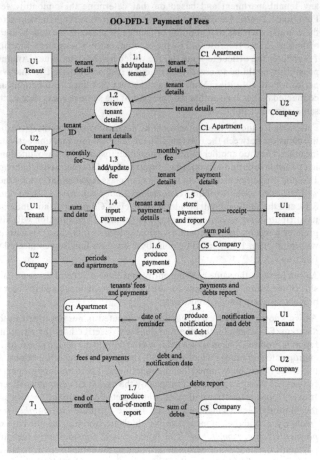

- Function 1.2 and 1.3 allow officers of the company to review the details of any tenant/apartment and based on that determine their monthly fee: Function 1.2 retrieves details about a certain apartment/tenant whose fee the company wishes to determine or change; it presents the details to the officer in charge (represented by the external entity **Company**); function 1.3 enables the officer to input the fee which he/she determines. Another possibility could be to create one function instead of these two that will perform both activities. Nonetheless, the fact that the two functions are connected makes it clear that they are part of the same process, that is, the same computer program.

- Functions 1.4 and 1.5 deal with accepting payments from tenants. Here too, the dataflow between the two functions means that one function activates the other. Here too another solution is possible: Instead of the two functions, it is possible to define only one (e.g., **input and update payment**). Function 1.5 adds the payment details to the object of class **Apartment** (where they will be added to the attribute *set payments {date, sum, form}*—see Figure 8.1), and the sum paid will be added to the class **Company** (thus updating its attribute *total annual payments from tenants*). The function will also produce a receipt for the tenant. (Again, in stead of including this activity within function 1.5, it could be done by a separate function connected to function 1.5.)

- As can be seen, the same external entity may appear several times on each side of the frame. This is done for the sake of convenience and in order to prevent crossing lined (dataflows).

- As we know, the way each function is executed is not described in the diagram. For example, the diagram does not describe how the payments report is produced (function 1.6); this will be done in the design phase, using appropriate techniques which deal with the process logic of functions. At this stage it may be assumed that the function will perform loops repeated for each of the apartments determined by the user (i.e., company officer). In every loop the function will retrieve an object of **Apartment**, specifically the monthly fees (which are stored in the attribute *set monthly fees {month, fee}* and the payment details (which are stored in the attribute *set payments {date, sum, form}*. The function will consider only fees and payments within the time period determined by the company officer. Based on these data, the function will calculate the tenant's debt, if there is any, and produce a payments report that will be sent to the tenant. As said, these issues are part of the system's design phase, and therefore are not expressed in the OO-DFD.

- Function 1.7 is activated at the end of each month. It calculates, for each apartment, the remainder of debt as based on data retrieved from the apartment's object and produces a debts report. In addition, it computes the sum of debts of all tenants and updates the class **Company** (specifically, its attribute *sum of amounts receivable from tenants*). While calculating the debt of an apartment, the function checks the amount and whether a notification was sent to the tenant last month (this information is saved in the attribute *set reminders {date, debt}* of the **Apartment** object). If needed (according to conditions specified in the users' requirements document), function 1.7 will then activate function 1.8, which will produce a notification of the debt that will be sent to the tenant. This example shows that a dataflow from one function to another does not necessarily always activate it; it depends on conditions which are part of the process logic of the activating function—conditions which are not shown in the diagram.

Clarifications to OO-DFD-2 (Figure 8.9)

- In this diagram we see two classes which did not appear in the root diagram: **Work** and **Contractor**. This is because they are used "internally" by the subfunctions of **Maintenance work** and not by any of the functions which appeared in the root diagram.

- Function 2.1 enables the users to add or update work requests coming from tenants. (Note that a request may be submitted by one or more tenants; this is not shown in the diagram but will be considered at the design phase, where an input screen will be designed that will enable to register more than one tenant for a request.) Once activated, the function verifies the details of the tenants (retrieving their objects from the class **Apartment**) and then creates a new object of **Work**, or updates an existing one (if a tenant wishes to update an existing request). We could distinguish between an addition function and an update function, but this is not needed because the practice in data processing is that a function which adds input data also enables changing the data; the distinction between the two subactivities will be done at the design stage (e.g., by providing different input screens for adding or changing data).

- Function 2.3 enables to add and update data of contractors who work with the company.

- The primary function of this OO-DFD is 2.2: **Performance of works**, which is defined as a general function. This function retrieves data stored in the class **Contractor**; retrieves from and updates the class **Work**; and updates the class **Company**. The details of this function are described in OO-DFD-2.2.

Figure 8.9. OO-DFD-2 of apartments building system

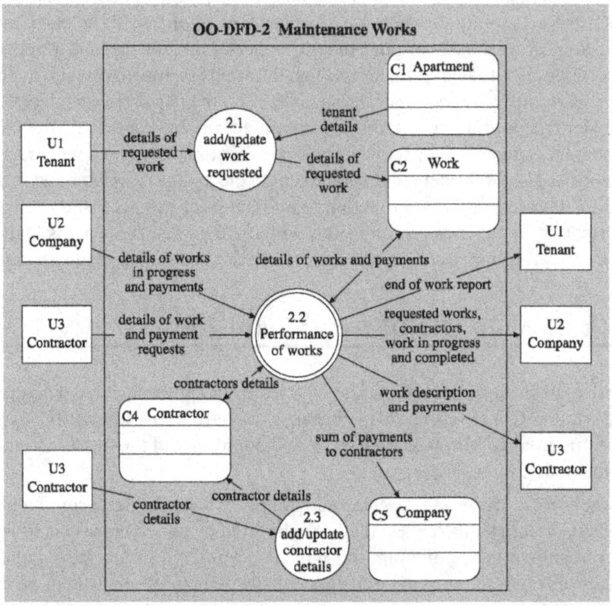

Clarifications to OO-DFD-2.2 (Figure 8.10)

- In this diagram there are seven elementary functions. Function 2.2.1 presents the authorized officer of the company with requested works that were not yet dealt with (those with status "requested"). The officer will select requested work he/she wishes to deal with. Note that function 2.2.1 does not get input from an external entity—this is correct, because once activated, the function retrieves information on the requested works from the **Work** class and presents it to the user, who then selects one of them to deal with. Hence, it should be understood that the dataflow from the function to the **Company** user entity means that the user-system interface that will be designed (in the design phase) will include a menu entry which will enable the user in charge (in this case a company officer) to activate

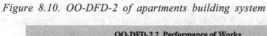

Figure 8.10. OO-DFD-2 of apartments building system

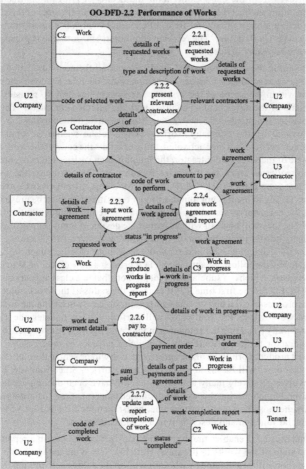

the function. Once the user selects a requested work, function 2.2.2 retrieves from the class **Contractor** the details of relevant contractors, depending on the type of requested work (which is an attribute of the class **Work**) and the contractors' fields of expertise (which is a set attribute of the class **Contractor**). The relevant contractors' information is presented to the company officer.

- As said in the users' requirements document, all the communication and possible negotiations between the company and the relevant contractors is not within the scope of the system. The system has only to register the details of the agreement or contract with the selected contractor. This is done by functions 2.2.3 and 2.2.4. It is assumed that function 2.2.3 is activated by the company's officer when he/she wishes to input the agreement details. Once activated, the user inputs the code of the work and name of the selected contractor; the function then verifies the existence of the requested work and the selected contractor by retrieving the work object from class **Work** and the contractor's object from class **Contractor**. (If any of them is not found, a proper error message must be presented to the user; but as we know, such messages are not included in the OO-DFDs; they will be dealt with as part of the design of input-output forms.) Then, the user inputs the details of the work agreement, and function 2.2.3 activates function 2.2.4 and forwards to it those details. Function 2.2.4 performs the following activities: (1) it creates a new object of **Work in progress**, which is a subclass of **Work**—note that this class appears in this OO-DFD for the first time; (2) it changes the status of the Work object to "in progress;" (3) it updates the **Contractor** object by inserting the code of the work which the contractor will perform; (4) it updates the class **Company** by adding the amount of money which will have to be paid to the contractor to the attribute *sum of amounts payable to contractors*; and (5) it produces printouts of the agreement: one will be sent to the contractor and another will be saved in the company's office. Since function 2.2.4 involves relatively many activities, it could have been decomposed into several functions; but this would have added more functions to the diagram. Another possibility could be to replace both functions 2.2.3 and 2.2.4 by one general function and describe it in a separate diagram.[17]

- Function 2.2.5 enables the user (a company officer) to obtain a report on the state of the works in progress. Here too, it may be assumed that the function will be activated by whoever will get the authority to produce such a report, and this will be done via the user-system interface. Besides being activated from the interface, this function needs no input data.

- Function 2.2.6 enables the company to handle payments to contractors. The company officer who initiates a payment to a contractor activates the function and inputs a code of the work for which he/she wants to make a payment. The function retrieves the respective work in progress object, which includes relevant details such as the *total sum to pay* and the past payments to the contractor (detailed in the attribute *set payments {date, amount}*). Based on these details the officer determines and inputs the amount to be paid. Following that, the function adds the payment details (date and amount)[18] to the **Work in progress** object and produces a payment order which is sent to the contractor.

- When the company officer wishes to report that a certain work is complete, he/she activates function 2.2.7 and inputs the work code. The function retrieves the details of the work in progress object, produces a report which is sent to the tenants who requested the work, and changes the status of the work to "completed."

Checking the Compatibility of the OO-DFDs and the Initial Class Diagram

To conclude this example, we demonstrate the verification of compatibility of the OO-DFDs and the initial class diagram.[19] At the class level we simply verify that all classes in the class diagram are indeed used in the OO-DFDs. At the attribute level we check, for each class, that all of its attributes are added/updated at least once (by any function) and retrieved at least once. For every class we create a table in which the rows are the attributes of the class and the columns are the elementary functions which either update the class ("update" functions) or retrieve from it ("retrieve" functions). For each of the dataflows from the "update" functions to the class and from the class to the "retrieve" functions, the DD specifies the data elements it includes. Based on that we mark, for each of these functions, the class attributes which they update or retrieve. An updated attribute is marked by "+" and a retrieved attribute by "-". Tables 8.2-8.4 show the checks for three of the classes: **Contractor**, **Work**, and **Work in progress**. We see that the first two classes are correct because each of their attributes is updated and retrieved at least once. However, in the **Work in progress** class we found an attribute, *actual completion date,* which is neither updated nor retrieved. After verification that indeed no function in the system needs to update or retrieve this attribute, it is decided to drop it from the class.[20]

Table 8.2. Compatibility check of class contractor

Attributes	Functions		
	2.3	2.2.4	2.2.2
Contractor name	+	+	-
Address	+		-
Set phone numbers	+		-
Set fields of expertise	+		-
*Set works contracted [**Work in progress**]*		+	-

Table 8.3. Compatilbility check for work class

Attributes	Functions				
	2.1	2.2.4	2.2.7	2.2.1	2.2.3
work code	+	+	+	-	-
*set who requested [**Apartment**]*	+			-	
date of request	+			-	-
type of work	+			-	-
description of work	+			-	
status(requested/in progress/completed)	+	+		-	-
date of status	+	+	+	-	

Table 8.4. Compatibility check for class work in progress

Attributes	Functions			
	2.2.4	2.2.6	2.2.5	2.2.6
*the contractor [**Contractor**]*	+	+	-	-
description of work	+		-	
starting date	+		-	
date to complete	+		-	
total sum to pay	+		-	-
set payments {date, amount}		+	-	-
actual completion date*				

* No function updates or retrieves this attribute

System Analysis with FOOM: Example of the Musical Programs System

In this section we present one more complete example of the analysis of an IS using FOOM methodology. First we will present the users' requirements[21] and then the initial class diagram, the OO-DFDs, and some compatibility checks.

Before we begin, we point out again that the analysis process is not exactly a sequential one but rather is iterative and interactive, in which the analysts interact with the users or their representatives; throughout the work process there is a constant improvement of the class diagram and the OO-DFDs. Here we can only see the final products.

The reader is asked to treat the example as a self-practice exercise. This means that before looking at solution diagrams, the reader is expected to study the users' requirements and based on them to create an initial class diagram and the OO-DFDs—and only then study the solution provided in this section and see if and why there are any differences.[22]

The Users' Requirements

An IS that will assist the managers and editors of music programs of a radio station needs to be created. The system will contain a database of musical pieces owned by the station. The data on the musical pieces will be input and stored when new disks or other music media arrive from distributors. For every musical piece the following details will be stored: an identification code (piece ID); which will be given to each piece by the station; the piece name (e.g., name of a song); the music type (e.g., classic, country, jazz); the length of play (in minutes and seconds); the royalties owner (who will be paid according to the number of times the piece will be played); and the composers and the performers. The system will enable to produce various catalogs from the database of musical pieces. Catalogs will be produced upon requests from the music director of the station and according to different criteria such as music types, performers, and composers. The catalogs will be used by the music director and the program editors and may also be sent to distributors.

Music programs may play musical pieces requested by listeners. A listener may send a request (by postcard, fax, or any other means) to hear a certain musical piece. A request will include the name of the requested piece, the name of the program in which the listener wishes to hear it, a range of dates within which he/ she wishes to hear the requested piece, and a dedication (to be read before the musical piece is played). The listener's request is registered with a status "waiting" and waits until the editor of that music program will take care of it.

One of the main objectives of the IS is to assist the editors in the editing of the music programs. To enable this, the system will maintain a database of music programs and of the actual programs that will be broadcast throughout the season. A music program is identified by a name and is characterized by the types of music that will be played in it. A program has duration (in hours and minutes) and a day or days and start time in which it will be broadcast every week. In addition, every music program is assigned an editor and a technician (who are employees of the radio station). The planning of the music programs for the season is done by the music director, while the editor of a music program is in charge of scheduling its actual broadcast during the season. This means deciding which musical pieces will be played in each of the actual broadcasts of the programs. The IS will enable adding and updating music programs and the scheduling of actual programs that will be broadcast, including the assignment of musical pieces that will be played and the handling of listeners' requests. In addition, the system will enable the production of reports on the music programs for the music director, the editors, technicians, and the listeners (via newspapers and other media).

The assignment of musical pieces to a program will be done as follows: The editor will select a program which he/she wishes to schedule; this means selecting a program name and a date it will be broadcast (based on the day or days in which the program will be broadcast every week). The system will retrieve the details of the program and present the editor with relevant information: First, it will present details of existing musical pieces of the types which are suitable to that program. Then it will enable the editor to see which musical pieces have already been played on past broadcasts of the program (and when). The system will also enable the editor to review listeners' requests for this program whose range of dates includes the date of the scheduled program. Based on all this information, the editor will then select musical pieces to be played in the scheduled program. (The number of assigned pieces will depend on the duration of the program, the length of each piece, "talk time," and commercials.) Printed messages with the date in which the pieces will be played will be sent to listeners whose requests have been accepted, and the requests database will be updated accordingly. When the scheduling of a program is complete (as determined by the editor), the system will produce a "blueprint" for the editor and the technician, according to which they will prepare the broadcast.

The radio station must pay royalties to the royalty owner of each musical piece according to the number of times it is played. In order to do this, the system must record every actual playing of a music piece. This will be done by the technician of the program (during or after playing each piece). (Note that not every piece assigned to a program must actually be played, and there is a possibility that a certain piece will be played in a program even if not assigned in advance.) The system should enable the music director to produce various playing reports of musical pieces according to various parameters, such as per program, dates of broadcast, royalty owners, composers, and performers. The reports will be used by the musical director and also be sent to the musicians union (which represents the royalty owners). The actual payments to the royalty owners will be done by the station's finance department. For that, the system will produce a summary report at the end of each month, which will state how many times each piece has been played in the past month. The report will be sorted by royalty owner, program, and musical piece. The report will be sent to the finance department and to the musicians union.

The Objects Model: Initial Class Diagram

The initial class diagram is presented in Figure 8.11. It consists of four classes: **musical piece** (C1), **music program** (C2), **scheduled program** (C3), and **listener request** (C4). Note the differences between **music program** and **scheduled program**. The objects of the former are the various programs planned by the radio station for the season; the objects of the latter are actually scheduled programs to be broadcast on certain dates. Obviously, each **music program** object will be associated with many **scheduled program** objects—as

Figure 8.11. Initial class diagram of the musical programs system

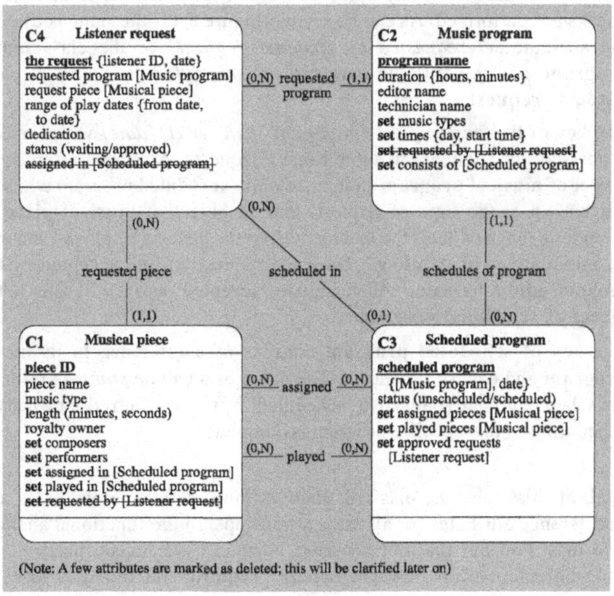

(Note: A few attributes are marked as deleted; this will be clarified later on)

many times as the program will be broadcasted. Note that a (new) **music program** may have no **scheduled program**, while a **scheduled program** must belong to one **music program**.

Without going into all details of the class diagram, here are a few highlights:

- It can be assumed that _piece ID_, the key attribute of a musical piece, is assigned when it is added to the system. Every piece also has simple attributes _piece name, music type, length,_ and _royalty owner_, and set attributes _composers_ and _performers_.

- Note the distinction between the set attributes _assigned programs_ and _played programs_ of class **musical pieces**. The values in the first set are determined by the program editor when the musical pieces for a program are scheduled; the values of the latter are determined by the technician when the pieces are actually played. The same is true for the inverse attributes in the class **scheduled program**.

- The attribute _set requested by [listener request]_ is marked as stricken out; this reference attribute is defined because of the many-to-many relationship between this class and the class **listener request**, but it is actually not needed by any user—as we will see when the compatibility checks are performed. As can be seen in Figure 8.11, the same is true for the attribute _set requested by [listener request]_ of the class **music program**, and the attribute _assigned in [scheduled program]_ of class **listener request**.

- The key of **listener request** consists of _{listener ID, date}_ which makes it possible for a listener to submit many requests. A request refers to an object of **musical program** (not an actually scheduled program which is not known at the time of request) and an object of **musical piece**. It includes a range of dates the listener wishes the piece to be played and gets an initial status of "waiting." Once the request will be accepted by the program editor, its status will change to "accepted" and it will refer to the object of **scheduled program**.

- The key of **scheduled program** consists of a reference to its **music program** and date of broadcast. The value of attribute _status_ is initially "unscheduled," and changed to "scheduled" by the program editor when the scheduling of that specific program is complete.

As noted, at this stage the class diagram includes reference attributes and inverse reference attributes for all the relationships. In the functional analysis stage we may find out that not all these attributes are indeed needed. For example, the relationship between **listener request** and **musical piece** is expressed by the inverse attributes *request piece [**musical piece**]* in the former class and *requested by [**listener request**]* in the latter class. We will see that no user of the system even needs to know, for a musical piece, who of the listeners requested to hear it. Therefore this attribute of **musical piece** will be dropped.

The Functional Model: OO-DFDs

The results of the functional analysis process are expressed by three OO-DFDs shown in Figures 8.12-8.14. Some clarifications for the diagrams are provided as follows.

Clarifications for OO-DFD-0 (Figure 8.12)

The root diagram includes three elementary functions and two general ones, each shown in its own OO-DFD. Function 1 is responsible for adding and updating data on musical pieces obtained from distributors (assumed to arrive on discs and other media). Function 2 enables the production of catalogs on the musical pieces in the database, according to parameters set by the music director. The name given to the three dataflows emanating from function 2 is just *catalogs*; however, the structure of the various catalogs will be determined in the design phase. Function 3 adds listeners' requests. Before a request object is added to the **listener request** class, the function verifies that the requested musical piece and the requested program do exist. Functions 3 and 4 are general and will be clarified separately.

It should be noted that in this example all four classes of the initial class diagram already appear in the root OO-DFD. In addition, note that function 4 obtains data of an external class **employees**. It is assumed that data on editors and technicians are already stored in an existing database (say of the human resources IS). The music programs system merely uses the data when those employees are assigned to the respective programs.

Clarifications for OO-DFD-4 (Figure 8.13)

The general function **edit music programs** is decomposed into eight elementary subfunctions. Note that this diagram is fully compatible with OO-DFD-0 in the sense that all the classes and external entities that were connected to function 4 in the root diagram also appear in this diagram.

Figure 8.12. OO-DFD-0 of musical programs system

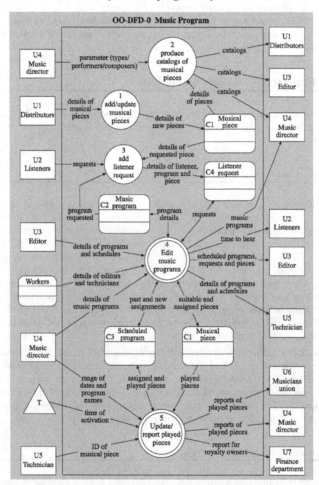

Figure 8.13. OO-DFD-4 of the musical programs system

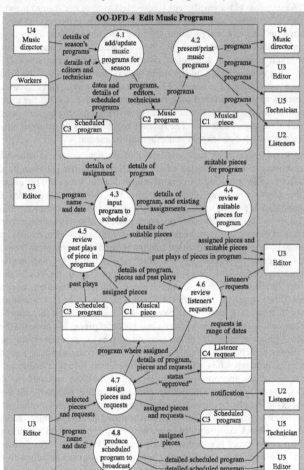

Function 4.1 deals with adding and updating the music programs of the radio station. The external class **employees** (on the left side of the frame) provides the details of the editors and technicians assigned to the programs. When the musical director creates a new program, the function creates (adds) a new object to the class **music program** and also new objects to the class scheduled program—each object for a specific date on which the program will be broadcast. This is done based on the times (days) the program will be broadcasted every week during the season. (This function, however, does not assign musical pieces to the **scheduled programs**.) Function 4.2 enables the user to present or print the music programs that will be distributed to the music director, editors, technicians, and listeners. The listener will probably be informed about the programs through newspapers and other public media.

Functions 4.3-4.7 deal with the assignment of musical pieces to scheduled programs. Function 4.3 enables the editor to select a specific program he/she wishes to work on, by imputing a program name and broadcast date. The function locates the **music program** object and retrieves the data needed for the assignment of music pieces, that is, the types of music and the program duration. In addition, it locates the scheduled program object and retrieves the existing assignments of pieces; this is so because the editor may have already assigned some musical pieces to this **scheduled program** but did not complete the task. Function 4.3 then activates function 4.4, which retrieves from the class **musical** piece the musical pieces which are suitable for this type of program. The function presents the details of the already assigned pieces and the suitable pieces to the editor. In addition, it activates function 4.5 which locates, in the class **scheduled programs**, the musical pieces which have already been played in this program, retrieves the details of these pieces from class **musical piece**, and presents them to the editor. (This will enable the editor to avoid playing too excessively the same musical pieces which have already been played in past broadcasts of the program.) The function 4.6 is activated, which retrieves listeners' requests for this program with the appropriate dates. The details of these requests are also presented to the editor. Using all this information, the editor makes the decision which pieces will be played on that scheduled program. Function 4.7 obtains the editor's assignments and adds them to the **scheduled program** object and the music program object. Actually, for every musical piece assigned, a reference to the object of that piece is added to the attribute *set assigned pieces [musical piece]*, and a reference to the object of **scheduled program** in added to the attribute *set assigned in [scheduled program]* of the musical piece object. If the assignments include pieces that were requested by listeners, the function adds references to the listeners' requests (in the attribute set *accepted requests [listener request]* and in the object of each of those listener requests it adds a reference to the **scheduled program** object and changes its status attribute to "accepted"). Finally, it produces a notification which is sent to those listeners.

Note again that the assignment process of musical pieces to a **scheduled program** does not have to be done all at once; the editor may work on a certain program without completing the assignments of musical pieces and continue sometime later. Every time the editor wishes to work on the assignment of a certain program, function 4.3 needs only to be activated, and the process will resume as explained. When the editor will indicate that the assignment is complete, function 4.8 will store the value "scheduled" in the attribute status of the **scheduled program** object.

Figure 8.14. OO-DFD-5 of the musical programs system

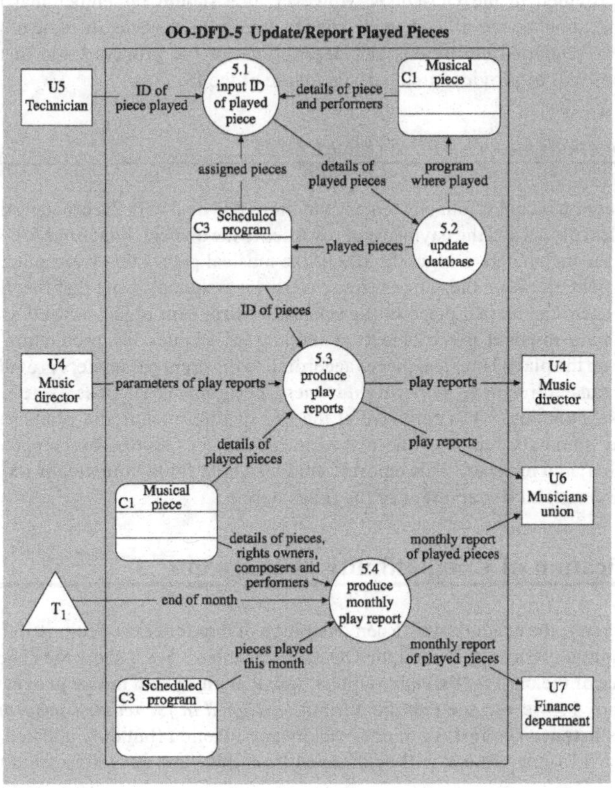

OO-DFD-5 Update/Report Played Pieces

Function 4.8 enables the production of detailed programs which have been scheduled, so that the editor and technician will use them in the preparation of the broadcast itself. It should be noted that functions 4.3-4.7 are connected to each other by dataflows, which means they activate one another once the first is activated by the program editor. But function 4.8 is not connected to the former. This means that the production of the scheduled program reports is not connected to the process of assigning musical pieces to the program. Function 4.8 will be activated by a program editor whenever he/she wishes; he/she will input a program name and date to be broadcasted, and the function will produce the desired report for the program editor's or technician's use.

So far we have seen a verbal (and not completely accurate) description of the assignment process and the other functions, all in accordance with the level of detail provided in the OO-DFDs. However, one should remember that the diagram cannot be specific when it comes to describing the process logic of the functions. Detailed definitions and descriptions of the process logic of the functions will be provided in the design phase of the IS.

Clarifications for OO-DFD-5 (Figure 8.14)

This diagram includes four elementary functions that deal with the broadcasting of musical pieces and the payments of royalties to the owners. Functions 5.1-5.2 enable the technician to input the IDs of the musical pieces that were actually played (whether from those that were or were not assigned). Note that function 5.2 registers the played piece in the **scheduled program** object as well as in each of the **musical piece** objects. Function 5.3 enables the production of reports on the played musical pieces according to different parameters provided by the music director (e.g., per right owners, performers, composers, etc.). In addition, Function 5.4 is activated at the end of each month and produces a monthly summary report of the played musical pieces, sorted by composer, performer, and program. This report is produced both for the **musicians union** and the **financial department** of the radio station.

Verification of Compatibility of Diagrams

We conclude the example with a demonstration of three checks of compatibility of the initial class diagram and the OO-DFDs. Tables 8.5-8.7 show the checks for three of the classes: **listener request, musical piece**, and **music program**. In Figure 8.5 we can see that the attribute *assigned in [scheduled program]* of class **listener request** is not retrieved by any function (but only updated by function 4.7); therefore it will be dropped from this class as well as from the

Table 8.5. Compatibility check for class listener request

Attributes	Functions		
	3	4.6	4.7
the request [listener ID, date]	+	-	
requested program [music program]	+	-	
requested piece [musical piece]	+	-	
range of play dates	+	-	
Dedication	+	-	
Status	+	-	+
assigned to [scheduled program] *			+

* *No function retrieves this attribute*

Table 8.6 Compatibility check for class musical piece

Attributes	Functions							
	1	4.7	5.2	4.4	4.5	5.1	5.3	5.4
piece ID	+			-		-	-	-
piece name	+			-		-		
music type	+			-				
length (minutes, seconds)	+			-				
royalty owner	+						-	-
set composers	+			-			-	-
Ser performers	+			-			-	-
set assigned in [scheduled program]		+			-			
set played in [scheduled program]			+					-
set requested by [listener request] *								

* *No function neither updates nor retrieves this attribute*

Table 8.7 Compatibility check for class musical program

Attributes	Functions			
	4.1	3	4.2	4.3
program name	+	-	-	-
duration {hours, minutes}	+	-	-	-
editor name	+		-	
technician name	+		-	
set music types	+	-	-	-
set times {date, start time}	+	-	-	
set requested by [listener request]*				
set consists of [scheduled program]	+			-

* *No function neither updates nor retrieves this attribute* dataflow coming from the updating function. This means that function 4.7 will only update the *status* attribute of that class. In Table 8.6 we see that the attribute *set requested by [listener request]* of class **musical piece** is neither updated nor retrieved by any function, so we drop it from the class. This is also true for the attribute *set requested by [listener request]* of class **musical program** (see Table 8.7).

Review Questions

1. What does an initial class diagram include? What does it not include?
2. What are the "direct" and the "indirect" ways to create an initial class diagram?
3. Discuss considerations and guidelines for determining whether a function is "general" or "elementary."
4. Explain and exemplify the different types of external entities.
5. Is an ATM a real-time entity? Explain.
6. Can an OO-DFD include a class which is only updated by a function (but no function retrieves data from it)? Explain.
7. What is "external class?"
8. What is the difference between an elementary dataflow and a general dataflow? Why is the distinction between the two types important?
9. What does a dataflow between two elementary functions mean?
10. What can be done if a certain OO-DFD includes too many functions?
11. What can be done if a certain OO-DFD includes too few functions?
12. In a certain OO-DFD, a dataflow links from an elementary function to a general function; how will this be expressed in the child diagram of the general function? Show an example.
13. In a certain OO-DFD, a bidirectional dataflow links two general functions; how will this be expressed in the child diagram of each of the general functions? Show an example.
14. Create a context diagram for the Customers and Suppliers system presented in Figures 8.4-8.6.
15. Why is it important to verify the compatibility between the initial class diagram and the OO-DFDs?

16. Explain and exemplify the issue of redundancy of relationship data in a many-to-many relationship between classes. How can such redundancy be avoided?

References

DeMarco, T. (1978). *Structure analysis and system specification*. Englewood Cliffs, NJ: Prentice Hall.

Gane, C., & Sarson, T. (1979). *Structured systems analysis, tools and techniques*. Englewood Cliffs, NJ: Prentice Hall.

Shoval, P. (1998). *Planning, analysis and design of information systems* (Vols. 1-3). Tel-Aviv, Israel: Open University Press.

Endnotes

[1]   Additional classes will be added in the design phase.

[2]   See Chapter IV.

[3]   This example was originally used in Shoval (1998).

[4]   Assume one family name representing whoever lives in the apartment.

[5]   This is similar, to a certain degree, to the possibility to have different computer programs which perform the same task.

[6]   General functions will be demonstrated later on.

[7]   Actually, it could appear inside the frame of the OO-DFD, next to the respective function.

[8]   The example in Figure 8.3 shows only a real-time entity fired by a function.

[9]   If we wish to show that data need to be input from an external entity and saved in a class, it should be done by a function that receives the input data from the entity and updates the class. Similarly, if we wish to pass data from one class to another, it should be done by a function, not by a direct connection.

[10]   Actually, the use of a class is not of paramount importance; instead, one may use an external entity instead. At any rate, this is not going to affect the new IS because we are not going to design or build the external components whether we call them external entities or external classes;

they serve only as a means to express input from external sources. Therefore, it also does not matter to us how exactly the data is organized in the external database, for example, is it in a class, a relational relation, or any other type of file.

11   It does not mean that the user entity will actually input the data; it is only the source of the data. At any rate, the user interface will be designed at the design phase.

12   For this reason it is preferable that the numbers of the connected functions will also be according to their order of execution.

13   Of course, diagrams with two or three functions as this one and others that will be shown later, are too small and trivial; but this is just for example.

14   It appears twice in the diagram only for convenience, to avoid crossing dataflows.

15   Of course, if such things are included in an OO-DFD it does not make the diagram erroneous; it only makes it full of trivial details that will be dealt with anyhow in the programming stage, as part of common programming practice.

16   Again we note that an OO-DFD of a real-world system would include more functions.

17   The readers are welcome to revised draw diagrams according to the two alternatives.

18   In this example only; in reality there would be more details on a payment.

19   Recall that this check should be done with the aid of the DD, which specifies the data elements that are contained in the dataflows. The next chapter deals with the DD in detail.

20   As we know, the diagrams shown in the various examples present the final results of the analysis process, so it is impossible to know what changes were made in order to prevent incompatibility. For example, let us assume that in a nonfinal OO-DFD-2.2 (Figure 8.10) the function 2.2.7 updated the **Work in progress** class by inserting the date the work was completed. During the compatibility check it was discovered that no function retrieves this data, that is, no one needs to know the date of completion. Therefore, this attribute should be removed from the class and from the DD. As a matter of fact, OO-DFD-2.2 does not include an update of this class.

21   We have already referred to this example in chapter VI, but the users' requirements have not been presented in detail. This example too has originally been used in Shoval (1998).

22   The reader is reminded that many correct solutions are possible, not only the solution provided here. At any rate, any solution must be examined

according to two criteria: (1) syntax of the models: the class diagram and the OO-DFDs must be syntactically correct according to the rules of each model; and (2) user requirement: all the users' requirements (as expressed in the requirements document) must be satisfied.

Chapter IX

Data Dictionary

This chapter explains the roles of a data dictionary (DD) in the development of the information system (IS) and describes its components. The chapter presents a possible implementation of the data dictionary both with the relational and the object oriented (OO) models.

A DD is a database or repository of data on the products of the analysis and design phases. It is initially created during the analysis phase, containing details about the components of the object oriented data flow diagram (OO-DFD) and the data elements carried by their various dataflows. But it will be updated and extended throughout the design phase to include details about the products of that phase too. The DD is essential in the development of large-scale systems because it enables its users (analysts and designers) to define, save, and retrieve, in a standard manner, various details of the analysis and design products, details which are not included in those products.

A DD can be implemented as a relational database consisting of tables, or as an OO database consisting of object classes. This chapter describes the components of a DD using both models. Obviously, at this stage we only describe the components which are created at the analysis phase.

A Relational Data Dictionary

The data dictionary consists of tables which store and enable to retrieve information of two major types: (1) information about the components of the OO-DFDs; and (2) information about the data elements carried by the dataflows.

Information about the Components of the OO-DFDs

The data dictionary should enable the analyst to document and retrieve information about any component appearing in any of the OO-DFDs. The components are (general and elementary) functions, external (user, time, and real-time) entities and classes. The information that might be needed on any component includes its identification, name, description, and the other components to which it is connected via dataflows. This information might be needed by the analyst while making modifications to the diagrams. To enable this, two relational tables are needed: a **components table** and a **dataflows table**.

Components Table

The structure of this table is as follows:[1]

Code	**number**	name	description

The table includes a record for each component of any OO-DFD. A component is uniquely identified by the component code and a number. The component codes are, as we know: F = a function;[2] U = a user entity; T = a time entity; R = a real-time entity; and C = a class. Besides its code and number, a component's record includes its name (as appearing in the diagram) and a description. The description may include some explanation about the component, if needed. For example, for a user entity it may explain who will actually be the users or the organizational unit; for a class—a short description on the objects that it will include (but there is no need to elaborate more because the details of the classes are defined in the class diagram). For an elementary function the explanation must be more detailed, it should describe what the function does and its process logic; these details will be used later on in the design phase. The necessary description can be provided in natural language (free text), but if the process logic is not simple and involves various conditions and actions, it might be better to describe it using structured English or pseudo code, or even create a flow chart.

In these cases, the description may be included in a separate file while the description field in the table will only contain a reference to it.

Dataflows Table

The structure of this table is as follows:

Source		target		dataflow name	type (e/g)
Code	number	code	number		

The table contains a tuple for each dataflow in the diagrams.[3] Note that a dataflow is identifiable by the components at its two ends: the source and the target (at least one of them must be a function).

This table, along with the **components table**, enables finding, for any component, the other components to which it is connected as their source or as their target. For example, to find which functions retrieve data from the class **apartment** (in all OO-DFDs) we may use the following SQL query:

Select target-code, target-number, dataflow name

From Components, dataflows

Where components.code = dataflows.source-code and components.number = dataflows.source-number and components.name = "Apartment" and components.code = "C";

Another example: to find which functions provide output to user entity **company**, we may sue the SQL query:

Select source-code, source-number, dataflow name

From components, dataflows

Where components.code = dataflows.target-code and components.number = dataflows.target-number and element name = "Company" and components.code = "U";

Information about the Data Elements Carried by the Dataflows

The data dictionary should include detailed definitions of the data elements carried by the elementary dataflows and passes from and to the components of the OO-DFDs. A data element is an elementary unit of data of a certain data type, for example, person ID number, first name, last name, phone number, birth date, grade, salary, and so forth. The data elements carried by a dataflow from a user entity to a function will eventually become fields in the input screen (or other input device that may be determined for that input); the data elements carried by a dataflow from a function to a user entity will eventually become fields in an output screen or a report; the data elements carried by a dataflow from a function to a class or from a class to a function will eventually become attributes which are updated or retrieved by the function, and which are also attributes of the class; the data elements carried by a dataflow from a function to another function will eventually become the parameters which are passed from the former to the latter.

There is no need to define the data elements carried by general dataflows, only by elementary dataflows, because general dataflows will eventually be decomposed into elementary ones.[4]

To enable the aforementioned definitions, three tables are needed: **data elements**, **elementary dataflows**, and **data elements on elementary dataflows**.

Data Elements Table

The structure of this table is as follows:

data element name	description	data type	length	range of values

- **Data element name:** Each data element has a unique name (usually one or two words).
- **Description:** explains what the element is. A description is only needed if the name of the element is unclear.
- **Data type:** for example, text (characters), numeric (integer), decimal (real), date, and so on.
- **Length:** the number of bytes.

- **Range of values:** if there is a limitation on the element's values. For example, > 0 means that the value must be positive.

The definitions of the data types, lengths, and ranges of values of the various data elements may be deferred to the design phase.

Elementary Dataflows Table

The structure of this table is as follows:

Source		Target		*list of data elements*	volume	method of delivery
code	number	code	Number			

While the dataflows table includes records of all the dataflows, this one includes only records of the elementary dataflows. The most informative data included in this table are the list of data elements carried by each elementary dataflow. This valuable information causes the table to be not normalized.[5] Actually, this field may be eliminated from this table because at any rate the next table (**data elements in elementary dataflows**) will provide these details. The fields "volume" and "method of delivery" will include data for only dataflows from and to user entities. The "volume" of each such dataflow is the sum of lengths of the data elements it carries; it will help the designer to determine the method and media for delivery of the input from the user or the output to the user. For example, if the volume of input data is huge, it might be determined that the input media must be some device (e.g., a scanner or a magnetic card reader) rather than a keyboard. This also determines the method of delivery (e.g., presenting a certain output on screen or by a printed report).

As said about data types and lengths of data elements, the definition of these details (i.e., of volume and method of delivery) may also be deferred to the design phase.

Data Elements in Elementary Dataflows Table

The structure of this table is as follows:

data element	source		Target		constraints
	code	number	code	number	

This table enables the finding out of which data elements are carried by which dataflow (as can be done in the former table assuming that it includes the filed list of data elements), and on which dataflow a certain data element is carried. Obviously, each data element will have as many records in the table as the number of elementary dataflows by which it is carried, and each elementary dataflow will have as many records as the number of data elements it carries. In addition, it is possible to define constraints (restrictions) on the appearance of a data element on a dataflow, as follows:

- **Optional:** meaning that the data element may not have a value. For example, for a data element "address" of a certain input dataflow, optional would mean that input of the address is not mandatory.

- **Multi-valued:** means that the data element may have many values. For example, for a data element "phone number" of a certain input dataflow it would mean that more than one phone number may be input. It is also possible to determine a minimal or maximal number of values—for example, "phone numbers (1-3)."

Optional Dictionary Tables

In addition to the previous three tables which enable defining the data elements carried by the dataflows, two more tables may be needed for special types of data elements: **Synonyms table** and **Aggregates table**.

Synonyms Table

In a large-scale system, there is a possibility that different users would use different names for a certain data element. For example, "pupil" can be used as a synonym of "student," or "ID number" as a synonym of "identification number." In such cases, one of the names should be chosen as the **standard** name of the data element, which will be used in the other tables where it appears, while the dictionary will store all its synonyms. For this, there is need for a **synonyms table** as presented hereafter. Note that the key of this table is "synonym name," while "standard name" is the data element name which is used in the other tables of the DD.

synonym name	standard name

Aggregates Table

Sometimes several data elements appear together on the dataflow, as a group. For example, the data elements: street, number, city, and zip code (and sometimes also state code or country) usually appear together and constitute a "data aggregate" called address. Another common example is the data aggregate "date" whose elements are day, month, and year. In such cases, space and time can be saved if the aggregate name is used instead of the individual data element names. This is enabled with the **aggregates table** which details the data elements of each aggregate. Note that the key of this table consists of both fields because a certain aggregate may include two or more data elements, while a certain data element may be included in more than one aggregate. It is also important to note that a certain data element may be part of an aggregate but also exists as an "independent" element. For example, "city" or "year" may be part of aggregates "address" and "date," respectively, but they may also serve as stand-alone data elements.

aggregate name	data element name

To summarize, Figure 9.1 presents the relational database schema of the DD using Microsoft (MS) Access. In addition to the tables and their fields, the foreign-key to primary-key relationships are also on display.

Figure 9.1. Relational database schema of the data dictionary

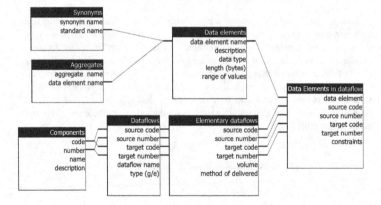

Examples of Data in a Relational Data Dictionary

Here is a small example of the DD tables (see Tables 9.1-9.7). Each table presents a few data records only, based on OO-DFD-1 of the **apartments building** system (Figure 8.8, Chapter VIII).

Table 9.1. Components table

Code	Number	Name	Description
F	1.1	add/update tenant details	The function enables the adding of new tenants, as well as the updating of existing tenants or their deletion.
F	1.2	review tenant details	...
U	1	Tenant	...
U	2	Company	...
T	1	Time	...
C	1	Apartment	The attributes of the class and its relationships with other classes are detailed in the class diagram.
...	...	...	...

Table 9.2. Dataflows table

Source		Target		Dataflow name	Type
code	number	code	number		
U	1	F	1.1	Tenant details	e
F	1.1	C	1	Tenant details	e
F	1.4	F	1.5	Tenant and payment details	e
F	1.5	U	1	Receipt	e
C	1	F	1.7	fees and payments	e
T	1	F	1.7	End of month	e
...	...	...	...	...	...

Table 9.3. Data elements table

Data element name	Description	Data type	Length (bytes)	Range of values
Apartment number	Identifies an apartment in the building and the family or tenants who live in it.	Numeric	2	$x > 0$
Family name	Does not identify an apartment	Text	30	
Month		Numeric	2	$13 > x > 0$
Monthly fee	How much a tenant needs to pay	Decimal	3(2)	...
Sum	How much has been paid	Decimal	3(2)	...
Remainder	...	Text	100	...
...	...	...	...	...

Table 9.4. Elementary dataflows table

Source		Target		Volume	Method of delivery
code	**number**	**code**	**number**	(bytes)	
U	1	F	1.1	150	Typing from keyboard via input screen.
F	1.1	C	1	150	...
C	1	F	1.4	150	...
F	1.5	C	5	50	...
F	1.5	U	1	100	...
...	...	...	...		...

Table 9.5. Data elements in elementary dataflows table

Data element	Source		Target		Constraints
	code	**number**	**code**	**number**	
Apartment number	U	1	F	1.1	
Apartment number	F	1.1	C	1	
Apartment number	F	1.5	U	1	
Number of tenants	U	1	F	1.1	optional
...	...	...	...		
Family name	U	1	F	1.1	
Family name	F	1.1	C	1	
...	...	...	...	...	
Sum	U	1	F	1.4	
Sum	F	1.4	F	1.5	
Sum	F	1.5	C	1	
Sum	F	1.5	U	1	
...	...	...	...	...	

Table 9.6. Synonyms table

Synonym name	Standard name
Tenant number	Apartment number
apartment	Apartment number
...	...

Table 9.7. Aggregates table

Aggregate name	**Data element name**
Phone number	Type
Phone number	Number
Date	Day
Date	Month
Date	Year
...	...

An OO Data Dictionary

Figure 9.2 presents the data dictionary in a class diagram. Here are several clarifications:

- The **components** class contains objects which are the various components of the OO-DFDs. We made no distinction between different kinds of components. However, we could subclassify **components** into **functions**, **classes**, and **external entities**. Furthermore, we could subclassify **functions** into **general** and **elementary functions**, and **external entities** into **user**, **time**, and **real-time entities**.

Figure 9.2. Class diagram of the data dictionary

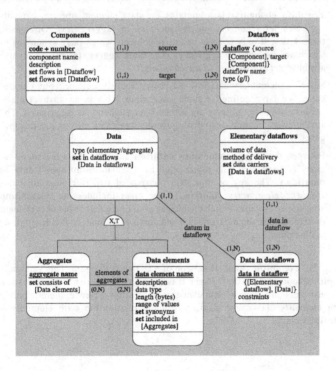

- As we know, each component is identified by the component code and number. Note the two set reference attributes of the class: one set (*flows in*) refers to the dataflows coming to this component from other components, and the other set (*flows out*) refers to dataflows going out from this component to other components.

- The **dataflows** class includes objects of all the dataflows, general and elementary. A dataflow is identified, as we know, by the source and target components. (We may assume that this class includes a function/method whose objective is to verify that at least one end of the ends of each dataflow refers to a function.)

- **Elementary dataflows** is, obviously, a subclass of **dataflows**. For each elementary dataflow we write the total volume of data it carries and the method of delivery. As we know, this is only relevant for dataflows coming from or going to user entities (but this is not shown in the diagram because we have not made the distinction between subclasses of **components**).

- The **data elements** class contains the data element objects. Note its attributes *set synonyms* and *set included in [aggregates]*. Obviously, these sets will only contain values for objects which have synonyms or which are included in aggregates. The class **aggregates** has an inverse attribute *set consists of [data elements]*.

- Since an elementary dataflow may carry both data elements and aggregates, we have defined a super class **data**. This is an abstract class, because all of its objects are either Data elements or aggregates. The attribute *type* enables us to distinguish between data elements and aggregates.

- Between the classes **elementary dataflow** and **data** there is a many-to-many relationship. It is represented by a "relationship class" **data in dataflows**. The key of this class consists of two reference attributes *{[data], [elementary dataflow]}*. The class includes the relationship attribute *constraints* which enables us to define whether the data element or aggregate in the dataflow is mandatory or optional, or if it is single or multi-valued.

Figure 9.3 exemplifies another version of a DD class diagram. This version is simplified (compared to the former): It assumes that there are no aggregates and no constraints on values of data elements in dataflows. Hence, there is only a **data elements** class, with a many-to-many relationship with **elementary dataflows** class.

Figure 9.3. A simplified class diagram of the data dictionary

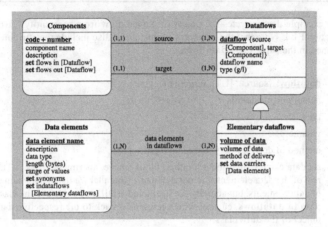

Examples of Data in an OO Data Dictionary

Here is a small example of the OO DD. The example refers to the (extended) class diagram in Figure 9.2. It shows only one object from each class, based on the same OO-DFD-1 of the **apartments building** system.[6]

An Object of Class Components

The example demonstrates the object **C1** which is the class **apartments**:

- **code+number**: C1
- name: Apartments
- description: stores objects of apartments.
- set flows in [Dataflows]: [F1.1], [F1.5], [F1.8][7]
- set flows out [Dataflows]: [F1.2], [F1.4], [F1.6], [F1.7].

An Object of Class Elementary Dataflow

The example demonstrates the object of the dataflow from user entity U1 to function F1.1. Note that the attributes of this object also include the attributes defined in the super class **dataflows**.

- **dataflow**: {source: [U1], target [F1.1]}
- name: tenants details
- type: e
- volume: 150
- method of delivery: keyboard and input screen.
- set data carries: apartment number, family name, apartment size,... (The rest of the data elements are not detailed.) Note that we listed here names of data elements, but actually the list includes OIDs of objects in the class **data in dataflows**, each of which references back to the respective data object of the **data** class.

An Object of Class Data Elements

The example demonstrates the object of the data element **apartment number**.

- type: elementary (note that this and the next attribute are taken from the super class **data**).
- set in dataflows: [data in dataflows]: [U1, F1.2]; [F1.1, C1]; [C1, F1.2];... (Each pair is a source and a target of a certain dataflow. Only a few of the dataflows in which this data element is carried are detailed.) Note that actually the set includes the OIDs of objects in the class **data in dataflows**, each of which references back to the respective object of the **elementary dataflows** class.
- **data element name**: apartment number
- description: identifies an apartment or a family living in the apartment.
- data type: numeric
- length: 3
- range of values: between 001 and 4500
- set synonyms: tenant ID, apartment

- set included in [aggregate]: this data component belongs to no aggregate; if it did, the OID of the aggregate object would have been written here.

An Object of Class Aggregate

The example demonstrates the object of the data aggregate **date**:

- type: aggregate
- set in dataflows: [data in dataflows]: [U1, F1.4]; [F1.1, F1.5]; [F1.5, C1]; ... (See comment in the former example.)
- **aggregate name**: date
- set elements of aggregate: [day], [month], [year] (Actually the set includes references to the OIDs of these data elements.)

An Object of Class Data in Dataflows

The example demonstrates an object which links the data element **apartment number** and the elementary dataflow from user entity U1 to function F1.1

- **data in dataflow** {[elementary flows], [data]}: [U1, F1.1]; [apartment number]
- constraints: mandatory

Review Questions

1. What is the objective of the components DD?
2. Assume you have a relational DD; explain by referring to specific tables, how one can find the following: (1) which elementary functions retrieve (read from) a certain class; (2) which functions provide outputs to a certain external entity; and (3) which functions update a certain class.
3. Assume you have an objects DD; answer the same questions as stated in Review Question two, by referring to specific classes in the class diagram.
4. Why is it not necessary to define which data elements flow on general dataflows?

Each of the following questions can be answered assuming a relational or an objects data dictionary. For each question, refer to specific tables or classes which need to be accessed:

5. How can you find out which dataflows carry/contain a certain data element?

6. How can you find out the volume of data carried by a certain elementary dataflow?

7. How can you find out which data elements are carried/contained by a certain elementary dataflow?

8. How can you find the standard name of a data element?

9. How can you find out which dataflows carry/contain a certain data aggregate?

10. How can you find out which are the data elements of a certain aggregate?

11. What type of relationship exists between the dataflows table/class and elementary dataflows able/class?

12. Practice exercise: Create a relational database schema for a DD, similar to the one presented in Figure 9.1. You may use any relational Data Base Management System (DBMS), for example, MS Access, MySQL, Oracle, and so forth. Then, populate the tables of the DD with data from one of the systems exemplified in chapter VIII. Note that for this you have to "invent" data elements which flow on the various elementary dataflows of the OO-DFDs.

13. Practice exercise: Create an objects database schema for a DD, similar to the one presented in Figure 9.2 or 9.3. Then populate the classes of the DD with data from the same system used in the previous exercise.

Endnotes

[1] Key fields are in bold and underlined.

[2] Note that general functions and elementary functions have the same code F; the function type is identifiable by its decimal number.

[3] A two-way dataflow will have two records in this table, in the opposite directions.

[4] Hence, the data elements carried by a general function are the union of data elements carried by its elementary dataflows.

⁵   This field must be defined as a character string of some large size to enable many data elements per dataflow.

⁶   In this example we see both the attribute names and values (data). However, the readers should bear in mind that in the dictionary database, the names of the attributes are saved in the database catalog, where the classes are described, while the objects contain only the data values.

⁷   Actually, the values of this set are Object Identification Numbers (OID) of the referenced objects (i.e., dataflows), but for the sake of demonstration we present the values of those objects (i.e., the dataflows as identified by their sources and targets). This comment applies also to the other reference attributes in the example.

Section III:
Information Systems Design
with FOOM

This unit is concerned with the phase of system design. As we know, design is a continuation of the analysis phase and it uses its products (i.e., the initial class diagram, the OO-DFD's and the data dictionary) as input for the design of the system components.

The products of the design phase, according to *FOOM* methodology, are: (a) a **complete class diagram** which includes, in addition to the data classes, menus, inputs, outputs and transactions classes. Each class contains, in addition to attributes and relationships, its functions; (b) detailed descriptions of the **methods** of the classes; (c) the **user interface**; (d) the **input** and **output screens/reports**. The products of the design phase will be used as input for the construction/programming of the system.

Chapter X (Transactions and Their Top-Level Design) starts with an overview of the design phase according to the *FOOM* methodology and presents the sub phases and their products. Then, the chapter focuses on the design of transactions. First it describes what transactions are and how they can be identified and extracted from the OO-DFDs. Afterwards, it explains how to map transaction diagrams to top-level descriptions, which detail their components and process logic. The transactions' top-level descriptions will eventually become detailed descriptions of respective class methods. The chapter ends with additions to the data dictionary and the class diagram due to the definition of the transactions.

Chapter XI (Design of the Man-Machine Interface: Menus, Inputs, and Outputs) describes a method for the design of the user interface—menus trees—for the entire system as well as for its sub systems. Then it describes how to design the inputs and outputs/reports of the systems. As results, new classes of menus, forms and reports are added to the class diagram.

Chapter XII (Detailed Design of the Transactions and Class Methods) describes how to map a top-level description of a transaction to a detailed description, and then how to "decompose" a detailed description of a transaction to various methods which are attached to proper classes. Two equivalent techniques for the description of methods are provided: pseudo-code and message charts. The chapter ends with a review on the products of the design stage, which serve as input to the system construction (programming) stage.

Chapter X

Transactions and Their Top-Level Design

This chapter starts with an overview of the design phase according to the functional and object oriented methodology (FOOM) and presents the subphases and their products. Then, the chapter focuses on the design of transactions. First it describes what transactions are and how they can be identified and extracted from the object oriented data flow diagrams (OO-DFD). Afterwards, it explains how to map transaction diagrams to top-level descriptions, which detail their components and process logic. The transactions' top-level descriptions will eventually become detailed descriptions of respective class methods. The chapter ends with additions to the data dictionary (DD) the class diagram due to the definition of the transactions.

Overview of the Design Phase According to FOOM

In the design phase we use the products of the analysis phase in order to design the components of the system. At the end of the design phase, the following products will be created: (1) a **complete class diagram** which will include, in addition to all the data classes, the interface, input (Forms), and output (Reports) classes; every class will include, in addition to its attributes, a list of its functions; (2) a detailed description of the **methods**, the functions of the classes. The methods will be described in pseudo code or with message charts; (3) the **user interface**—in the form of a menus tree; and (4) the **input and output screens/ reports**. The products of the design phase will enable the creation of the information system (IS) in an object oriented environment.

In order to create these products, the design phase is carried out in several subphases, which are:

1. identification of the transactions of the system and creation of their top-level descriptions;

2. design of the user interface—a menus tree—and addition of the Menus class;

3. design of the input and output screen/reports and addition of the Forms and Reports classes; and

4. detailed design of the transactions and their decomposition into class methods, described in pseudo code or message charts.

This chapter deals with the first subphase, while the other subphases will be dealt with in the following chapters.

Identifying the Transactions

What is a Transaction?

A transaction is an independent computer process which performs a task for a user of the system in order to assist in the completion of a business process.[1] A transaction may include a series of activities performed by a computer program which support in achieving the user's task. For example, a transaction may enable the user to input new data, update the database, retrieve data from the database, perform various computations (e.g., summarizing, sorting, comparing), produce reports, and so on. The activities included in a transaction are performed in a certain order or process logical, according to the user's task.

Hence, an IS is made up of transactions, each assisting in performing a certain business task. All the transactions taken together express the functionality of the system. In a business/organizational IS, most of the transactions will be activated by users[2] who interact with the system; that is, a certain user may interact with a certain transaction and together carry out the user's task. But some of the transactions may not be activated by users but rather "automatically" by the system, at certain points of time or time intervals, or as a result of real-time events.

Obviously, the transactions of the system should be derivable from the OO-DFDs which define the users' needs. Eventually they will become the application programs, implemented as class methods. The first task in the design of transactions is to discover them in the OO-DFDs, identify their components, and describe their process logic, thus providing a top-level (general) description. In this subphase, the object scheme is also added a new class called "transactions." Later on, each top-level description will be detailed and then decomposed into various methods that will be attached to the proper classes.

As said, the transactions do exist in the OO-DFDs. They have to be discovered, extracted, and described. First, let us define a transaction in terms of its OO-DFD components:

A transaction consists of one or more elementary functions which are connected directly to each other by dataflows. It also includes the classes and external entities which are connected to those functions. A transaction must include at least one external entity (of any kind) which enables its activation.

Let us look more closely at the definition of the transaction:

- A transaction includes one or more elementary functions which are connected **directly to each other** by dataflows. As we know, a dataflow connecting two functions means that one function activates (triggers) the other; that is, they all execute in the same process, which is the transaction. Functions that are not directly connected are separated by classes. The lack of a direct connection between functions means that they are not activated in the same process; that is, they belong to different transactions.

- A transaction may consist of a single elementary function, if it is not directly connected to any other function. Such a transaction is probably simple and does not perform many activities. On the other hand, a transaction may consist of many elementary functions; there is no "formal" limitation on the number of functions, as long as they are connected directly, but it is preferable to have relatively simple transactions so that the interaction of a user with a transaction will be simple and easy. If it will turn out that a certain transaction is not simple enough, it may have to be changed, which actually means that the respective OO-DFD will have to be changed, in order to keep all analysis and design products updated and consistent at all times.[3]

- All the functions included in a transaction are **elementary**. A general function is not a part of a transaction, since it is decomposed into subfunctions. As we know, a general function may be decomposed into many subfunctions, elementary or general ones; some of them may be directly connected to each other (via dataflows) while some may be "separated" by classes. This means that the elementary subfunctions of a general function may eventually belong to different transactions.

- A transaction includes the external entities and the classes which are connected to its elementary functions; an external entity can be a source of data input to a function or destination of information output by a function; the class can be updated by a function used by a function to retrieve data from it. Note that a certain external entity or class may belong to more than one transaction, while an elementary function may belong to one transaction only.

- It is possible that the components of a certain transaction appear in more than one OO-DFD. This is the case if at a certain level there is a general function connected (directly) to an elementary function or to another general function. The elementary functions of a transaction which "belongs" to different OO-DFDs are easily identifiable by following the connectors at the right or left sides of the OO-DFDs.

- A transaction must include at least one external entity (of any kind) which enables its activation. As we know, an external entity can be a user entity (U), a time entity (T), or real-time entity (R):

  o The existence of a user entity in a transaction means that the transaction will be activated by a user because he/she either needs to input data into the system or retrieve information from it, or do both. A transaction which includes a user entity is called **user transaction**. This is the most common type of transaction in IS, where various users interact with the various transactions of the system. Obviously, a user transaction must be accessible from the user interface (that will be designed later on). A transaction may include more than one user entity, both as sources of data or destinations of information. This does not necessarily mean that more than one user will activate the same transaction and interact with it concurrently; a transaction will probably be activated by a certain user who will be authorized to activate it; the various user entities only signify where the input data comes from or where the output information goes to, not who actually activates the transaction and interacts with it.

  o The existence of a time entity means that the transaction will be activated "automatically" on a certain point of time or time intervals, as indicated on the triggering dataflow—without the involvement of a user. This type of transaction is called **time transaction**. As we know, not many transactions in an IS are likely to be time transactions. Obviously, a time transaction will not be accessible to users via the user interface.

o   The existence of a real-time entity means that the transaction will be activated by a device that senses the environment and sends messages to a function which interprets the messages real time and reacts accordingly. This type is called **real-time transactions**. Real-time transactions are certainly rare in IS but more typical to real-time, embedded systems.

o   A transaction that includes both user entities and a time entity may be defined as a **mixed transaction**, which means that it can be activated by both a user who interacts with the system, and "automatically" by the system in predefined time intervals. However, the existence of both user entities and a time entity in a transaction does not necessarily mean that it should be activated in both modes. There are two possibilities: (1) that indeed it is a **mixed transaction**, which may be activated in both modes. For example, assume a certain transaction that produces a certain report on a timely basis (say once a week) but which can also be activated by an authorized user to produce the report anytime the user wished to get it. (2) That it is only a **time transaction**, which will be activated "automatically" and on that occasion will perform the input operation (if a user entity is on the "input" side) or produce the output (if a user entity is on the "output" side). For example, assume a certain transaction that is activated once a month and produces a monthly report which is sent to various users.

Since a given transaction that includes both user entities and a time entity can be interpreted in different ways, the system analyst along with the user must determine the desired mode of its activation. Note that a mixed transaction must be accessible to its user(s) from the user interface, in addition to being activated automatically by the system. Note also that if a mixed transaction or time transaction includes a user entity on the "input" side, it cannot be assumed that there is a real user "waiting" with data to be input once the transaction is activated automatically; rather the data to be input must be prepared on an appropriate input device and be ready to be activated with the transaction. (For example, assume a batch of sales forms are prepared to be read by an optic or magnetic reader.)

Examples of Transactions

Following the definition of a transaction, it is straightforward to identify and extract the transactions from the OO-DFDs. In most cases, all the components of a transaction will be found in one OO-DFD; in some cases, a transaction may be "spread" over more than one OO-DFD. In order to "see" the transaction more easily in the diagrams it is possible to color all the functions belonging to the same transaction in one color. Another way to see clearly the transactions is to present them in a separate diagram.

We will demonstrate a few transaction diagrams which were extracted from OO-DFD-1 of the **Apartments Building** system (Figure 8.8 of Chapter VIII). In this OO-DFD we identify five transactions; their diagrams are presented in Figure 10.1.

Here are some explanations on the components of some of the transactions and what they are meant to do. At this stage the explanations are actually narrative descriptions of the **possible** meaning of the transactions and their process logic. More precise descriptions of the transactions and their process logic will be provided later on, using pseudo code:

- **Transaction (a)** exemplifies a simple user transaction; it includes only the elementary function 1.1, one user entity U1, and one class C1. The task of the transaction is to enable the user to add or update details of the tenants of an apartment. The transaction will not necessarily be activated by a tenant, as may be implied from the user entity **tenant**. It may be activated by an authorized officer of the maintenance company in charge of this activity. Alternatively, it may indeed be activated by a tenant (for example, if the system will be implemented via the Internet, enabling the tenants to access the system from their apartments). The decision about who will activate the various user transactions will be made later on at the stage of interface design (see Chapter XI). Once activated, function 1.1 will display an input screen (form) by which the user will be able to choose between adding a new tenant and updating details of an existing one. The function will enable the user to key in the new data in proper fields/windows or update existing data presented in those fields. Then the function will add a new tenant (**apartment**) object or update the existing object, and the transaction will terminate.

- **User transaction (b)** includes two elementary functions 1.2 and 1.3, a user entity U2 and the class C1. The meaning of the transaction can be interpreted as follows: The transaction will be activated by an authorized officer of the company when he/she decides to set or update the monthly

Figure 10.1. Transaction diagrams extracted from OO-DFD-1 of the apartments building system

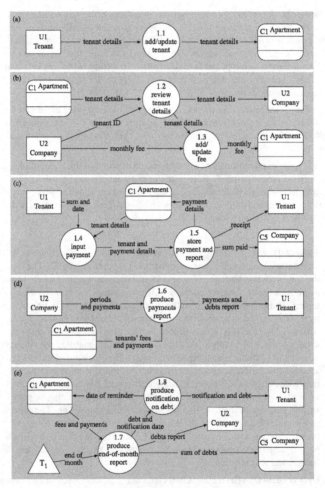

fees of a tenant. Once activated, function 1.2 will retrieve from class C1 and present on screen a list of apartment IDs and family names; the user will select a certain apartment/tenant and consequently all details of that apartment and tenant will appear on the screen presented to the user. The officer will review the details, perhaps consider other things (which are not in the system), and based on that he/she will determine the monthly fee and input the fee and the effective month using the input screen. Then function 1.2 will trigger function 1.3 and forward to it these details; function 1.3 will in turn update the apartment object accordingly. Note that the previous explanation is not a one-to-one description of the diagram, it may be slightly different or more detailed because it describes not just the components of the transaction but rather the transaction as a whole unit or process.

- **Transaction (e)** demonstrates a time transaction that is activated at the end of each month. (The exact day and hour will be set separately at the implementation phase.) Although the transaction includes user entities, which means that potentially this is a mixed transaction, it is determined by the analyst and user that it is actually just a time transaction. Once activated, function 1.7 will perform a series of activities for each apartment object: First it will retrieve the monthly fees and payments made by the tenant since the beginning of the year; based on that it will calculate the debt as of the end of this month (if any), print a line in the debts report (which will eventually be forwarded to the authorized company officer), and update the **Company** class with the amount of debt. In addition, the function will activate function 1.8, whose task is to check if a notification on the debt should be sent to the tenant. (The details of the check are not specified yet, but note that they have been documented in the DD where function 1.8 is described.) If so determined by the function, a notification is printed (detailing the debt) and sent to the tenant and the apartment object is updated accordingly. Note that this process will be repeated for all apartments. This is evidenced from what the transaction is intended to do, even though the diagram shows no "loop."

As we have seen more than once, the transaction diagram (which is extracted from the OO-DFD) only details its components but it does not "tell the story," that is, it does not prescribe a specific meaning and process logic. Generally, a transaction diagram can be interpreted in different ways; but the analyst and the user must determine and specify the proper meaning and process logic according to which the transaction should work. The process logic of a transaction will be specified in pseudo code. Initially we will create general, top-level descriptions of the transactions; later on they will be more detailed.

Top-Level Descriptions of Transactions

The process logic of the transactions must be determined by the analyst in cooperation with the user (or his/her representative), because the transaction is aimed to assist the user performing a business function. The process logic of a transaction can be described using various structured techniques, such as those used to describe programs or other sequences of activities. In FOOM we use Structured English or pseudo code.[4]

A top-level description of a transaction consists of two types of commands: (1) commands which define the main activities that the transaction performs; and (2) commands which define the process logic according to which the activities are performed.

The commands which define the main activities of a transaction are based on its functions and other components, as follows:

- Each function appearing in a transaction is translated to a command **"execute function..."** followed by the function number and name.
- Each dataflow from a user entity to a function is translated to a command **"input from U..."** followed by the user number and name and the dataflow name.[5]
- Each dataflow from a function to a user entity is translated to a command **"output to U..."** followed by the user number and name and the dataflow name.
- Each dataflow from a class to a function is translated to a command **"read from C..."** followed by the class number and name and the dataflow name.
- Each dataflow from a function to a class is translated to a command **"write to C..."** followed by the class number and name and the dataflow name.
- Each dataflow from a function to a function is translated to a command **"move to F..."** followed by the function number and the dataflow name.

The process logic of the transactions is defined with structured-programming patterns:

- **Sequence:** Commands which are performed in sequence are detailed one after the other, either in the same line or in separate lines.

- **Conditions (braches):** Commands which are performed according to conditions are specified using the pattern "if <condition> then <action> else <action>", where <action> may stay of any of the previous commands. Alternatively, if the conditions are complex and to avoid nesting of " if… then…. else…" patterns, the "Do case… end case" pattern may be used, within which the various conditions and actions can be detailed one after the other.
- **Iterations (loops):** Commands which may be repeated many times, depending on certain conditions, are specified using a "Do-while... end-while" pattern, with a mechanism to determine the end-of-loop condition.

It should be emphasized again that a top-level description of a transaction is not a one-to-one mapping from the transaction diagram. Certain changes, usually additions, may take place due to the process logic determined for the transaction. For example, wherever the previous mapping rules say "dataflow name" there may be some variations due to the specific interpretation of the transaction which may imply more specific details about what a dataflow included. At the same time, note that the transaction's top-level description does not include all possible and needed details; in particular, it does not detail exactly the activities involved in its functions. Such details will be added, as already mentioned, at the step of detailed description of transactions.

In the sequel we show a few examples of top-level descriptions of transactions. The first three examples are based on the transactions diagrams presented in Figure 10.1. The examples include explanations, which are brought in parentheses and italic font within the example text.

Example 1: Top-Level Description of Transaction (a) of Figure 10.1

Begin transaction 1.1 *(The ID of the transaction is made of the numbers of its functions.)*

Input from U1 Tenant: type of operation desired *(It is assumed that an input screen is displayed and the user is asked to select "add" or "update" a tenant.)*

If action = "add" then input from U1 Tenant: new tenant details to add

Else *(if action = "update")* then input from U1 Tenant: tenant details to update *(It is assumed that upon selection of "update" the function first asks the user to input an apartment number or tenant family name; based on that it retrieves the details of that tenant and presents them on the input screen/form, enabling the user to key in the changes. Note that the transaction diagram does not show a "read' dataflow from class C1 to function 1.1; it is implied because, as we know, any add or update activity is preceded by a find/read activity.)*

Execute F1.1: Add/update tenant details

Write to C1 Apartments: new or updated tenant details

End transaction.

Example 2: Top-Level Description of Transaction (c) of Figure 10.1

Begin transaction 1.4/5

Input from U1 Tenant: Apartment number or family name

Read from C1 Apartment: tenant details *(The function finds and retrieves the apartment object.)*

If not-found then present error message and ask user to input again an apartment ID

Else input from U1 Tenant: payment details *(The exact details are specified in the DD.)*

Execute F1.4 Input payment *(Actually, this function does the previous activities; it is brought here just for the completeness of the description.)*

Move to F1.5: tenant and payment details

Execute F1.5: Store payment and report *(Actually, this function does the following activities; again, it is brought just for the completeness of the description.)*

Write to C1 Apartment: payment details

Write to C5 Company: sum paid

Output to U1 Tenant: receipt

End transaction.

Example 3: Top-Level Description of Transaction (e) of Figure 10.1

Begin transaction 1.7/8

(This is a time transaction that will be activated at the end of each month; the dataflow from T1 to F1.7 is not included in the description.)

Do-while there are apartment objects in class C1: *(The transaction performs a loop on all the apartment objects.)*

    Read from C1 Apartment: details of fees and payments since the beginning of year

    Execute F1.7 Produce end-of-month report *(The function name is misleading; it actually calculates the tenant's debt; the method of calculation is not described yet at this stage; generally, it sums up the actual payments and compares them to the sum supposed to be paid according to the monthly fees. In addition the debt of the tenant is accumulated.)*

    Output to U2 Company: debts report *(A line is printed in the debts report detailing the debt of the current tenant.)*

    Move to F1.8: debt of tenant and date of past reminder

    Execute function 1.8: produce remainder to ower *(The function checks the   condition for sending a reminder considering the size and age of the debt and the month in which the past reminder was sent; these details are not included here; they are recorded in the DD and will be included in the detailed description.)*

    If remainder = "T" then Write to C1 Apartment: date of reminder; Output to U1 Tenant: notification and debt details *(This applies only to tenants who need to be reminded.)*

    Else; *(no action for a tenant who needs not be reminded)*

End while

Write to C5 Company: sum of debts *(The accumulated sum of debts of all tenants is added to the attribute **total amounts receivable** of the Company class.)*

End transaction.

Example 4: Top-Level Description of Transaction 4.3-7 of Figure 8.13 (Chapter XIII)

The following example refers to the transaction that appears in OO-DFD-4 of the musical programs system (see Chapter VIII). This is a rather complex transaction including functions 4.3-4.7. It deals with the scheduling of music programs by the editor. The diagram of the transaction is presented in Figure 10.2. The top-level description of the transaction follows, along with comments.

Begin transaction 4.3-7

Input from U3 Editor: program name and date

Read from C2 Music program: details of program *(A search is conducted for the program which the editor wishes to schedule, that is, assign musical pieces. Among other things, the music program object includes the types of music suitable for this program.)*

Read from C3 Scheduled program: details of assignment *(The Scheduled program object is retrieved. It contains the details of the musical pieces that have already been assigned to the program.)*

Execute F4.3: Input program to schedule *(This function name is misleading; actually this command is written only for the completeness of the description because the input has already been received in the "Input from..." command.)*

Move to F4.4: details of program and existing assignments *(The forwarded data will be used by the following functions.)*

Read from C1 Musical piece: suitable pieces for program *(The suitable pieces are retrieved according to previous parameters, which include the types of music suitable for this program.)*

Execute F4.4: Review suitable pieces for program *(This function presents to the editor the details of the musical pieces already assigned to this program and other suitable pieces retrieved from the Musical pieces class.)*

Output to U3 Editor: assigned and suitable pieces *(This command is actually redundant; what it does is already said in function 4.4.)*

Move to F4.5: details of suitable pieces

Read from C3 Scheduled program: past plays *(retrieves lists of musical pieces already played in past broadcasts of the program, so that the editor will be aware of which pieces have already been played and how many times)*

Read from C1 Musical piece: assigned pieces *(retrieves the details of the above musical pieces)*

Execute F4.5: Review past plays of pieces in program *(This function actually presents to the editor the details of the musical pieces that were actually played in past broadcasts of this program.)*

Output to U3 Editor: past plays of pieces in program *(Again, this command is redundant due to the previous one.)*

Figure 10.2. Transaction diagram of transaction 4.3-7 of the musical programs system

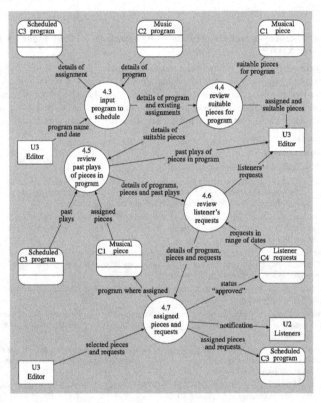

Move to F4.6: details of program, pieces and past plays

Read from C4 Listener request: listeners' requests within the range of dates *(Only requests with status "waiting" whose range of date includes the date of the scheduled program are retrieved.)*

Execute F4.6: Review listeners' requests *(The function presents to the editor the above listeners' requests. The command is the same as the next one.)*

Output to U3 Editor: listeners' requests

Move to F4.7: details of musical pieces assigned and played, and listeners' requests *(All the passed information, which is also displayed to the editor, will assist in assigning musical pieces to the scheduled program.)*

Do-while the editor wishes to assign more musical pieces: *(The loop executes as long as the editor wishes to assign musical pieces to the program. The editor may assign only some pieces in a work session with the transaction, pause, and resume the work some other time.)*

Input from U3 Editor: selected musical piece and listeners' requests *(Assume that the editor is reviewing the information presented on his/her screen, including lists of suitable musical pieces, pieces already assigned to the program being scheduled, pieces that have been played in past broadcasts of the program and listeners' requests. Based on all this, the editor decides which musical piece to assign.)*

Execute F4.7: Assign pieces and requests *(It may be assumed that the actual assignment of a musical piece is done by clicking on its name appearing in any of the lists presented on the editor's screen.)*

Write to C3 Scheduled program: assigned piece *(The selected piece is added to the set of assigned pieces.)*

Write to C1 Musical piece: program where assigned *(The scheduled program is added to the set of programs the piece was assigned to.)*

Do-while there are listener requests for this piece: *(An assigned piece may have been requested by one or more listeners.)*

Write to C3 Scheduled program: approved listener request *(The listener whose request has been fulfilled is added to a set of approved requests.)*

Write to C4 Listener request: status = "approved"

Output to U2 Listeners: notification of approved request

End while *(end of inner loop dealing with approved listener requests)*

End while *(end of outer loop dealing with the assignment of pieces)*

If editor completed all the assignments of pieces to this program then write to C1 Musical piece: status = "scheduled"

Else; *(The status remains "unscheduled".)*

End transaction.

As we know, when the structured description of a process is very complex, it may be presented in a hierarchical form, with one "main" procedure (or module) and one or more subprocedures. Each subprocedure is given a name by which it is referenced from the main procedure (using the command "Do <procedure name>). Since the description presented previously is fairly complex, it will be presented again, this time by using a main procedure and three subprocedures.

Begin transaction 4.3-7

Do "Present program for assignment"

Do "Present suitable pieces"

Do "Assign pieces"

If editor completed all the assignments of pieces to this program then write to C1 Musical piece:
> status = "scheduled"

Else; *(The status remains "unscheduled.")*

End transaction.

Begin Present program for assignment

Input from U3 Editor: program name and date

Read from C2 Music program: details of program *(A search is conducted for the program which the editor wishes to schedule, that is, assign musical pieces. Among other things, the music program object includes the types of music suitable for this program.)*

Read from C3 Scheduled program: details of assignment *(The Scheduled program object is retrieved. It contains the details of the musical pieces that have already been assigned to the program.)*

Execute F4.3: Input program to schedule *(This function name is misleading; actually this command is written only for the completeness of the description because the input has already been received in the "Input from..." command.)*

Move to F4.4: details of program and existing assignments *(The forwarded data will be used by the following functions.)*

End Present program for assignment.

Begin Present suitable pieces

Read from C1 Musical piece: suitable pieces for program *(The suitable pieces are retrieved according to previous parameters, which include the types of music suitable for this program.)*

Execute F4.4: Review suitable pieces for program *(This function presents to the editor the details of the musical pieces already assigned to this program, and other suitable pieces retrieved from the Musical pieces class.)*

Output to U3 Editor: assigned and suitable pieces *(This command is actually redundant; what it does is already said in function 4.4.)*

Move to F4.5: details of suitable pieces

Read from C3 Scheduled program: past plays *(retrieves lists of musical pieces already played in past broadcasts of the program, so that the editor will be aware of which pieces have already been played and how many times)*

Read from C1 Musical piece: assigned pieces *(retrieves the details of the above musical pieces)*

Execute F4.5: Review past plays of pieces in program *(This function actually presents to the editor the details of the musical pieces that were actually played in past broadcasts of this program.)*

Output to U3 Editor: past plays of pieces in program *(Again, this command is redundant due to the previous one.)*

Move to F4.6: details of program, pieces and past plays

Read from C4 Listener request: listeners' requests within the range of dates *(Only requests with status "waiting" whose range of date includes the date of the scheduled program are retrieved.)*

Execute F4.6: Review listeners' requests *(The function presents to the editor the above listeners' requests. The command is the same as the next one.)*

Output to U3 Editor: listeners' requests

Move to F4.7: details of musical pieces assigned and played, and listeners' requests *(All the passed information, which is also displayed to the editor, will assist in assigning musical pieces to the scheduled program.)*

End Present suitable pieces.

Begin Assign pieces

Do-while the editor wishes to assign more musical pieces: *(The loop executes as long as the editor wishes to assign musical pieces to the program. The editor may assign only some pieces in a work session with the transaction, pause, and resume the work some other time.)*

　　Input from U3 Editor: selected musical piece and listeners' requests *(Assume that the editor is reviewing the information presented on his/her screen, including lists of suitable musical pieces, pieces already assigned to the program being scheduled, pieces that have been played in past broadcasts of the program and listeners' requests. Based on all this, the editor decides which musical piece to assign.)*

　　Execute F4.7: Assign pieces and requests *(It may be assumed that the actual assignment of a musical piece is done by clicking on its name appearing in any of the lists presented on the editor's screen.)*

　　Write to C3 Scheduled program: assigned piece *(The selected piece is added to the set of assigned pieces.)*

　　Write to C1 Musical piece: program where assigned *(The scheduled program is added to the set of programs the piece was assigned to.)*

　　DO-while there are listener requests for this piece: *(An assigned piece may have been requested by one or more listeners.)*

　　　　Write to C3 Scheduled program: approved listener request *(The listener whose request has been fulfilled is added to a set of approved requests.)*

　　　　Write to C4 Listener request: status = "approved"

　　　　Output to U2 Listeners: notification of approved request

　　　End while *(end of inner loop dealing with approved listener requests)*

　End while *(end of outer loop dealing with the assignment of pieces)*

End Assign pieces.

In conclusion, we wish to remind that the detailed description of a transaction, which will be created later on, will contain more details and will be more accurate. In addition, it will refer to specific input and output screens and reports that will be designed in the next step of the design phase. Generally, the detailed description of each transaction will enable the designer to identify activities or procedures that will be defined as methods. Certain methods will be removed from the "main" body of the transaction and attached to proper classes; remaining parts, that is, the main part of the transaction will become the "transaction method," which will be attached to a new class: Transactions. This abstract class will include no objects, only transaction methods—one for each transaction. (This will be detailed in Chapter XII.)

Data Dictionary of the Transactions

The DD of the system must be updated with information on the transactions and their components. As we did in Chapter IX, here too we show the needed updates for both a relational DD and an OO dictionary.

The Relational Data Dictionary

Two new tables will be added to the data dictionary, as follows:

Transactions Table

This table has a record for each transaction. Its structure is as follows:

transaction ID	transaction name	type (U/T/R/M)	ref. to diagram	ref. to description	activation conditions	users and authorizations

Transaction ID is a unique number or code which can be used to identify a transaction, instead of the combination of function numbers included in the transaction which we have been using so far in the examples. In addition, each transaction may be given a name which represents what it does. The **type** field indicates whether it is a user, time, real-time, or mixed transaction. The next two fields include references to files which store the transaction's diagram (if one has nee created, since it already exists in the OO-DFDs) and the top-level description. The last two text fields enable describing specific conditions for the activation of the transaction (e.g., the average and pick time frequency of activation, or preconditions for activation), and the users who will be permitted to activate the transaction.

Components of Transactions Table

The structure of this table is as follows:

transaction ID	component code	number

It enables finding the various components of a transaction and the different transactions in which a certain component participates. Obviously, each elementary function in the system will appear only once in this table, while general functions will not appear at all. External entities and classes may appear many times, according to the number of transactions in which each of them participates. Note that the key of this table consists of all its fields/attributes.

In addition to these new tables, the **Elementary dataflows** table will be added a new field **belongs to transaction**.

The OO Data Dictionary and the Transactions Class

A new class titled **Transactions** will be added (see Figure 10.3). Most of the attributes of this class are equivalent to respective fields in the Transactions table. Two specific attributes are *set components of transaction [Components]* and *set elementary dataflows [Elementary dataflows]*. At this stage we treat the new **Transactions** class as part of the DD. However, it will also be part of the complete class diagram of the application. As we will see (in chapter XII), each object of this class will include a transaction method which will include the "main" part of the transaction code, with messages to specific methods that will be attached to other classes. This is indicated in Figure 10.3 by transactions.method (ID) at the lower compartment of the class rectangle.

Besides this new class, the class **Components** will be added an attribute *set included in transactions [Transactions]*, and the class **Elementary dataflows** will be added an attribute *belongs to transaction [Transactions]*.

Figure 10.3. The transactions class

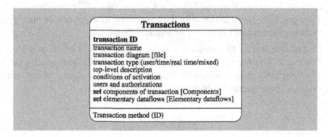

Review Questions

1. What are the products of the design phase? What are its substages?

2. What is a transaction from a user's point of view?

3. What is a transaction in terms of OO-DFD components?

4. Why are general functions not included in transactions?

5. Explain and exemplify why a transaction can belong to more than one transaction.

6. What are the similarities and differences between a transaction in FOOM and a use case in UML?

7. What is a user transaction, a time transaction, and a mixed transaction? Show examples of transaction diagrams of each type.

8. Prepare a few transaction diagrams of the Apartments Building system. How many transactions, in total, are there in that system? List the elementary functions in each of the transactions.

9. Prepare a few transaction diagrams of the Musical Programs system. How many transactions are there in that system? List the elementary functions in each of the transactions.

10. List the types of commands included in a top-level description of a transaction.

11. Prepare top-level descriptions of the transactions prepared in Review Question 9 for the Apartments Building system.

12. Prepare top-level descriptions of the transactions prepared in Review Question 10 for the Musical Programs system.

13. Extend the relational DD created in Review Question 12 of chapter IX, by creating a Transactions table and a Components of Transactions table. Then populate these tables with data about the transactions of one of the systems: Apartments Building or Musical Programs.

14. Extend the objects DD created in Review Question 13 of chapter IX, by creating a Transactions table and a Components of Transactions table. Then populate these tables with data about the transactions of one of the systems: Apartments Building or Musical Programs.

References

Babin, G., Lustman, F., & Shoval, P. (1991). Specification and design of transaction systems: A formal approach. *IEEE Transactions on Software Engineering, 17*(8), 814-829.

Shoval, P. (1988) ADISSA: Architectural design of information systems based on structured analysis. *Information System, 13*(2), 193-210.

Shoval, P. (1991). An integrated methodology for functional analysis, process design and database design. *Information Systems, 16*(1), 49-64.

Endnotes

[1]   The term "transaction" is taken from the ADISSA methodology (Babin, Lustman, & Shoval, 1991; Shoval, 1988, 1991). One may find some similarity between a transaction and a Unified Modeling Language (UML) use case. However, while a use case consists mainly of an actor and functions, a transaction also includes classes and external/user entities. As we know, a use case can also be described in a narrative description; here, a transaction is described in pseudo code.

[2]   In a system which serves many users, it is likely to assume that there is a sharing of responsibility and an authorization policy that allows certain users to access and activate only certain transactions and prevents them from activating others.

[3]   This shows that in spite of having moved from the analysis phase to the design phase, changes of the analysis products are still possible (although relatively minor ones); that is, analysis and design are not entirely sequential processes, they are more like spiral processes.

[4]   It is assumed that the reader is familiar with this technique. Anyhow, we will show examples which will make it clear. Other structured techniques, which are not used here, may be appropriate for this purpose; for example, flowcharts, sequence diagrams, and collaboration diagrams. Following the aims of FOOM, we opt to minimize the different techniques and notations and prefer using pseudo code only, here as well as at the next step of detailed design of transactions.

[5]   But not from a time entity, because the time interval is not data input to the system, it only signifies the time of activation.

Chapter XI

Design of the
Man-Machine
Interface:
Menus, Inputs,
and Outputs

This chapter deals with the design of the interfaces between the users and the system. First, it describes a method for the design of menus trees—for the entire system as well as for its subsystems. Then it describes how to design the inputs and outputs/reports of the systems. As a result, new classes of menus, forms, and reports are added to the class diagram.

Designing the Menus Tree Interface

A menus interface enables the user to choose the desired options from lists of available options presented on screen. The lists of options, that is, menus, may appear in various forms, for example, text, icons, buttons, and so forth. The advantage of a menus interface is that even naïve, inexperienced users are able to operate it and find what they are looking for. If the menus are organized in a hierarchy, as a tree of menus, the user may start the search from the root menu which proposes the main options; the user then can successively make selections down the tree until the desired option is found and selected. This kind of interface is suitable for a variety of users, especially occasional or inexperienced ones, who are not familiar with the information system (IS) and its capabilities. A menus interface also enables enforcing an authorization policy: Certain users may be given access only to the options which they are allowed to perform. However, a menus tree may be too tedious and time consuming for experienced, routine users, who already know what they are looking for and would like to get direct access to the desired options. For them, a "direct manipulation" interface is needed, for example, special function keys or shortcuts which directly activate the desired operations. In this chapter we concentrate on the design of a menus tree interface.

As we know, a menus tree consists of a hierarchy of menus. The root (or main) menu contains the primary options, which reflect the main issues or services which the system provides. The user selects an appropriate option from this menu, and as a result the system displays a secondary (or child) menu which includes the suboptions, that is, more specific issues/services. This process may go on—depending on the "depth" of the menus tree in the direction explored by the user—until at some point the user selects an option which does not lead to another child menu, but rather activates the desired operation. Hence, any menu may contain two types of items: "selection" and "trigger." A "selection" item causes the display of a submenu; a "trigger" item causes the activation of an operation, that is, a transaction of the application. It is likely that a menu at the top of the menus tree (particularly the root menu) will include mostly "selection" items, while menus at lower levels will include more "trigger" items. Note that a menus tree is not necessarily balanced, that is, the depth from the root menu to the lowest level menu may vary, depending on the breakdown of issues/ services provided by the system. This issue will be elaborated later on.

As said, there are many ways and forms of presenting menus on screen. In other words, a menu item may appear to the user in various forms. For example, as a text box consisting of one or more words which describes briefly the option, or an icon which portrays the option, or both. A "user friendly" system would enable the user to get more explanations about the options ("help") which can be invoked by the user (e.g., by hitting the respective menu item). Menus may be presented in lines or columns. For example, a root menu may consist of text boxes displayed on the top line of the screen; once a "selection" item is selected, the submenu may "pull down" in a column under the selected option; the selection of a "selection" item from this menu may cause a submenu to "pop up" at a certain location on screen, and so forth. Besides varieties of forms of presentation, there are issues of aesthetics of menus. This includes proper use or colors, size of text and icons, location of items on screen, and so on. All these aspects of menus design will not be discussed in this chapter. We concentrate on the **functional design** of the menus interface, namely the various menu items which should be included in the user interface and their proper organization in the menus tree.

The Method for Designing the Menus Interface[1]

The menus tree is created from the three object oriented data flow diagrams (OO-DFD) in a process consisting of two main stages: In the first stage, which is algorithmic, a menus tree is created from the diagrams based on the general and elementary functions that are connected to user entities. In the second stage, which involves interaction between the designer and users, the aforementioned menus tree is improved until a satisfactory design to the users is achieved.

The Algorithmic Steps of the Menus Tree Design Process

Step 1: Deriving an Initial Menus Tree From the OO-DFDs

A menu is created for every OO-DFD which has at least one user entity. The menu may contain items of two types: "selection" and "trigger," which are determined according to the types of functions which are connected to the user entities: For every **general function** connected to a user entity (one or more, from the "input" or "output" side of the diagram), a "selection" item is defined, because when the user will select this item, a child menu will be displayed. For every **elementary function** connected to a user entity, a "trigger" item is defined, because when the user will select it, it will cause activation of the transaction to which that function belongs. At this stage, every menu is given an ID number which is identical to the OO-DFD number from which it was originated, and every item in the menu is given the number and name of the function from which it was created. A "selection" line is marked by an "S" and a "trigger" line is marked by a "T." Next to the "T" we write the number of the transaction to which the function belongs. (The data dictionary (DD) records the transaction numbers and the transaction to which each elementary function belongs.)

Note that the menus tree obtained by now is a subset of the OO-DFDs. As such, its structure reflects the functional structure of the system. Clearly, only OO-DFDs which have no user entities at all will not have a constituent menu. Any menu created may have a different number of items of the two types, depending on the number of functions connected to user entities and their types (general or elementary). The root menu is likely to include mostly "selection" lines because most of its functions are general, while lower level menus are likely to include more "trigger" items because the respective OO-DFDs include more elementary functions. Obviously, a leaf menu includes only "trigger" items.

We will now demonstrate step 1 of the process using the **Apartments Building** system. The OO-DFDs of this system have been presented in Figures 8.7-8.10 (Chapter VIII). The initial menus tree of this system, resulting from step 1 of the algorithm, is presented in Figure 11.1. It consists of four menus, one for each of the OO-DFDs, because in each of them there are functions which are connected to user entities. Based on the transaction numbers (which are written next to the "T" items only) we can see that the system includes 13 transactions involving users.[2] Note that in some cases, the same transaction number of a transaction is written next to more than one line, indicating that more than one elementary function connected to user entities belongs to the same transaction. This duplicity will be dealt with in the next step.

Step 2: Combining "Trigger" Items Belonging to the Same Transaction

As noted, a menu may happen to have several "trigger" items belonging to the same transaction. However, the menu is meant to enable the activation of an entire transaction, including all of its functions, not just single functions within transactions.[3] This means that the redundant "trigger" (T) items should be combined into a single line.

Figure 11.1. Initial menus tree of the apartments building system

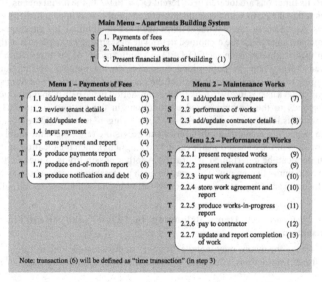

Main Menu – Apartments Building System

S 1. Payments of fees
S 2. Maintenance works
T 3. Present financial status of building (1)

Menu 1 – Payments of Fees

T	1.1 add/update tenant details	(2)
T	1.2 review tenant details	(3)
T	1.3 add/update fee	(3)
T	1.4 input payment	(4)
T	1.5 store payment and report	(4)
T	1.6 produce payments report	(5)
T	1.7 produce end-of-month report	(6)
T	1.8 produce notification and debt	(6)

Menu 2 – Maintenance Works

T	2.1 add/update work request	(7)
S	2.2 performance of works	
T	2.3 add/update contractor details	(8)

Menu 2.2 – Performance of Works

T	2.2.1 present requested works	(9)
T	2.2.2 present relevant contractors	(9)
T	2.2.3 input work agreement	(10)
T	2.2.4 store work agreement and report	(10)
T	2.2.5 produce works-in-progress report	(11)
T	2.2.6 pay to contractor	(12)
T	2.2.7 update and report completion of work	(13)

Note: transaction (6) will be defined as "time transaction" (in step 3)

For example, in menu 1 (Figure 11.1) items 1.2 and 1.3 belong to the same transaction (number 3). As it looks, item 1.2 triggers function 1.2 which enables reviewing the tenant's details, while items 1.3 triggers function 1.3 which enables adding or updating a monthly fee. But since the two functions are part of the same transaction, there is no need for two separate items which "independently" trigger the component functions of the transaction. On the contrary, the user who is authorized to activate this transaction (say an officer of the company) wishes to activate the transaction as a whole, and the various functions of the transaction will be activated "internally," according to the process logic of the transaction. (Note that this may include activation of other functions belonging to a transaction which happen to not be connected to user entities and therefore are not present in the initial menu.) Therefore, all "trigger" items in all initial menus are combined.

The combination of items obliges us to give the combined item a new number and name. Temporarily, the number of a combined item is a concatenation of its original item numbers. For example, items 1.2 and 1.3 are replaced by item 1.2/3. The name of the unified item should express the essence of the transaction it activates, so it may be identical or similar to the name of the transaction. Later on, at the interactive stage of the menus design process, the items of the various menus may be given different names according to the users' preferences.

There may be cases where a certain transaction spans more than one OO-DFD, that is, its functions are located in different OO-DFDs.[4] In the initial menus tree it means that the items with the same transaction number may appear in different menus. As we know, the redundant items need to be combined; the question is: in which menu to place the combined item? The best strategy is to place it in the menu that originated from the OO-DFD in which "most" of the transaction is located. "Most" can be determined according to the number of functions belonging to that transaction in each of the respective diagrams. The rationale for this is that a user is likely to look for the transaction in the path of menus which corresponds to the decomposition of functions in the system: If most of a transaction is located in a certain OO-DFD, its "trigger" item should be located in the respective menu. If no difference can be visible (e.g., the same number of functions of the transaction appear in two diagrams), then the location of the menu item can be determined arbitrarily. Another possibility is to include the same item in the two menus. This may be even preferable to users who may be able to locate and trigger the transaction by following more than one search path.

Step 3: Removing Items Belonging to "Time" and "Real-Time" Transactions

At this stage the menus may include "trigger" items which belong to "time" or "real-time" transactions. For example, it is possible that a certain transaction has been defined as a "time" transaction in spite of including elementary functions which are connected to user entities.[5] The items which belong to such transactions should be removed from the menus tree. (But note that this does not apply to "mixed transactions," which may be activated from the menus interface as well as on a timely basis.)

In the example of the **Apartment Building** system (Figure 11.1) there is only one transaction—transaction 6—which has been defined as "time transaction." It appeared in the initial menu because functions 1.7 and 1.8 (that belong to it) are connected to user entities. However, it has already been determined that this transaction is not to be activated by a user, only in predefined time intervals (and as a result of its activation, reports will be sent to a user); hence, items 1.7/8 will be removed from menu 1.

Step 4: Elimination of "Degenerate" Menus

As a result of all the previous steps, "degenerate" menus may have been created, that is, menus containing a single item only. A degenerate menu does not offer any choice to the user, and therefore needs to be removed from the menus tree. If the item in the degenerate menu is a "trigger" (marked "T") it replaces the "selection" line in the parent menu. This means that the respective transaction will be activated from the parent menu. If the item in the degenerate menu is a "selection" (marked "S"), there is no need for any additional changes (except for elimination of the degenerate menu). This means that upon the selection of the parent item (in the parent menu) the "grandchild" menu (which now becomes the "child" menu) will be presented.

Figure 11.2 presents the menus tree of the **Apartment Building** system at the end of step 4 of the algorithmic stage. As we can see, each "T" item is associated with one transaction number. Note the numbers and names of the unified "trigger" items. Note also that the items of the "time transaction" 6 have been eliminated. (In this example, no menu has become "degenerate.")

Since no degenerate menus have been created in the previous example, we will demonstrate such cases using another example, the **Customers and Suppliers** system. The OO-DFDs of this system have been presented in Figures 8.4-8.6 (Chapter VIII). Figure 11.3 presents the menus tree of the system created in each of the algorithmic steps: Part (a) presents the menus created in step 1. As can be seen, this system has only 4 transactions. Part (b) presents the menus after step 2 and 3 together. The two "trigger" items of transaction 1 have been unified and the "trigger" items of transactions 3 and 4 (defined as "time transactions") have been removed. As a result, the two menus 1 and 2 became "degenerate" and they need to be removed. Part (c) of the figure presents the only menu that remains in this small system.

Figure 11.2. The menus tree at the end of the algorithmic stage

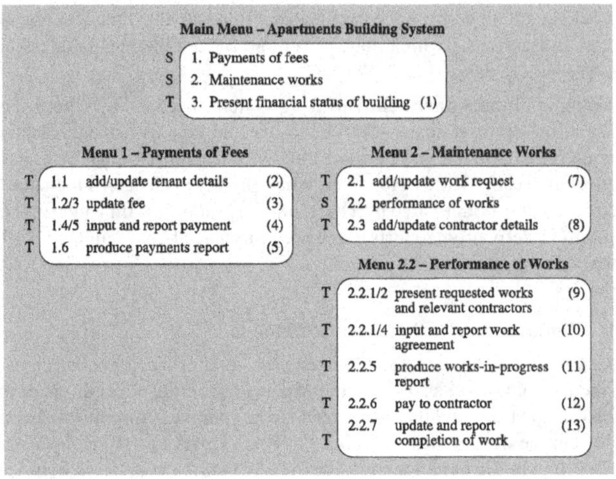

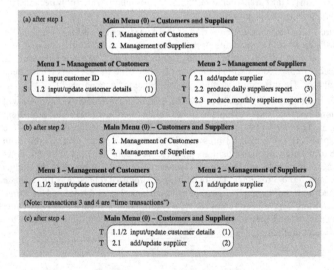

Figure 11.3. The menus tree of the customers and suppliers system

The Interactive Stage of the Menus Tree Design Process

The purpose of the interactive stage is to improve the menus tree which has been created thus far "automatically." This stage is performed in cooperation between the analyst/designer and the users (or their representatives), using appropriate software tools purposed for the design and creation of menus.[6] Using such a tool, the menus thus far created can be changed and improved according to the users' preferences.[7]

Unlike the previous stage, this one is not structured. In the sequel we outline a few guidelines for possible improvements of the menus tree.

- **Unification or Splitting of Menus:** It is possible that at the end of the algorithmic stage we obtained menus with too few or two many items. "Narrow" menus (with only two or three lines) are especially not desirable; a "narrow" menu can be eliminated by moving its items up the tree, replacing their parent "selection" item. A "wide" menu (with many items, say above 10) may be split into two menus, such that each of them will include items which are tightly related. Consequently, the "selection" item in the parent menu must be split into two "selection" items, each for its respective child menu.

- **Renaming Menu Items:** Instead of the line numbers and names of the menu items, which are based on the functions numbers and names, more appealing numbers and names can be given, according to the users' preferences. For example, instead of existing item numbers it may be decided to use serial numbers for the items within each menu, or to eliminate any numbers at all and use only item names. (Numbers are not needed anyhow if items are selectable with a pointing device.) As for the names of the items, whether "selection" or "trigger," they should be as short as possible, but still reflective of the selections proposed or transactions activated. Obviously, the symbols "S" and "T" are removed from the menus.

- **Help and Navigation Mechanisms:** A help mechanism should provide explanations to users who are not sure about the meaning of a certain menu item. Hence, for each menu item, a proper textual explanation should be added.[8] In addition, the menus should include a navigation mechanism (e.g., hotkeys) that will enable a user to easily move from a given menu up to its parent menu, the root menu, or any specific menu. Another option should be the elimination of the display of menus (relevant for an experienced user) and the option to use function keys which directly trigger desired transactions.

- **"Aesthetic" Design of Menus:** This involves, as already said, designing the graphic form of the menus, adoption or creation of icons instead of or in addition to the items' texts, and so forth. These aspects are beyond the scope of this book.

The Activation of "Time" and "Real-Time" Transactions

"Time" and "real-time" transactions are not activated by users and are not accessible from the user interface. The activation of the "time transactions" of an application should be the responsibility of the person or organizational unit in charge of the day-to-day operation of the system. "Time transactions" can be activated by a "scheduler" program which resides in the computer and runs at all times. Assume that the scheduler program maintains a list of all "time transactions" running by the computer.[9] Since each such transaction has a time interval for its activation, the program can compute for each transaction its next time (date/hour/minute) and be prompted at certain time intervals (e.g., every hour); it would then check if any transactions (at the top of the table) have to be activated at that time and act accordingly. Afterwards, the program would calculate the next activation time of the transaction (according to the time interval stored in its table of "time transactions") and move it to the proper place in the sorted time table.

A "real-time" transaction is automatically activated when its sensor receives proper input from its environment. Our assumption is that the system will be implemented with a sensor that will be able to receive and analyze the inputs, and when the input corresponds with certain predefined activation conditions, a signal will be sent and activate the transaction.

Designing Menus for Subsystems

Until now we have thought of the users of the IS as one group where every user can access (i.e., activate) all the transactions of the system via the menus tree. This may work for small systems with few users and transactions. But a large-scale system may have many (even an unlimited number of) users. The users may belong to different organizational units, each with its objectives and responsibilities in the organization. Moreover, a system may have users from within the organization (employees) or from the outside (e.g., customers and suppliers). A large-scale system may consist of many transactions which are aimed to support the various different users. In such systems there is no need (and it is also undesirable) to expose all of the system's transactions to all users, because of security, privacy, and managerial reasons. This means that not all users should be exposed to all menus and menu items of the system. We need to create a mechanism which will enable to the "opening" of only certain parts of the system to certain types of users, by creating "partial" menus of the system for them. Such a mechanism is needed in addition to any other means to protect the system from access by unauthorized persons (such as login authorizations and passwords). We are looking for a mechanism to define and create menus trees, submenus of the "global" menus tree, tailored for specific groups of users. The other protection mechanisms can and should be applied on any group of users who have access to some part of the system—a subsystem—via a submenus tree.

Let us first define a subsystem: A subsystem consists of a set of transactions which serve a group of users of a certain type, who have a certain organizational responsibility or special characteristics for which certain transactions are defined. The subsystem includes a submenus tree which enables the users of that subsystem to operate (activate) their transactions. The subsystem includes also a subset of the global database schema which is used by those users. As said, usually a subsystem serves a certain organizational unit. For example, in the **Student Management System** of a university we may define the following subsystems: student admission, academic affairs (including registration to courses, reporting of grades, etc.), tuitions, dormitories, executive reports, and so forth. Clearly, the users of a certain subsystem need to have access to certain transactions which "belong" to their subsystem, but need not know about or have access to other subsystems and their transactions.

Subsystems of a system can be defined when the system is being developed, at the design phase. In addition, a new subsystem can be defined anytime during the lifetime of a system. In any such case, a menus tree for the subsystem is defined as follows.

1. First, an administrative/manager decision must be made about the need to define a subsystem, its objectives and users. Sometimes a subsystem will correspond to a certain organizational unit, but not necessarily. Based on that, a decision must be made about which of the systems' transactions will belong to this subsystem. A certain transaction may belong to more than one subsystem, if users who belong to different subsystems are authorized to activate it.[10]

2. Based on the aforementioned decision, we review the global menus tree and mark the "trigger" (T) items of the transactions of that subsystem.

3. Then we mark the respective "selection" (S) items at the parent menus of the marked "T" items.

4. Then we mark the "selection" items at the parent menus of the marked "S" items; this is repeated until we reach the root menu.

5. All marked items constitute the initial submenus tree of the subsystem. It is possible that this process generated "degenerate" menus (consisting of single "T" or "S" items). Such menus should be eliminated, as described for the global menus tree.

6. Eventually, the interactive stage of the menus tree design process should be performed, in order to improve the resulting submenus tree.

It must be noted that in the case of a large-scale system, it is possible that a global menus tree (for the entire system) will not be implemented at all, but rather it will remain only a design artifact (a "virtual" menus tree). Rather, only submenus trees will be created for the various subsystems. Note also that not only a certain transaction may belong to more than one subsystem, it is reasonable that a certain user will "belong" to more than one subsystem. For example, a user at a certain managerial level or position may have access to transactions belonging to different subsystems.

The Menus Class

After the menus are designed, a new class **Menus** is added to the class diagram. The objects of this class are all the menus that were designed for the system. Figure 11.4 presents the class diagram. The **Menus** class contains two types of attributes: attributes bearing the content of the menu objects, and attributes dealing with the display options of the menus. The figure only presents the content-bearing attributes, that is, *menu name*, the key attribute, and *set menu items*; each member of this set is a triplet consisting of: (1) ID code—as we know, a menu item does not have to have an ID, therefore this attribute may remain null; (2) name—includes the text of the item that will be displayed on screen; and (3) type—either "S" for a selection line or "T" for a trigger line. Attributes dealing with display options, which are not presented in the figure, may include, for example, reference to the parent menu, reference to the icon representing the menu (if any), shortcuts, and so forth. It might be assumed that attributes of this kind will be implemented by using appropriate class libraries of the CASE tool or the interface development environment used by the developers.

Figure 11.4. The menus class

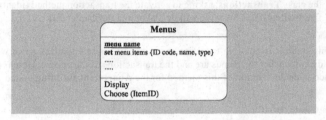

Figure 11.5. Two menu objects of the menus class

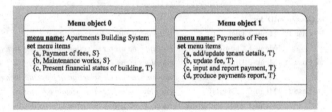

Figure 11.5 presents two objects (that is, menus) of the **Menus** class, taken form the **Apartments Building** example: the root (main) menu, and Menu object 1.

The **Menus** class may include various methods that will be implemented using the class libraries of the interface development environment, for example, a method for creating a shortcut for a menu, a method for the updating of the menus hierarchy, a method for creating a new menu, and so forth. We exemplify only two methods (Figure 11.4):

A.   **Display** method presents a menu object on screen, detailing its various menu items (each of which may be of type "S" or "T").

B.   **Choose (ItemID**11**)** method is activated by the Display method once the user selects one of the above menu items. Once activated, the method sends a message in accordance with the selection made by the user: If a selection ("S") item has been selected, a message is sent to the Display method of class **Menus,** asking to display the selected submenu (identified by ItemID). If a trigger ("T") item has been selected, a message is sent to the class **Transactions**, asking to activate the transaction method (identified by ItemID). This issue will be elaborated in Chapter XII.

At this stage it is possible to define the method Choose (ItemID), since we already know what the menus are and the transactions of the system. Here is a pseudo-code description of this method for the **Apartment Building** system:

Begin Choose (ItemID)

Do while not "exit"   *("exit" may be implemented as a "button" enabling the user to exist the system)*

   Menu-0.Display   *(displays the main menu of the application)*

   Menu-0.Choose (ItemID)   *(accepts the user's selection, which may be an "S" or a "T" item of the main menu)*

   On Case ItemID do:

      Case 1:   Menu-1.Display   *(displays menu 1: Payments of fees)*

           Menu-1.Choose (ItemID)   *(accepts the user's selection of from this menu)*

      Case 2:   Menu-2.Display   *(displays menu 2: Maintenance works)*

           Menu-2.Choose (ItemID)   *(accepts the user's selection of from this menu)*

      Case 3:   Menu-2.2.Display   *(displays menu 2.2: Performance of works)*

           Menu-2.2.Choose (ItemID)   *(accepts the user's selection of from this menu)*

      Case 4: Transaction.transaction1   *(a message to class Transactions to activate transaction 1)*

      Case 5: Transaction.transaction2   *(a message to activate transaction 2)*

      Case 6: Transaction.transaction3   *(a message to activate transaction 3)*

      Case 7: Transaction.transaction4   *(a message to activate transaction 4)*

      Case 8: Transaction.transaction5   *(a message to activate transaction 5)*

      Case 9: Transaction.transaction7   *(a message to activate transaction 7)*

      Case 10: Transaction.transaction8   *(a message to activate transaction 8)*

      Case 11: Transaction.transaction9   *(a message to activate transaction 9)*

      Case 12: Transaction.transaction10   *(a message to activate transaction 10)*

      Case 13: Transaction.transaction11   *(a message to activate transaction 11)*

      Case 14: Transaction.transaction12   *(a message to activate transaction 12)*

      Case 15: Transaction.transaction13   *(a message to activate transaction 13)*

   End Case

End while

End.

Note that if the user selects a "selection" item from a displayed menu, it causes the display of the respective submenu, and then an additional user selection from the submenu, invoking the Choose method again. However, if the user selects a "trigger" item, a message is sent to the abstract class **Transactions**, where the selected transaction method is activated and starts to execute (as will be detailed in Chapter XII). Once the execution is completed, the main menu is displayed.

Designing the Inputs and Outputs

The design of the inputs and the outputs[12] is based on the Input/Output commands appearing in the transactions' top-level descriptions. As we know, the feeding in of input data and the production of output information is done within the various transactions of the system. Every input is expressed in the OO-DFD by a dataflow from a user entity to an elementary function, and every output is expressed by a dataflow from an elementary function to a user entity. In the top-level descriptions of transactions, the Input/Output commands are expressed as follows:

- **Input from User…:**[13] the name of the input dataflow
- **Output to User…:** the name of the output dataflow

A transaction may include several input or output commands, each appearing in a proper place, according to the process logic of the transaction. So far, the medium for feeding the inputs or producing the outputs have not yet been determined. For example, it has not yet been determined whether a certain input will be fed using a keyboard, by a barcode reader, or a magnetic card reader. Similarly, it has not yet been determined whether a certain output will be printed, presented on screen, or sent by e-mail. At this stage of inputs and outputs design, the following decisions need to be made for every input and output dataflow/command:

- For every input dataflow/command, it should be determined which input medium (device) will be used and how will the data be fed in. Based on that, the respective input device should be designed in detail. For example, it may be determined that a certain input will be performed using a keyboard and input screen; hence the screen must be designed in detail.

- For every output dataflow/command, it should be determined which output device will be used. Based on that, the respective output device should be designed in detail. For example, it may be determined that a certain output will be performed by a printed report; hence the report must be designed in detail.

In spite of what has been said, not every input command will necessarily become an independent input screen; it is possible that several input commands will be combined and implemented by a single input screen. Similarly, it is possible that several output commands will be combined and implemented by a single report. Moreover, it is possible that several input and output dataflows/commands (within a certain transaction) will be combined and implemented by one interactive input/output screen, which enables both feeding input data and presenting output to the user.

The decisions on the appropriate input and output media (devices) should be made in cooperation between the designer and the users' representatives, because it may have various implications, such as budgets to acquire the necessary devices, the infrastructure, work methods, and so forth. When considering the appropriate input and output devices for each transaction, it is necessary to take into account the nature of the transaction (for example, whether it is a user transaction where the user must feed in the data while interacting with the transaction, or a time transaction which requires preparation of the input data in advance, using specialized "off-line" devices, e.g., scanners). Other important factors include the frequency in which the transaction is activated; the amount of data that needs to be input or produced; the required level of accuracy; and the fitness of the devices to the users. Besides, existing devices in the organization need to be taken into account too, as well as other financial constraints.

The specific design of each input or output screen is done with appropriate software tools (similar to what has been said about the menus interface design). When designing a specific input or output, it is necessary to make sure that it includes all the data elements that need to be input or output. This is done with assistance of the DD, which specifies for each input and output dataflow the data elements it contains. For every data element in an input screen, it should be determined whether the data will be fed in by keying in the data or by selecting the data from a list, using the mouse. Based on these decisions, the headlines, titles, and field names need to be determined. In addition, the right controls[14] need to be chosen for every input.

We will demonstrate the task of input and output design using a transaction from the **Apartments Building** system. First, let us have a look again at the top-level description of transaction 1.4/5 which deals with Tenant Payments. (This description has been shown in example 2 of chapter X; comments have been removed; the input/output commands are in bold.)

Begin transaction 1.4/5

Input from U1 Tenant: Apartment number or family name

Read from C1 Apartment: tenant details

If not-found then present error message and ask user to input again an apartment ID

Else **input from U1 Tenant: payment details**

Execute F1.4 Input payment

Move to F1.5: tenant details and payment

Execute F1.5: Store payment and report

Write to C1 Apartment: payment details

Write to C5 Company: sum paid

Output to U1 Tenant: receipt

End transaction.

Assume that the user who is in charge of this transaction is an officer of the company who activates the transaction whenever he/she wishes to update the system on a tenant's payment. The officer is sitting in front of a workstation and interacts with the transaction. The payment details will be input using an input screen, keyboard, and mouse device, and the output will be produced by a printer. Here is a more detailed explanation of the designer's considerations:

One input screen will be designed for all of the transaction's input activities. The input screen will be presented to the user once the transaction is activated. The screen will have an appropriate title (e.g., "Accept Payment from a Tenant") centered at the top. The body of the screen will include various input fields as follows: First, we need input fields for the apartment number and/or the family name of the paying tenant; this will satisfy the first input command (**Input from U1 Tenant ID: Apartment number and family name**). Each input field needs to be of a certain length and defined over a certain data type (e.g., numeric and text, respectively). Next to each input field we need an appropriate title. Assume that the user will feed in data for at least one of these fields and then press a "Send" button. In response, the transaction will verify that the apartment/family really exists in the database (using the Read/Find command of the **Apartment** class). This kind of input involves actual keying in the apartment number or family name; if a family name is used, there may be more than one family with that name, so the apartment number of the respective family name must be retrieved and presented on the screen in the respective field, and the user must be given an option to acknowledge the right apartment/family or ask to see the next apartment with the same family name (using other buttons, e.g., "OK" and "Find

Next"). This method of input is amenable to human errors (e.g., keying in an existing apartment number or family name) for which there must also be designed a window for an error message (e.g., "no such apartment/family") and a button to clear the input windows.

An alternative design that may save such errors is that once the transaction is activated by the user it first searches the **Apartment** class and presents on screen a list of all the apartment numbers and family names, using a scroll window, and then the user can select the proper apartment and family by using the mouse device. This method of input is free from keying in errors and eliminates the need for error messages and certain buttons.

At any rate, once the proper apartment/tenant is selected, new input fields with appropriate titles will be opened on the same input screen, including fields to input the payment details (e.g., date of payment, sum, and payment method); this will satisfy the second input command (**Input from U1 Tenant: payment details**). These fields may appear on the input screen from the beginning but be defined as inactive (that is, it will not be possible to key data in them) until the proper apartment/tenant is selected. Figure 11.6 presents an input screen designed for the inputs of this transaction.[15]

For the output command of this transaction (**Output to U1 Tenant: receipt**) we will design a receipt printout that will include the appropriate information (such as receipt number; apartment number and family name; date of payment; and the other payment details—all according to the data elements defined in the DD for the respective output dataflow.) An example is presented in Figure 11.7.

Figure 11.6. Design of the input screen for tenant payments

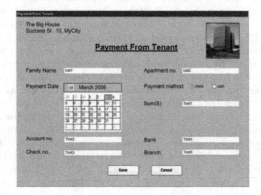

Figure 11.7. Design of the printout of a payment receipt

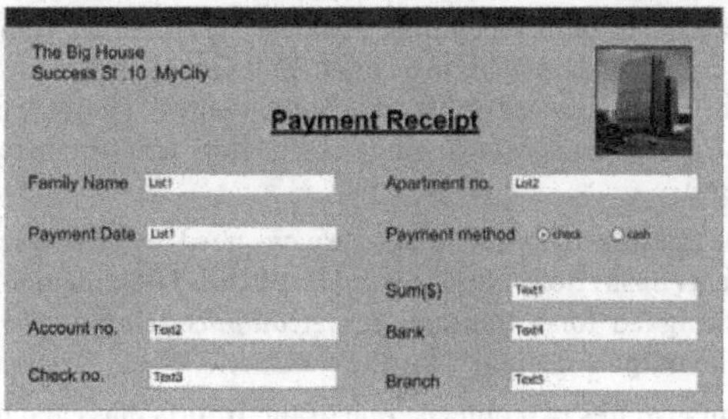

We have demonstrated the design of an input screen and an output report for one user transaction. As we know, there are various input and output devices, and various ways to design every input and output. As said, the decision regarding the devices depends on the type of each transaction; the frequency of its activation; the amount of data that must be input or output; the source of the input data and the way the data can be collected; the target of the output and its location; and so on.

The Data Dictionary and the Inputs and Outputs Classes

After having designed the inputs and outputs, two new classes are added to the class diagram: **Inputs** (also termed **Forms**) and **Outputs** (also termed **Reports**). These classes belong both to the DD and the class diagram of the application (similar to the **Transactions** class; see Chapter X). The objects of each of these classes are the input and output screens (or forms and reports) that were designed for the system. Figure 11.8 presents the diagrams of these two classes.

The attributes of these two classes are similar: Every input and output is identified by the transaction to which it belongs along with a serial number. It also has a *title* (headline) which is identical to the name of the screen or report, the *input* or *output device*. The next attribute is a reference to a file containing the figure or the prototype of the input/output, as designed with the software tool.

Source of input and *target of output* are textual attributes describing the respective external entities. The sets *input fields* (for Inputs) and *output fields* (for Outputs) consist of tuples including the attributes *field name* and *explanation*, which describes the data fields to be input, for example, the method of filling in the data[16] (for input screens) or presenting the output[17] (for output screens). The explanation attribute may also include explanatory text (tip) to be displayed upon user request.

To complete the updates to the data dictionary, we need to add two set reference attributes to the **Transactions** class: *set inputs [Inputs]* will include references to the inputs designed for a transaction; *set outputs [Outputs]* will include references to the outputs designed for the transaction.[18]

Figure 11.9 demonstrates two objects; one of the **Inputs** class and the other of the **Outputs** class; these are the Input and Output objects that were presented in Figures 11.6 and 11.7, respectively.

The Inputs and Outputs classes include a method named *Display* which presents the form/report on the screen. In case of the **Output** class, the method presents (that is, produces) the output using the appropriate output device. In case of an **Input** class, the method presents the input (e.g., the input screen), then the user fill in the data, using the respective input device, and the method returns the input data in a variable called ReturnObject. This data can then be used by other components of the transaction which handle the input.

In conclusion of this chapter, let us review what we have achieved.

- We have designed the user interfaces in the form of menus trees—this includes a menus tree of the entire (global) IS and submenu trees for the subsystems. We added a **Menus** class to the class diagram, whose objects are the designed menus.

Figure 11.8. The inputs/forms and outputs/reports classes

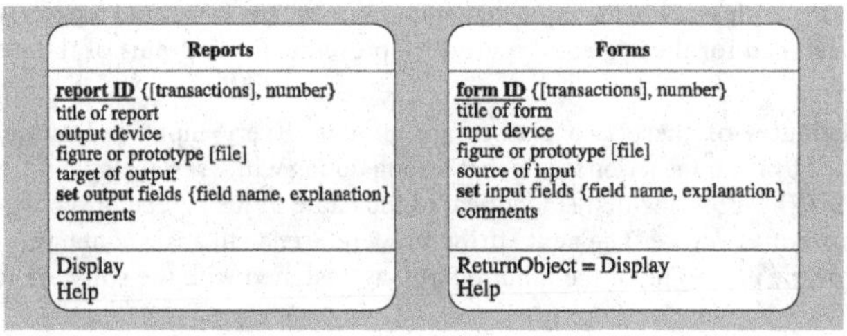

Reports	Forms
report ID {[transactions], number} title of report output device figure or prototype [file] target of output **set** output fields {field name, explanation} comments	**form ID** {[transactions], number} title of form input device figure or prototype [file] source of input **set** input fields {field name, explanation} comments
Display Help	ReturnObject = Display Help

Figure 11.9. Objects of the inputs/forms class and output/reports class

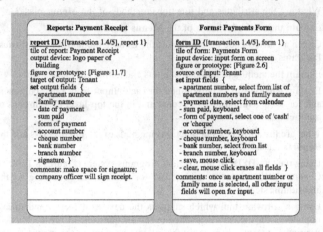

- We have designed all the inputs and outputs of the system, per its transactions. We added an **Inputs** class and an **Outputs** class, whose objects are the various inputs and outputs.

Review Questions

1. What are the four algorithmic steps in designing the menus tree interface?

2. What is a "degenerate" menu and how can it be created? Distinguish between three different cases.

3. What are "redundant" menu items and why are they created?

4. How can it happen that a certain transaction may have "triggers" in different menus? What is the solution for this?

5. What is the objective of the interactive stage of the menus tree design process? Detail a few possible guidelines applicable to this stage.

6. How is a time transaction activated? How is a real-time transaction activated?

7. Detail the process of designing a submenus tree for a subsystem.

8. What are the attributes and functions/methods of the **Menus** class?

9. Explain the method Choose of the **Menus** class.

10. Create a pseudo-code description of the Choose method for the Musical Programs system.

11. Explain the method to design the inputs and outputs of the system.

12. Explain what has to be determined for each "Input from U…" command and for each "Output to U…" command in the top-level descriptions of transactions.

13. What are the attributes and functions/methods of the **Forms** class and the **Reports** class?

14. Using the OO-DFDs of the Musical Programs system (Figures 8.12-8.14, Chapter VIII), create a menus tree for the system according to the algorithmic steps.

15. Using a software tool which supports the design of menus and forms, implement the menus tree created in review question 14 for the Musical Programs system. Then, apply the interactive stage of the menus design process until you obtain the final menus tree of that system.

16. Following review question 15, use the software tool to design the input/output forms and reports for a few transactions of that system.

References

Shoval, P. (1988). ADISSA: Architectural design of information systems based on structured analysis. *Information System, 13*(2), 193-210.

Shoval, P. (1990). Functional design of a menu-tree interface within structured system development. *International Journal of Man-Machine Studies, 33*, 537-556.

Shoval, P. (1995). Experimental comparison between automatic and manual menu-interface design methods. *Interacting With Computers, 7*(1), 73-89.

Endnotes

1   The method for designing the menus tree is based on the architectural design of information systems based on structures analysis (ADISSA) methodology (Shoval, 1988, 1990, 1995).

2   The system may include also time or real-time transactions which do not involve user entities and therefore their transaction numbers do not appear here; this point will be clarified later on.

3   The various functions within a certain transaction will be activated "internally," once the transaction is activated, depending on the process logic of the transaction.

4   This happens in cases when a general function is connected to another general or elementary function; elementary subfunctions of a general may belong be connected to other elementary functions located in a different diagram.

5   The transaction type is defined in the DD.

6   Such as Visual Basic, VB.net, Visual Java, PowerBuilder, and Delphi.

7   If a computer aided software engineering (CASE) tool that supports the methodology is used, it may be assumed that the initial menus tree has already been created with the tool, which is then used for improvements of the menus.

8   The help mechanism can be implemented in different ways. For example, when a user clicks the right mouse button pointing to a certain menu item, a help window opens next to it.

9   It may include "time transactions" for various applications.

10 For example, a transaction that finds a student's registration to courses. This transaction may be activated both by employees working for an academic department (and subsystem) as well as by employees working for the tuitions department.

11 ItemID is the ID code of a menu item.

12 The method for designing the inputs and outputs is also based on the ADISSA methodology.

13 The "..." stands for the user entity ID.

14 Such as text box, list box, or combo box.

15 The design was made using MS Visio. Note that the example also includes input fields for the bank and account data which are not included in the class **Apartment**.

[16] Such as text box, list box, check box, or combo box.

[17] Such as a label, picture, or locked textbox.

[18] The inverse attributes of each of these reference attributes is part of the key attribute of **Inputs** and **Outputs** classes, respectively.

Chapter XII

Detailed Design of the Transactions and Class Methods

*This chapter describes how to map a top-level description of a transaction into a detailed description, and then how to "decompose" a detailed description of a transaction into various methods which are then attached to proper classes. Two equivalent techniques for describing methods are provided: **pseudo code** and **message charts**. The chapter ends with a review on the products of the design phase, which serve as input to the system construction (programming) phase.*

Steps in the Design of Transactions and Class Methods

The main objective of this stage is to define the class methods and attach them to proper classes. This involves two main steps.

In the first step, we convert the top-level descriptions of the transactions[1] into **detailed descriptions**. A detailed description of a transaction is expressed in pseudo code and it details the various procedures performed by the transaction, as derived from the process logic of the elementary functions of the transaction and the dataflows between the functions and the external entities and the data classes.

In the second step, the detailed description of each transaction is "decomposed" into various procedures; some of them are defined as methods which are removed from the main transaction description, attached to proper classes, and replaced by messages to those methods. The remaining parts of the transaction (which are not defined as class methods) are defined as the "main" method of the transaction, which is attached to the class **Transactions**. Eventually, each transaction of the system becomes a "main" method which is attached to the **Transactions** class, and includes messages to other methods which are attached to proper classes.

Hence, all the application programs of the information system (IS) are actually defined as methods of the **Transactions** class and other classes. When the user wishes to run (execute) an application program, he/she makes selections from the menus interface. Once the user selects a trigger ("T") menu item, the menu object sends a message to the **Transactions** class to activate the desired Transaction method. The method is executed according to its internal process logic; as said, during the execution it may send messages to the methods of other classes, which may in turn send messages to other class methods. When the "chain of activations" of the various methods ends, the transaction terminates, and the control returns to the Menus Choose method (as described in chapter XII).

From Top-Level to Detailed Transaction Descriptions

In Chapter X we saw how the transactions are identified in the object oriented data flow diagrams (OO-DFD) and then described using pseudo code. A top-level description of a transaction includes, as we know, the main activities that take place in the transaction as based on its components and its process logic.

The transition from a top-level description of a transaction to a detailed description is based on the commands included in the initial description: Every command is being either elaborated or replaced by specific commands, as follows:[2]

- Every **"execute function..."** command, which states that a certain function needs to be executed, is replaced by a detailed description of the function, according to its internal process logic. These details do not appear in the OO-DFD, as we well know, but they should appear in the data dictionary (DD), specifically in the part where the elementary functions are described. If the existing description is missing or not precise enough, the analyst/designer may get the missing details from the user (or the user's representative). The amount of detail may vary from function to function; in some cases an elementary function may be very simple and easy to describe; in other cases it may be more complex, involving various activities, conditions, loops, and so forth.

- Every **"input from U..."** command, which states that data need to be received from a user, is replaced by a reference to a predefined input screen or a different input device, as defined for that input. Note that at this stage we have already designed all inputs and outputs, and defined the **Inputs (Forms)** and **Outputs (Reports)** classes and their objects.

- Every **"output to U..."** command, which states that information needs to be produced for a user, is replaced by a reference to a predefined output screen or a different output device, as defined for that output.

- Every **"read from C..."** command, which states that data of a certain object or objects need to be retrieved, is replaced by a more detailed command that includes the conditions for retrieval (if any). Note that the data elements (attributes) that need to be retrieved have already been defined in the DD.

- Every **"write to C..."** command states that data of a certain object or objects need to be updated. As we know, write/update may mean adding a new object, changing an existing object, or deleting an object. Therefore, the "write" command is replaced by a more detailed command which specifies the type of the update and its conditions (if any). Note again that the data elements that need to be updated have already been defined in the DD.

- Every **"move to F..."** command indicates the activation of the following function. The data (parameters) that need to be passed to the function are specified in the DD. Therefore, there is no need to add more detail for this command.

Here are several examples for the transition from top-level descriptions of transactions to their detailed descriptions.

Example 1: Transaction 1.4/5 of the Apartments Building System

The objective of transaction 1.4/5 of that system is to handle payments received from tenants. In order to make things easy to follow, the **top-level description** of the transaction[3] is brought again here:

Begin transaction 1.4/5

Input from U1 Tenant: Apartment number or family name

Read from C1 Apartment: tenant details

If not-found then present error message and ask user to input again an apartment ID

Else input from U1 Tenant: payment details

Execute F1.4 Input payment

Move to F1.5: tenant and payment details

Execute F1.5: Store payment and report

Write to C1 Apartment: payment details

Write to C5 Company: sum paid

Output to U1 Tenant: receipt

End transaction.

For the "input" commands of this description, an input screen called "Payment Form" was created (see Figure 11.6 in Chapter XI). In addition, a "Payment Receipt" was designed for the output command (see Figure 11.7, Chapter XI). As for the inputs of this transaction, it has already been made clear that the input screen includes a scroll window displaying the apartment numbers and family names, from which the user can choose the proper apartment and family using the mouse device. This means that the entire list of apartments is first retrieved from the **Apartments** class, and only then the user can choose one of them. Consequently, the rest of the input fields will be opened, to keying in the payment details.

The **detailed description** of the transaction follows. The description is relatively short, since the transaction is "simple" and the functions it includes do not perform any complicated task besides receiving some input data, updating several values of an object, and producing an output (receipt)—which means that there are no special procedures to be explained here.

Begin transaction 1.4/5

Do while "update" was not chosen:

Read C1 Apartment - Retrieve all apartment objects from the class and save their *apartment number* and *family name* attributes. *(Assume that these details are saved in the system's memory.)*

Input from U1 Tenant - Use Input 1.4/54 "Payment Form". *(At this point only the apartment number and family name scroll window is "open," displaying the apartment numbers and family names. The user chooses an apartment number or a family using the mouse device.)*

(Note that the command "Execute F1.4 ... " is not detailed; it is actually performed using the above input screen. As result of the user's choice, the remaining windows on the

screen become active; the user keys in the payment details; afterwards, the user would press the "update" button.)

End while *(The loop terminates once "update" is pressed.)*

(Note also that the command "Move to F1.5..." is redundant because all data retrieved from C1 and input U1 is available within the procedure.)

(Similarly, the command "Execute F1.5..." is redundant because the update is performed by the next command "Write to C1...".)

Write to C1 Apartment – Update the apartment object by adding the payment details to its respective attributes.

Write to C5 Company – Update the singular class with the paid amount. The sum is added to attribute *total annual payments from tenants*.

Output to U1 Tenant – Use Output 1.4/55 ("Payment Receipt").

End transaction.

Example 2: Transaction 4.3-7 of the Musical Programs System

Transaction 4.3-7 in the Musical Programs system is in charge of assigning musical pieces to programs. Here is again its **top-level description:**[6]

Begin transaction 4.3-7

Do "Present program for assignment"

Do "Present suitable pieces"

Do "Assign pieces"

If editor completed all the assignments of pieces to this program then write to C1 Musical piece: status = "scheduled"

Else;

End transaction.

Begin Present program for assignment

Input from U3 Editor: program name and date

Read from C2 Music program: details of program

Read from C3 Scheduled program: details of assignment

Execute F4.3: Input program to schedule

Move to F4.4: details of program and existing assignments

End Present program for assignment.

Begin Present suitable pieces

Read from C1 Musical piece: suitable pieces for program

Execute F4.4: Review suitable pieces for program

Output to U3 Editor: assigned and suitable pieces

Move to F4.5: details of suitable pieces

Read from C3 Scheduled program: past plays

Read from C1 Musical piece: assigned pieces

Execute F4.5: Review past plays of pieces in program

Output to U3 Editor: past plays of pieces in program

Move to F4.6: details of program, pieces and past plays

Read from C4 Listener request: listeners' requests within the range of dates

Execute F4.6 Review listeners' requests

Output to U3 Editor: listeners' requests

Move to F4.7: details of musical pieces assigned and played, and listeners' requests

End Present suitable pieces.

Begin Assign pieces

Do while the editor wishes to assign more musical pieces:

      Input from U3 Editor: selected musical piece and listeners' requests

      Execute F4.7: Assign pieces and requests

      Write to C3 Scheduled program: assigned piece

      Write to C1 Musical piece: program where assigned

      DO-while there are listener requests for this piece:

            Write to C3 Scheduled program: approved listener request

            Write to C4 Listener request: status = "approved"

            Output to U2 Listeners: notification of approved request

      End while

End while

End Assign pieces.

The previous was the top-level description of the transaction. Assume that at the stage of inputs and outputs design, an input-output screen (whose number 4.3-7.1) has been designed for this transaction, which enables the displaying of various details about the program to be scheduled, the suitable musical pieces, the listeners' request, and so forth, and the user to make selections from the screen or key in data as needed. In addition, an output/report (whose number is 4.3-7.2) was designed as a postcard which will be sent to a listener whose request has been approved.

The **detailed description** of the transaction follows. We can see that this description also consists of a main procedure that calls three subprocedures. The names of the procedures were not changed, but their descriptions are more detailed.

Begin transaction 4.3-7

Do "Present program for assignment"

Do "Present suitable pieces"

Do "Assign pieces"

Input from U3 Editor - Use Input 4.3-7.1. If the editor decides that the assignment of musical pieces to this program is complete, he/she is supposed to press to "end scheduling" button.

If "end scheduling" pressed then Write to C3 Scheduled program: status = "scheduled"

Else; *(the status remains "unscheduled")*

End transaction.

Begin Present program for assignment

Read from C2 Music program: program names - Upon activation of the transaction, all objects of class **Music program** are retrieved and their names are kept in an array (vector) in memory.

Input from U3 Editor: program name to schedule - Use Input 4.3-7.1. The list of the musical program names is displayed in a scrolling window; the user (editor) chooses the program he wishes to edit.

Read from C2 Music program: details of program - As result of the user's choice, the selected **Music program** object is retrieved and kept in memory; the attribute *set time {day, hours}* enables to compute the dates of all future broadcasts of this program till the end of season; the dates will be presented in a scrolling window.

Input from U3 Editor: date of program to schedule - Use Input 4.3-7-1. The above dates are presented in a scrolling window. The user chooses the desired date.

Read from C3 Scheduled program - The object of the chosen **Scheduled program** is being searched for. If the object already exists (i.e., the editor already started scheduling this program in the past), then the object's details are retrieved and displayed in respective windows of the input screen. If not (i.e., the editor never started scheduling this program) - those windows of the input screen remain empty.

(Note that the command "Execute F4.3..." is redundant; the data about the program to schedule have already been retrieved in the previous command.)

Move to F4.4: details of program and existing assignments - The parameters passed to the next procedure include the attributes of the **Scheduled program** object and *music types* of the **Music program**.

End Present program for assignment.

Begin Present suitable pieces

Read from C1 Musical piece: suitable pieces for program - A search is performed for musical pieces whose music type is at least one of the types listed in attribute *set music types* of the **Music program** object. The numbers and names of each of these pieces are kept in memory, to be displayed later on screen. Already scheduled pieces are not included again.

(The command "Execute F4.4..." is redundant; it is carried out by the next output command.)

Output to U3 Editor: suitable pieces - Use Input 4.3-7.1. (This is actually an input/output screen.) The details of the above suitable pieces are displayed in a scrolling window; from these the editor will choose, later on, the pieces he/she wishes to assign to this scheduled program.

(The command "Move to F4.5..." is redundant; the data from the past commands are available to the next commands within this procedure.)

Read from C3 Scheduled program: past played pieces - Find a certain number of objects of the latest broadcasts of this program (the number is determined by the editor) and keep the IDs of the musical pieces that have been played in them; these will be used to retrieve the relevant details of these pieces and then presented to the editor (so that he/she will be aware of already played pieces).

Read from C1 Musical piece: details of past played pieces - Find all the objects of **Musical piece** that have been kept as result of the above Read command; for each of them keep its number and name, to be displayed later on screen.

(The command "Execute F4.5..." is not detailed; it is performed by the next output command.)

Output to U3 Editor: past plays of pieces in program - Use Input 4.3-7.1. The details (i.e., numbers and names) of the past played musical pieces are displayed in a scrolling window.

(The command "Move to F4.6..." is redundant, as explained earlier.)

Read from C4 Listener request: Search objects of the class **Listener request** which qualify to the following conditions: (1) their *requested program* attribute references to the **Music program** being scheduled; (2) their attribute *range of play dates* includes the date of the **Scheduled program**; (3) their *status* is "waiting". Keep the details of these objects (including the requested musical piece and dedication), to be presented later on screen.

(The command "Execute function 4.6..." are expressed by the next output command.)

Output to U3 Editor: listeners' requests - Use Input 4.3-7.1. The details of the listeners' requests that were retrieved and kept in the previous Read command are displayed in a scrolling window of the screen.

Move to F4.7: details of the program, pieces and requests - The parameters passed to the next procedure include the attributes of the **Scheduled program** object, the numbers and names of the assigned pieces, suitable pieces, played in the past pieces, and requested pieces, along with their listeners' dedications. All these are displayed in the respective windows of the input screen.

End Present suitable pieces.

Begin Assign pieces

Do-while the editor has not pressed the "stop" button. *(The loop executes as long as the editor wishes to assign more musical pieces to the scheduled program. He/she may assign only some pieces in a work session with the transaction, pause—by hitting the "stop" button— and resume the work some other time.)*

Input from U3 Editor: selected musical piece and listeners' requests - Use Input 4.3-7.1. The editor reviews the information presented in the windows of the screen, as described previously, and based on that he/she decides which musical piece to assign. Assignment of a piece is done by choosing/clicking on a name of a musical piece appearing in any of the windows: suitable pieces, played in the past pieces, or requested pieces, and moving it to the window of the assigned pieces. *(The command "Execute F4.7..." need not be detailed because is actually performed by the former command.)*

Write to C3 Scheduled program: assigned pieces and requests – Adds the ID of the assigned piece to the attribute *set assigned pieces* of the **Scheduled program** object.

Write to C1 Musical piece: program where assigned - The ID of the Scheduled program object is added to the attribute *set assigned in* of the selected **Musical piece** object.

Do-while there are listener requests for this assigned piece *(An assigned musical piece may have been requested by more one or more listeners. The loop is performed for each of the listeners who requested the assigned piece.)*

Write to C3 Scheduled program: listener's ID - The attribute *set approved requests* of the **Scheduled program** object is updated by adding a reference to the **Listener request** object.

Write to C4 Listener request: status = "approved" - The attribute *status* is updated so that this request will not be retrieved again in further assignments.

Output to U2 Listeners: notification - Use Output 4.3-7.2 *(As said, this output was designed as a postcard to be sent to the listeners whose requests have been granted.)*

End while *(This inner loop terminates when there are no more listener requests for this assigned musical piece.)*

End while *(This outer loop terminates when the editor presses the "stop" button, since he/she is no longer interested in assigning more musical pieces to this scheduled program. When the transaction will be activated again, all assigned pieces, which are saved in the **Scheduled program** object, will be retrieved and displayed in the respective window of the input/output screen.)*

End Assign pieces.

Example 3: A Transaction in an Academic Library System

The following example is taken from an IS of an academic library. Here is a verbal description of the transaction dealing with lending out books to students.[7]

A student who wishes to borrow books comes to the lending out counter with his/her reader card (a magnetic card with the student's ID) and the books. On the cover of every book there is a barcode label with the book's ID. First of all, the magnetic card reader reads the student's details and the system checks the reader's record in order to make sure he/she is allowed to borrow books. Based on the student's record, the system determines whether the student is eligible to borrow books and how many and notifies the librarian. If the student is allowed, each book is lent out by reading its barcode; the lend details are saved, and the reader is given a printout specifying the books that were lent and when they are due back. Once the last book has been lent out to the reader, a "blank" barcode reading is performed in order to signal the system.

Here are the rules regarding the lending out of books: an old-time (over three years) undergraduate student may borrow as many as eight books if he/she owes no money to the library. If there is a debt of up to $200 he/she may only borrow five books, and if the debt is bigger—none at all. If the old-time student is studying for a higher degree, the number of books allowed is double that of an undergraduate student in the same situation. A new student (less than a year), who owes less than $80, may borrow up to two books. If the debt is bigger than $80, he/she may

Figure 12.1. Diagram of a transaction of the academic library system

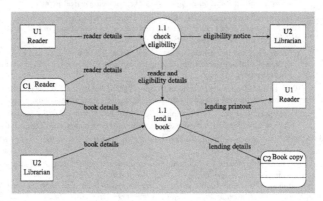

borrow no books, unless he/she is a graduate student, in which case one book is allowed. If the new reader has no debt, then if he/she is a graduate student he/she may borrow up to five books, while if the student is an undergraduate student he/she may borrow only three books.

Figure 12.1 presents a diagram of the transaction. Note that details such as the conditions for lending out books are not included in the diagram (and the OO-DFD from which it is extracted). It should be assumed that these details are saved in the DD. In the transaction diagram we see only two functions; one deals with checking the student's eligibility to borrow books, and the other—with the actual lending of books.

Before presenting the top-level description and then the detailed description of the transaction, let us discuss the classes and the inputs and outputs involved in this transaction.

The Classes: The transaction involves data classes: C1 is the **Reader** class, whose objects are the various readers (i.e., students). Class C2 is **Book copy**, whose objects are the books of the library. (We do not see here the class **Book** which certainly exists in this system. An object of book presumably includes attributes such as title, authors, publisher, and so forth, and it may have one or more book copies. But this transaction only handles the lending out of copies of books.) A partial class diagram for this example is presented in Figure 12.2. Every lending of a book is represented in this diagram by a many-to-many relationship between **Reader** and **Book copy**, and two respective set reference

Figure 12.2. Partial class diagram of the academic library system

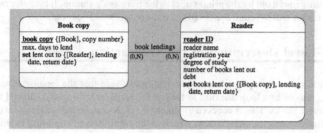

attributes: in **Reader** it is *set books lent out {[Book copy], lend date, return date}*; in Book copy the inverse attribute is *set lent out to {[Reader], lend date, return date}*.[8] Note that class **Reader** contains, among other things, the attributes *degree of study, registration year,* and *debt.* Upon lending out of a book, each of the set attributes (of the **Reader** object and of the **Book copy** object) is updated by adding a tuple of values: Reference to the Book copy and the lending date is added to the Reader object; and reference to the Reader and the lending date is added to the Book copy object. At this stage the attribute *return date* of both objects remains null; it will be updated by a separate transaction dealing with book returns.

The Inputs and Outputs: Assume that at this stage the inputs and outputs of the system, including those of this transaction, have already been designed as follows:

- **Input number 12.19 from U1 Reader to function 1.1:** The reader details are read from a magnetic card by a card reader.

- **Input number 12.2 from U2 Librarian to function 1.2:** The book details (actually, details of a book copy) are read from a barcode attached to the inside cover of the book by a barcode reader. Assume that the barcode includes the book ISBN and copy number.

- **Output number 12.1 from function 1.1 to U2 Librarian:** The eligibility notice is presented on the librarian's screen. It includes the reader details (e.g., reader ID, name, registration year, degree of study, number of books eligible, number of books lent out, and debt) and a notice: In case of eligibility the notice is "This reader may lend out X books," where X = number of books eligible—number of books lent out. In case of ineligibility the notice is "This reader may not lend books at this stage."

- **Output number 12.2 from function 1.2 to U1 Reader:** The lend details are printed out by the printer next to the librarian's station. It includes the reader's details and the details of each of the books lent out.

Top-Level Description of the Transaction

The transaction's top-level description follows. Note that the lending of the books is done by a loop that runs as long as the reader is willing and allowed to lend more books. This is checked by function 1.1. As can be seen, the top-level description does not include details such as the conditions of eligibility to lend books—these will be included, however, in the detailed description.

Begin transaction 12
Input from U1 Reader: reader details
Read from C1 Reader: reader details
Execute F1.1: check eligibility
Output to U2 Librarian: eligibility notice
Do while reader is willing and eligible to lend more books
    Input from U2 Librarian: book details
    Execute F1.2: lend book
    Write to C1 Reader: lend details
    Write to C2 Book copy: lend details
    Output to U1 Reader: lend printout
End while
End transaction.

Detailed Description of the Transaction

The detailed description that follows considers the various conditions for lending out books to readers. It consists of a main procedure which calls two subprocedures: one which checks the eligibility of the reader to lend books; the other deals with the actual lending of books.

Begin transaction 12
Input from U1 Reader: reader details - Use input 12.1 (magnetic card reader)
Read from C1 Reader: read reader's details
Do **"Eligibility check"** *(This procedure, which elaborates on function 1.1, returns a variable named "elig" with the number of books the reader is eligible to lend at the present time.)*

If elig <=0 then output to U2 Librarian: ineligibility notice - Use Output 12.1

Else output to U2 Librarian: eligibility notice - Use Output 12.1

    Do while elig > 0 *(as long as the reader is eligible to lend more books)*

        Input from U2 Librarian: book details - Use Input 12.2 (barcode reader)

        If input <> "F" then Do **"Lend out book"** *(This function deals with lending the book to the reader and updating the reader's eligibility. The process is performed only if the barcode was that of a book to be lent, not of a fictitious book, which returns an "F" value.)*

        Else *(if input = 'F')* output to U2 Librarian: end of process notification - Use Output 12.1

    End while

End transaction.

Begin Eligibility Check

years = current year – *registration year (Assume that current year is taken from the system, while registration year is an attribute of reader.)*

If years > 3 then Do-Case:

        Case-1: if debt = 0 then N=8

        Case-2: if debt <=200 then N=5

        Case-3: debt > 200 then N=0

    End case

    If *degree of study* = "Grad" then N=N*2

    Else;

Else *(if years <= 3)* Do-Case:

        Case-1: if debt = 0 and degree of study = "Grad" 1 then N=5

        Case-2: if debt = 0 and degree of study = "Under" then N=3

        Case-3: if debt >= 40 and degree of study = "Grad" then N=1

        Case-4: if debt >= 40 and degree of study = "Under" then N=0

        Case-5: if debt < 40 then N=2

    End-Case

elig = N- *number of books lent out*

End Eligibility check.

Begin Lend out book

Write to C1 Reader: lend details -   a) add 1 to attribute *number of books lent out*;

                                      b) add a tuple to attribute *set books lent out*

                                      with OID of Book copy and *lend date*

Write to C2 Book copy: lend details - add a tuple to attribute *set lent out to* with OID of Reader and *lend date*

Output to U1 Reader: lent printout - Use Output 12.2

elig = elig – 1 *(returns the value of eligible to the main procedure)*
End Lend out book.

From Detailed Descriptions of Transactions to Class Methods

In this stage, the detailed description of each transaction is "decomposed" into methods which are attached to proper classes. Before elaborating on that, let us remember the discussion in the Functions Section of Chapter II, which dealt with functions or methods of classes. We made a distinction between two major types of methods:

Basic Methods enable performing the four basic operations: create, read, update, and delete (CRUD):

- **Create** adds an object. It is possible to set the attribute values of the created object in several ways: some may receive default values (if such values were predefined); some may receive values while being created, through user input; and some may remain null until they are updated by some other method.

- **Read** locates/finds an existing object of the class. The method receives (as a parameter) the identification of the sought object and returns the object or a message saying that the object does not exist. In addition to the basic Read method, there may be specific methods to find one or many objects according to certain search criteria—depending on the specific application and its users.

- **Update** changes values of attributes of an existing object. Generally, a class may have different specific update methods, if it has attributes which have to be updated in different manners or at different times. Each of these methods may be activated, most likely, in response to an event occurring in the real world.

- **Delete** removes an object from the class. The method receives a value that enables it to identify the object to be deleted. It also returns a message informing the sender whether the object has been deleted or not found.

We assume that every data class has basic methods. There is no need to design/define them, and it may be assumed that all classes inherit the basic methods from a superclass where these methods are defined.

The appendix at the end of this chapter provides a few examples of basic methods. Actually, we do not detail the methods themselves, only their structure. Each method has a name, parameter, and returning values. We also provide examples for the use of the methods.

Application-Specific Methods[10] are defined according to the specific needs of the application (i.e., the users). Such methods may perform various specific tasks, beyond tasks which can be performed by the basic methods. It is reasonable that a specific method would include messages to basic methods which will perform for it the basic CRUD operations. It is also reasonable to assume that the same basic method might be activated by more than one specific method.

Before detailing the process by which a transaction description is decomposed into methods, here is an example which clarifies the distinction between basic methods and specific methods:[11] Assume that we need to register a student to courses. Registrations take place at the beginning of every semester. A student may register to one or more courses. This can be achieved by a specific method of the class **Student**, which includes the attribute *set registered to courses {[Courses], grade}*. The objective of the method is to add tuples to this set, one per each course the student registers to. At this stage only the courses' OIDs are to be added, but the grades are null. Once the method is activated, it first finds the student's object—using the basic method Read of **Student**. Then it performs a loop as long as there are more courses the students registers to. In every iteration of the loop, the method sends a message to the user (assume that it is done through a message to a method of a class **Forms** which displays a form on screen), requesting the user to key in a course code. Once the course code is returned to the update method, it sends a message to the Read method of class **Course** in order to verify that the course exists. If the Read method returns an error message, the update method will send an error message to the user (via the previous form) requesting the user to key in another course code. If the Read method finds the course object, it returns its OID to the update method. Now this method needs to make sure that the student is not already registered to this course, so it runs a search **inside** that set attribute. If it finds the aforementioned course's OID in the set, the method will send an error message to the user; if not—it will perform the addition to the set. Then it will send a message to the class **Course**, to its specific method *add a student to course*; the message includes the course OID (by which the course object can be found) as well as the student's OID, so that that method will be able to add the student's OID to the attribute *set registered students {[Students], grade}*. Every iteration of the main loop of the update method (of **Student**) ends with a message to the user (on screen) asking whether he/she wants to register to more courses. If the answer is yes, a new update loops begins; otherwise the update terminates.

Generally, the detailed description of a transaction is "decomposed" into methods and messages according to the following rules:

- A command "Input from User…" is translated into a message to the Display method of the **Forms** class; the message will include the ID of the specific Form object. The Display method will enable, as we know, feeding in the input needed by the transaction. (If the input is retrieved through an input screen, the input fields will be presented in appropriate windows, in accordance with the input screen's design.) The method will return an object containing the input values (or null, if no data were input).

- A command "Output to User…" is translated into a message to the Display method of the **Reports** class; the message will include the ID of the specific Reports object and the output values. The display method will enable the production of the output, according to its design.

- A command "Read from Class…" is translated into a message to the method of that class, whose task is to search and retrieve one object or more, according to conditions defined in the transaction. Therefore, the message will include the class name, the name of the Read method, and the search conditions (if there are any). Note that the Read method of the target class is assumed to exist already (as a Basic method).

- A command "Write to Class…" is translated into a message to the method of that class, whose task is to perform the specific Write command, according to the description of the transaction. As we know, a Write command can mean adding a new object (using the Create basic method), or removing an existing object (using the Delete method), or changing an object (using the Update or Change method). Sometimes the Write command may apply to a single object (e.g., creating a new object); while sometimes it may apply to certain objects (e.g., changing a certain attribute of objects of a class according to certain conditions). Hence, the message will include the class name, the name of the specific Create/Delete/Update methods, and the conditions (if there are any).

- A detailed description of a transaction may include commands which describe a certain procedure (possibly derived from an "Execute func-tion…" command in the top-level description). Here we need to review the procedure and determine if it can be defined as a specific method that can be detached from the "main" part of the transaction and attached to one of the classes involved in the transaction. This may be a class which is used by that procedure (i.e., which the procedure retrieves from or updates). For example, assume that the description of a certain transaction includes a procedure (i.e., certain commands) which performs the task of updating the average grade of a student as a result of reporting a new course grade (as has been demonstrated earlier). It makes sense to define this procedure as a specific method that will be attached to class **Student**. Hence, the original procedure will be a message to the new method of the designated class. The message may include parameters that will transfer any data required by the method to fulfill its task. The method may return the result of its operation.

If a procedure cannot be assigned to any class (for example, because it involves several classes, or perhaps because it involves no classes—just some general calculations), it remains in the transaction. The remaining parts of the transaction, which have not been identified as basic or specific methods and replaced by messages (to those methods), are defined as the "main" method of the transaction. This method is attached to the **Transactions** class.

Hence, we wish to repeat: The **Transactions** class will contain one "main" method for each transaction. A Transaction method will be activated by a user who uses the interface and makes selections among menu items, until activating a desired "T" menu item. At that point the Choose method of the **Menus** class sends as message to the respective Transaction method. Once activated, the Transaction method executes according to its process logic. This may include the sending of messages to basic or specific methods of various classes. A certain specific method may, in turn, send messages to other class methods, according to its process logic. Eventually, the transaction method completes its task, and control is returned to the Menus main method (as described in chapter XI).

In the sequel we provide a few examples for the mapping of detailed descriptions of transactions into methods and messages. We use the same examples that have been used in the previous section. The examples are brought in pseudo code.[12]

It is important to point out that the pseudo code we use to describe methods is not a programming language; it is not a formal language, and does not follow syntactic rules. The pseudo-code description of methods is aimed to provide guidelines to the programmers who will program and test the methods. Therefore, the pseudo code must include also comments and explanations which the programmers will use when creating the program code. To understand the structure of the methods in the following examples, the reader is referred to the Appendix at the end of this chapter.

Example 1: Transaction 1.4/5 of the Apartments Building System

As you may recall, this is a relatively simple transaction; and so is its pseudo code. (The line numbers are not a part of the method description; they are only meant to make the explanation easier to follow.)

1.   **Begin Transaction.Method 1.4/5**
2.   Do while "update" was not chosen:
3.   apart-numbers, family-names = Apartment.GetObjects (All)
4.   payment-details = Forms.payment form.Display (apart-numbers, family-names)
5.   End while
6.   Apartment.Add payment (payment-details)
7.   Company.Change (Add, total annual payments from tenants, sum paid)
8.   Reports.Payment receipt.Display
9.   **End.**

Explanations:

1.   This is the Transaction method. As we will see, the body of the method includes messages to other class methods.

2.   Recall that the method performs a loop as long as the user does not press the "update" button of the *payments form*, that is, as long as the user did not complete keying in the payment details.

3.   Within the loop, a message is sent to class **Apartment** to its method *GetObjects*. The parameter (All) means that the method retrieves all apartment objects. But only their apartment numbers and family names are kept in respective arrays (in memory).[13]

4.   A message is sent to the Display method of class **Forms**, in order to display its object *payment form*. The parameters apartment-numbers and family-names pass these data so that the receiving method can display them in the respective windows of the form (as can be seen in Figure 11.6, Chapter XI). Then the user chooses an apartment number or a family name. As a result, the other input fields of the form become active so that the user can key in the rest of the payment details. The method returns the payment details which are kept in variables named payment-details. Note that at the programming stage, payment-details will be defined in more detail using specific variables for the specific fields; here we do not need to go into such details.

6.   After the payment data have been received, a message is sent to class **Apartment** to its method *Add payment*, with the parameter payment-details. *Add payment* is assumed to be a specific method that has to be defined (but its description is not provided here); its task is to add the details of the new payment to the apartment object; specifically to its attribute *set payments*.

7.   Following that, a message is sent to the Change method of class **Company**. The method's parameters include the type of change (Add), the attribute

to which it applies (*total annual payments from tenants*), and what has to be added (*sum paid*). Note that the structure of the parameters of this method (as well as of other methods) is not consistent with the structures used in programming languages. Moreover, we do not use any formal language and notations for our methods and parameters; our objective is to provide simple and easy-to-comprehend guidelines so that the programmers who will read them will be able to convert them easily to program code.

8. Finally, a message is sent to the Display method of the **Reports** class in order to produce the payment receipt.

Example 2: Transaction 4.3-7 of the Music Programs System

A detailed description of this transaction has been presented in the previous section. This is a fairly complex transaction; it includes several classes and there is an intense interaction between the user (the editor) and the IS, using input/output screens. After reviewing the detailed description of the transaction, we have come to a decision as to how to decompose it into methods and messages: The procedure **Present program for assignment** will be defined as a specific method of class **Music programs**; the procedure **Present suitable pieces** will be defined as a specific method of class **Scheduled program**; and the procedure **Assign pieces**, along with the rest of the commands included in the transaction's description, will be defined as the "main" method, that is, the method Transactions.Method 4.3-7. As we will see, the main method and the specific methods include, among other commands, messages to other basic and specific methods of various classes involved in the execution of the method. What follows are both the main/Transaction method and the aforementioned specific methods.[14]

Begin Transaction.Method 4.3-7

SchProgramObject = MusicProgram.PresentProgramToSchedule

> (*The transaction begins by sending a message to PresentProgramToSchedule, which is a specific method of the class **MusicProgram**. The details of the method will follow. The method returns the details of the program to which the editor wishes to assign musical pieces; these are kept in a variable SchProgramObject. These details include, among other things, the music types of the program, references to musical pieces already assigned, and references to approved listener requests—this is true for a program which the editor already started to schedule in the past.*)

SuitablePieces, PlayedPieces, RelevantRequests =

ScheduledProgram.PresentRelevantPieces (SchProgramObject)

*(A message is sent to PresentRelevantPieces, a specific method of class **ScheduledPorgram**, whose details follow. The message contains, as a parameter, the details of the program to schedule. The method returns three lists of musical pieces: suitable pieces, pieces played in past broadcasts of this program, and pieces requested by listeners. All this information will be presented to the editor, and based on it he/she will decide which musical pieces to assign to this program.)*

Do while not "stop"

(Now starts a loop in which the editor assigns musical pieces to the program. The loop will terminate when the editor will press the "stop" button on the input form. Recall that the editor may assign only some musical pieces in a work session, pause by hitting the "stop" button, and resume the work some other time.)

PieceObj, ApprovedRequests = Forms.Schedule Program.Display (SuitablePieces, PlayedPieces, RelevanPieces)

*(A message is sent to the Display method of class **Forms** to act upon the input/output form Schedule Program. This method [whose details are not shown here] enables the editor to choose a musical piece from any of the lists displayed in scroll windows of the form. Assume that the choice is done by clicking on a piece name and moving it from its window to the window containing the assigned pieces. The OID of the selected piece is kept in one variable (PieceObj) and the OIDs of the listener who requested this piece are kept in the other variable (ApprovedRequests).)*

ScheduledProgram.SchProgramObj.Change (Add, set assigned pieces, PieceObj)

*(This is a message to the method Change of class **ScheduledProgram**.   T   h   e method acts on the scheduled program object. The meaning of the parameters of this method is as follows: Add is the operation, set assigned pieces is an attribute of the object, and PieceObj is the OID of the musical piece to be added to the set.)*

MusicalPiece.PieceObj.Change (Add, set assigned in, SchProgramObj)

*(This is a message to the method Change of class **MusicalPiece**; similar to the former case, this method adds the OID of the scheduled program to set assigned in of the assigned musical pieces.)*

For i = 1 to end of ApprovedRequests do:

(A loop is performed for all the listeners who requested the above assigned musical piece. Recall that ApprovedRequests is an array which contains the OIDs of approved listener requests.)

ScheduledProgram.SchProgramObj.Change (Add, set approved requests, ApprovedRequests(i))

*(This is a message to the Change method of class **ScheduledProgram**. Its task is to add the OIDs of the approved listener requests to the attribute set approved requests of the scheduled program object.)*

ListenerRequest.ApprovedRequests(i).Change (Replace, status, "approved")

*(Now, a message is sent to the Change method of class **ListenerRequest**, in order to update the status of the request from "waiting" to "approved," so that this request will not be retrieved again in future assignments.)*

Reports.CardToListener.Display(ApprovedRequest(i),   SchProgramObj)

*(Now a message is sent to the Display method of class **Reports**, to be applied on the output CardToListenert; it prints a postcard that will be sent to the listener. The postcard will contain the details of the request and the scheduled program, based on the parameters   passed to it.)*

Next i *(This inner loop terminates after all approved requests have been processed.)*

End While *(The outer loop terminates after the editor presses the "stop" button.)*

Out = Forms.Schedule Program_Stop.Display()

*(After the editor presses the "stop" button, the Display method of class **Forms** is activated in order to open two buttons: "Exit—Schedule Complete" and "Exit—Schedule Not complete": The former will be hit if the editor determines that the scheduling of the program is complete; he/she will hit the other button if he/she plans to continue scheduling this program at another time. The editor's decision is kept in the return variable Out.)*

If Out = "Schedule Complete" then ScheduledProgram.SchProgramObj.Change (Replace, status, "scheduled")

(If the "Schedule Complete" button was pressed, the status of the scheduled program is changed accordingly.)

Else; *(There is no status change.)*

End.

Begin MusicProgram.PresentProgramToSchedule

*(This is a specific method of class **MusicProgram** which is called from the main method and returns a variable named SchProgramObj which includes the details of the program to schedule.)*

MusicPrograms = MusicProgram.GetObjects (program name)

*(Upon activation of the method, a message is sent to a basic GetObjects of class **Music Program** in order to find all objects of music programs. The method returns an array of program names which are kept in the variable MusicPorgrams.)*

ProgramObj = Forms.Schedule Program.Display (MusicPrograms)

*(Now a message is sent to the method Display of class **Forms**, to be activated on the input form Schedule Program. The message contains, as parameter, the names of the music programs; assume that the list of program names will be displayed in a scroll window, and the editor will then choose one program from the list. The OID of the chosen program is returned and passed to the variable ProgramObj.)*

SchedDates = MusicProgram.ProgramObj.Get-programs-to-schedule

*(Now a message is sent to a specific method Get-programs-to-schedule of class **MusicPrograms**, which is activated on the ProgramObj chosen by the editor. Assume that this specific method [whose details are not brought here] goes over the set times {day, hour}, based on that computes the dates of all future broadcasts of this program until the end of the season; before inserting a computed date in the return variable the method still has to check if the program planned for that date has already been scheduled by the editor. For this it goes over the values of the set which consists of [Scheduled program] and for each value it sends a message to the class **ScheduledProgram** to find the object; if the object is not found it means that the program for that date has not been scheduled yet; if the object is found the method checks its status: if the status is "unscheduled," it returns its broadcasting date to the sender. Eventually, the return variable of this method [i.e., the variable SchedDates of Get-programs-to-schedule] contains a list of future broadcast dates of the program from which the editor will be asked to choose one.)*

SchedObj = Forms.Schedule Program.Display (SchedDates)

(A message is sent to method Display of class Forms, to be activated on the form object Schedule Program [the same form used earlier]; the parameter includes the above dates

of the future broadcasts of the program. Assume that the dates are displayed in a scroll window, from which the editor will choose one which he/she wishes to work on. The OID of the chosen program is passed to the variable SchedObj.)

SchProgramObj = ScheduledProgram.GetObjects (SchedObj)

> *(Now a message is sent to the basic method GetObjects of class **ScheduledProgram**, with the OID of that object; the method finds and returns the ScheduledProgram object, which is kept in the variable ScheProgramObj. Note that the object contains, among other things, references to musical pieces already assigned, and references to approved listener requests—this is true for a program which the editor already started to schedule in the past. The variable is returned to the main Transaction method.)*

End.

Begin ScheduledProgram.PresentRelevantPieces (SchProgramObj)

SuitablePieces = MusicalPiece.GetObjects (music types in SchProgramObj)

> *(When this method is activated, a message is sent to the GetObjects method of class **MusicalPiece**. The parameter includes a list of music types of the program. The method searches and retrieves all the musical pieces whose type is one of the above. The numbers and names of each of these pieces are kept in the variable SuitablePieces, to be displayed later to the editor.)*

PastPrograms = ScheduledProgram.GetLatestBroadcasts

> *(This is a message to a specific method of the class ScheduledProgram [whose details are not shown here]. The method retrieves a certain number of previously broadcasted program objects, in order to enable the extraction of the musical pieces played in them. The OIDs of these programs are kept in the return variable.)*

PastPieces = MusicalPiece.GetLatestPieces (PastPrograms)

> *(Following the result of the previous message, a message is sent to a specific method of class **MusicalPieces** [whose details are not shown], whose task is to retrieve the musical pieces played in those previously broadcasted programs. The return variable PastPieces keeps the numbers and names of these pieces.)*

RelevantRequests = ListenerRequest.GetRelevantRequests (SchProgramObj)

> *(Now a message is sent to a specific method GetRelevantRequests of class **ListenerRequest** [whose details are not shown]. The parameter passed to this method is the scheduled program object, which includes its broadcasting date. This method retrieves requests for the program with status "waiting" which satisfy the condition, that is, the range of play dates includes the broadcasting date of the program. The return variable includes, for each listener request, the dedication.)*

End.

Example 3: Transaction 12 of the Academic Library System

A detailed description of this transaction has been presented in Example 3 of the section, From Top-Level to Detailed Transaction Descriptions. We have seen that the description consists of a main procedure which calls two subprocedures: Eligibility check and Lend out book. The main procedure is defined as the Transaction/main method, while the two subprocedures are defined (with minor modifications) as specific methods: The method Eligibility check is attached to class **Reader**, and the method Lend out book is attached to class **Book copy**. Here are the pseudo-code descriptions of the three methods:

Begin Transaction.Method 12

reader-ID = Forms.Magnetic card reader.Display

> *(This is a message to the Magnetic reader card input. The reader's ID is saved in the return variable.)*

reader-object = Reader.GetObjects (reader-ID)

> *(Search and retrieve the reader object. The object contains the values of the various attributes, including registration year, debt, degree of study, and number of books lent out. These details are needed for the eligibility check.)*

elig = Reader.reader object.Eligibility-check

> *(A message is sent to the specific method Eligibility-check of class **Reader** to operate on the reader object. The object's details include registration year, debt, degree of study, and number of books lent out. These details are needed in order to calculate the number of books the reader is eligible to lend out at any point in time. The method returns a variable "elig" which contains the number of books the reader may lend.)*

If elig <= 0 then Reports.Eligibility notice.Display (reader object, "not eligible")

> *(If the reader is not eligible to lend even a single book, a message is sent to method Display of class **Reports** to display the Eligibility notice on the librarian screen. The parameter includes the reader object and the message "not eligible.")*

Else Report.Eligibility notice.Display (reader object, "eligible")

> *(Otherwise, the eligibility notice will be "eligible.")*

> Do while elig > 0

> > *(The loop is performed as long as the reader is eligible to lend more books.)*

> > BookCode = Forms.Barcode reader.Display

> > *(The meaning of this message is to read the barcode of the book.)*

> > If input <> 'F' then Book copy.Book copy object.Lending (BookCode);

> > > elig = elig - 1

> > > *(If a barcode of a book was read—not a false barcode which returns an "F" value— a message is sent to the specific method Lending of class **Book copy**. Upon completion of that method [i.e., a book has been lent out] the reader's eligibility decreases by one book.)*

> > Else Reports.End-of-lending notice.Display; elig = 0

> > > *(If a false barcode was read, a message is sent to **Reports** class to display the end-of-lending notice. In addition, the variable elig is set to 0 in order to terminate the process.)*

> End while

End.

Begin Reader.Eligibility-check

years = current-year – registration-year

If years > 3 then Do Case:

           Case 1: if debt = 0 then N = 8

           Case 2: if debt <= 200 then N = 5

           Case 3: if debt > 200 then N = 0

     End Case

     If degree of study = "Grad" then N = N*2

     Else;

Else Do Case *(If years of study is 3 or less.)*

    Case 1: if debt = 0 AND degree of study = "Grad" then N = 5

    Case 2: if debt = 0 AND degree of study = "Under" then N = 3

    Case 3: if debt >= 40 AND degree of study = "Grad" then N = 1

    Case 4: if debt >= 40 AND degree of study = "Under" then N = 0

    Case 5: if debt < 40 then N = 2

  End Case

elig = N - number of books lent out

End.

Begin Book copy.Lending

Reader.reader object.Change (Replace, number of books lent out, ++1)

    (A message is sent to the reader object in order to change the value of the attribute number of books lent out; it will be increased by 1.)

Reader.reader object.Change (Add, set books lent out, (Book copy object, lending date))

    (This message too is sent to the reader object; the Change method will add a tuple of values to the set books lent out. The tuple includes a reference to the book object and the lending date. At this stage there is no return date; it will be updated by a separate transaction, whose details are not brought here.)

Book copy.book copy object.Change (Add, set lent out to, (reader object, lending date))

    (This is a message to the Change method of Book copy which will add a tuple of values to the set lent out to. The tuple includes a reference to the reader object and the lending date. Again, at this stage there is no return date.)

Reports.Lending printout .Display (reader object, book copy object)

    *(The message is sent to the **Reports** class in order to print a line in the Lend printout; the Display method prints a line detailing the book name. Note that this command is performed within the loop of the Transaction method, so eventually the lend report will include a line for each book lent out.)*

End.

Message Charts

A message chart provides a visual presentation of a method, and is equivalent to a description in pseudo code. A message chart can be viewed as a variation of a "traditional" program flowchart because it employs the same process logic patterns and the same symbols; only the class symbol is added. The chart is displayed inside a folder-like rectangle. The label part of the folder contains the class and method names. The chart consists of the following symbols:

- **Ellipse:** Signifies the "begin" or "end" of the method.
- **Diamond:** Signifies a condition or a loop.
- **Rectangle:** Contains a command or a sequence of commands.
- **Class rectangle:** Signifies the class receiving a message to activate one of its methods. The class rectangle has three parts: (1) the upper (label) part contains the class name; (2) the middle part contains the name of the specific class object on which the method is to be activated. An object name is specified only if the method acts on a specific object; and (3) the lower part contains the name of activated method, its parameters and the return value—depending on the specific method.
- **Arrow:** Signifies a flow of control (if pointing to an "ordinary" rectangle), or a message being sent to a method (if it is pointing to a class rectangle).

As we already know, a transaction may consist of a "main" method (the Transaction method) which may contain messages to basic and specific methods of other classes. Therefore, a complete description of a complex transaction may include several message charts: a "main" chart for the Transaction method and subcharts for the specific methods. Moreover, since a specific method may include messages to other specific methods, there may be a hierarchy of message charts describing a whole transaction.

Being semantically equivalent, the two techniques for describing methods—pseudo code and message charts—may be used interchangeably. For example, a Transaction (main) method may be described by a message chart, while its submethods may be described by pseudo code, or vise versa. Moreover, there is no necessity to use message charts at all, in particular for relatively simple methods. But for complex methods, message charts may be more clear and comprehensible than pseudo code.

Here are a few examples of message charts:

Figure 12.3. Message chart of transaction 1.4/5

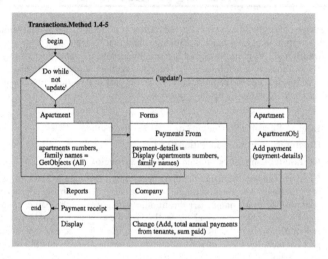

Example A

Figure 12.3 presents an example of a message chart of Transaction 1.4/5 of the Apartments Building system. It can easily be seen that the chart is equivalent to the pseudo-code description of this method.

Example B

Figures 12.4-12.6 present three message charts of Transaction 4.3-7 of the Music Programs system: Figure 12.4 is the message chart of the Transaction (main) method, while Figures 12.5 and 12.6 are message charts of two of its specific methods. Clearly, these charts are equivalent to the pseudo-code descriptions presented earlier. We could of course also present message charts of other specific methods included in the transaction (just as we could have done using that pseudo code).

Figure 12.4.

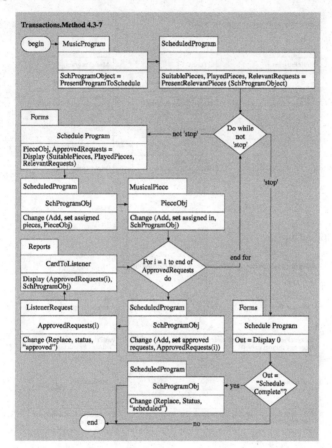

Figure 12.5.

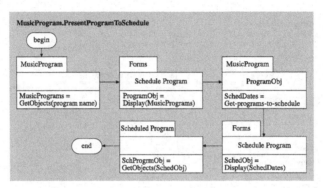

Figure 12.6.

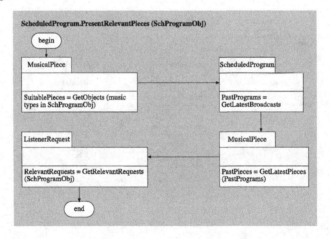

Example C

Figures 12.7-12.9 present three message charts of Transaction 12 of the Academic Library system. Figure 12.7 is the chart of the Transaction (main) method, while the other two charts describe the Eligibility check method of class **Reader**, and the Lend out book method of class **Book copy**.

Figure 12.7.

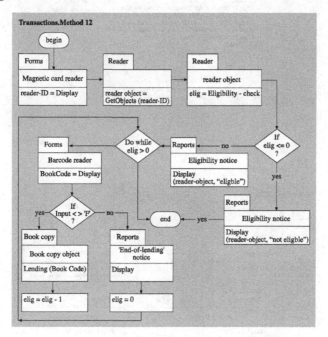

Figure 12.8.

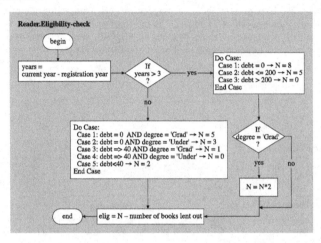

Figure 12.9.

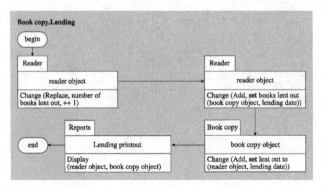

Summary of the Design Phase

In conclusion of the design phase, we review its products:

- A complete class diagram, consisting of the data classes, **Menus** class, **Inputs (Forms)** and **Output (Reports)** classes, and the **Transactions** class. Each of the data classes includes various attributes and relationships to other classes. In addition, each class includes a list of function names, that is, names of its specific methods which have been defined as a result of the process transactions decomposition.

- The **Menus** class includes detailed designs of the menus objects, and a pseudo-code description of the Choose method which enables the users to interact with the menus interface.

- The **Inputs (Forms)** and **Outputs (Reports)** classes include detailed design of the inputs and outputs/reports of the system.

- The **Transactions** class contains, for each transaction, a description of its main method—using pseudo code or a message chart.

- Each of the specific methods of the classes are described in detail using pseudo code or a message chart.

Before the design phase terminates, it is necessary to verify the consistency of the static product (i.e., the class diagram) and behavioral products (i.e., the methods). Special attention should be paid to making sure that every attribute of every data class is updated by at least one method and retrieved by at least one method. If this is not the case, then there is an attribute which is either never updated or never retrieved. This verification is repeating a similar activity performed at the end of the analysis phase (see the Keeping the Initial Class Diagram and the OO-DFDs Compatible section in Chapter VIII). The difference is that while at the analysis phase we verified the consistency of the initial class diagram with OO-DFDs, here we do it for the final class diagram and the various methods. The consistency check can be performed on every class (similar to what we have done in the analysis phase) and all methods which access it to "read" or to "write." That is, we list the attributes of a class and all the methods operating on that class; looking into the details of each method, we mark every attribute of the class which is retrieved by the method and every attribute which is updated by the method. Eventually, each attribute must be retrieved by at least one method and updated by at least one method. If this is not the case, we need to make sure that the relevant methods are defined correctly, or perhaps the attribute in question may be removed (and consequently, the method(s) which retrieve(s) that attribute or update it needs to be modified too).

The next phase of the development process is construction (i.e., programming). The aforementioned products of the design phase provide everything the programming teams need in order to create the system in an OO programming environment.

Review Questions

1. What are the steps in the design of transaction and class methods?

2. What is the "main" method of a transaction and how does it relate with other class methods?

3. Describe the transition from a top-level description of a transaction to a detailed description. How is each command in the top-level description handled?

4. What is the difference between a basic method and an application-specific method?

5. Describe the transition from a detailed description of the transaction to methods and messages. How are the various commands in the detailed description handled? What makes up a Transaction method?

6. How is a transaction activated and executed from the point of view of a user?

7. What components/symbols are included in a message chart?

8. Explain the similarity and the difference between a message chart and a pseudo-code description of a method.

9. Explain the similarity and the difference between a message chart and a program flowchart.

10. Explain what is a hierarchy of message charts or pseudo-code descriptions of transactions.

11. What are the final products of the design phase?

12. Explain the consistency checks of the design products. In what way is it different from the consistency checks of the analysis products?

References

Shoval, P. (1988). ADISSA: Architectural design of information systems based on structured analysis. *Information System, 13*(2), 193-210.

Shoval, P. (1998). *Planning, analysis and design of information systems* (Vols. 1-3). Tel-Aviv, Israel: Open University Press.

Endnotes

[1]   As described in Chapter X.

[2]   The rules for the transition of top-level descriptions of transactions to detailed descriptions are based on Architectural Design of Information Systems based on Structures Analysis (ADISSA) (Shoval, 1988, 1998).

[3]   This transaction was described in Chapter X and then again in Chapter XI. Here, the comments were left out.

[4]   Assume that this is the number of the input screen, that is, input number 1 of transaction 1.4/5.

[5]   This is the number of the output designed for this transaction.

[6]   The description has already appeared in Chapter IX, and the transaction's diagram has been presented in Figure 10.2, Chapter X. The version of description shown here is the one that consists of procedures. The remarks that appeared in the original description were left out.

[7]   This is just one transaction of the library system, but more details are not needed for the sake of this example. The example was originally used in Shoval (1998).

[8]   This is one possible class diagram for this case; an alternative could be having a "relationship class" **Lend out**, in which each lending of a book to a reader creates an object, which contains the lending details.

[9]   We gave the transaction an arbitrary number 12.

[10]   In short we call it specific method.

[11]   This example was originally presented in Chapter II.

[12]   In the next section, we will use message charts.

[13]   Obviously, this is not a "standard" way to define a message and its parameters; but as said, our notation is not formal and is mainly aimed to direct the programmers who will eventually code the methods according to the rules of the programming language that will be utilized.

[14]   The lines are not numbered, but comments and explanations follow almost every line/command.

Appendix:
Examples of Basic Methods

In this chapter, as well as in chapter II, we have made a distinction between basic methods and application-specific methods. We have assumed that every class includes basic methods that can perform the CRUD functions, so that we need only to define the application-specific methods, extract them from the transactions' descriptions and attach them to the proper classes.

We have been showing examples of various basic and application-specific methods in pseudo code, along with comments, and we have pointed out that this pseudo code is not a formal language and, unlike a programming language, it does not follow syntactic rules. Rather, the pseudo-code description of methods is aimed to provide guidelines to the programmers who will program and test the methods; therefore the pseudo code includes also comments and explanations.

In this appendix we define a few basic methods. The objective is to see the structure of such methods and their parameters.

A Method to Add A New Object to A Class:

Structure of method: ClassName.Construct (object)

Example: Student.Construct (StudentObj)

This method gets as a parameter the values of the attributes of new object and adds it to the class. It may be assumed that the data values of the new object have been added via some input device and already reside in memory in the variable 'object'. But note that 'object' is not necessarily a single variable of a certain data type, like in programming languages; rather it represents all the values of attributes that will become the new object. The method 'Construct' is not detailed here; but it should be assumed that it performs the relevant integrity checks for adding a new object, according to the relationship types and multiplicities defined in the class diagram for that class. Hence, the method is assumed to return a value 'True' if the new object has been added successfully, or 'False' if the object could not be added because of an integrity constraint.

A Method to Delete an Object

Structure of the method: ClassName.object (Delete)

Example: Student.StudentObj.Delete

The method deletes an existing object which is identified by the value of 'object'. As before, the method 'Delete' is not detailed, but it should be assumed that it performs the relevant integrity checks for deleting an object from a class, according to the relationship types and multiplicities defined in the class diagram for that class. Hence, the method is assumed to return a value 'True' if the new object has been deleted successfully, or 'False' if the object could not be deleted. Note the different notation of this method compared to 'Construct': In 'Construct' the parameter includes the data values of the new object; in 'Delete' the method operates on the object identified by 'object', which is actually its OID. It should be assumed that the OID has been obtained by an earlier 'Find' method.

A Method to Find an Object or Objects

Structure of method: returnObject = ClassName.GetObjects (conditions and attributes)

Example: some-students = Student.GetObjects. (name = "Smith" and city = "Chicago")

The method gets as parameter search conditions, which refer to values of the class attributes; it returns to 'retunObject' the data of the objects which satisfy the conditions. Note again that the return value is not a single variable; it may include the data values of one or more objects that satisfy the search conditions. If no search conditions are passed, that is, 'GetObjects()', all the objects of the class will be returned. On the other hand, it is possible that no object is returned if none satisfies the conditions.

A Method to Retrieve Certain Attributes of an Object

Structure of method: return values = ClassName.object.Get (list of attributes)

Example: stud-number, name = Student.StudentObj.Get (ID number, name)

The method operates on a certain object of a class, identified by 'object'. Its parameter is a list of attributes whose values will be returned to the variables listed in 'return values'.

A Method to Change/Update Attributes of an Object

Structure of the method: ClassName.object.Change (action, attribute, value1, [value2])

This method operates on an object which has to be changed. It receives several parameters: 'action' is the type of change: 'Add' adds a value to an attribute; 'Replace' puts a new value instead of an existing one; 'Del' erases the existing value. The action will be performed on the 'attribute'. 'value1' is the value to be added, replaced, or deleted. 'value2' is relevant only for 'Replace'—it includes the new value of the attribute. Note that if 'attribute' is a reference attribute, then 'value1' and value2' must include OIDs of objects to be added, deleted, or replaced. Note that 'attribute' may also be a tuple, or a set, or any combination of attribute types.

Examples:

Student.StudentObj.Change (Add, city, New-York)

Student.StudentObj.Change (Del, set phones, 054-8765432)

Student.StudentObj.Change (Replace, set phones, 054-8765432, 052-3456789)

The next example assumes that there is a many-to-one relationship between classes **Student** and **Department** with respective reference attributes: 'belongs to' is an attribute of Student, and 'student list' is an attribute of Department. In order to add a student to a department we need to change the values of the reference attributes of the involved objects. (It is assumed that the OIDs of the student and department have already been found by the respective 'Find' methods.) Hence, we apply these two 'Change' methods:

Student.StudentObj.Change (Add, belongs to, DepartmentObj)

Department.DepartmentObj.Change (Add, students list, StudentObj)

The next example shows an opposite operation: we want to disconnect a student from a department:

Student.StudentObj.Change (Del, belongs to, DepartmentObj)

Department.DepartmentObj.Change (Del, students list, StudentObj)

If we want to disconnect all the students from a certain department, we need to delete all references to the student objects in the department's object, and then delete the reference to that department in all its student objects. The next example shows a part of a specific method which carries out this task, dealing mainly with the "Change" methods. Note that the 'GetObjects' method retrieves all student objects belonging to the department (i.e., the department whose OIS is in 'DepartmentObj'). Then, a loop is performed for those students; in each iteration of the loop, the reference to the department is removed from the student's object. Note also the parameter 'All' of the 'Change' method applied on Department, which means that it deletes all values of this set attribute.

Department.DepartmentObj.Change (Del, students list, All)

all-dept-students = Student.StudentObjets.Change (belongs to = DepartmentObj)

For each Object in all-dept-students do:

      Student.StudentObj.Change (Del, belongs to, DepatmentObj)

Next object.

A Method to Count How Many Values Include an Attribute of an Object

Structure of method: return value = ClassName.object.Count (attribute)

Example: number-of-students = Department.DepartmentObj.Count (students list)

Note that if the attribute is simple, the return value can be 0 or 1. If it is a set attribute, the number of members in the set is returned.

Glossary

4GL
Fourth Generation Language

ADISSA
Architectural Design of Information Systems Based on Structures Analysis

CAD
Computer Aided Design

CAM
Computer Aided Manufacturing

CASE
Computer Aided Software Engineering

CRUD
Create, Read, Update, Delete

DBMS
Data Base Management System

DD
Data Dictionary

DDL

Data Definition/Description Language

DFD

Data Flow Diagram

DML

Data Manipulation Language

ER

Entity Relationship

ERD

Entity Relationship Diagram

FOOM

Functional and Object-Oriented Methodology

GIS

Geographical Information System

IS

Information System

MS

Microsoft

ODL

Objects Definition/Description Language

OID

Object Identification

OMG

Object Management Group

OMT

Object Modeling Technique

OO

Object-Oriented

OOA

Object Oriented Analysis

OOD

Object Oriented Design

OO-DBMS

Object-Oriented Data Base Management System

OO-DFD

Object-Oriented Data Flow Diagram

OOSE

Object Oriented Software Engineering

OPL

Object-Oriented Programming Language

OR-DBMS

Object-Relational Data Base Management System

PL

Programming Language

SC

Structure Chart

SQL

Structured Query Language

SSA

System Structure Analysis

SSD

System Structure Design

UM
   Unified Method

UML
   Unified Modeling Language

VB
   Visual Basic

About the Author

Peretz Shoval is a professor of information systems with the Department of Information Systems Engineering of Ben-Gurion University. He earned his BA (economics) and MSc (information systems) from Tel-Aviv University, and PhD (information systems, 1981) from the University of Pittsburgh, where he specialized in expert systems for information retrieval. In 1984, he joined Ben-Gurion University in Israel, where he started the Information Systems Program at the Department of Industrial Engineering and Management, and later on created and headed the Department of Information Systems Engineering. Prior to moving to academia, Shoval held professional and managerial positions in computer and software companies. Shoval's research interests include information systems analysis and design methods; data modeling and database design; and information retrieval and filtering. He has published more than 100 papers in journals, conference proceedings, and book chapters, and authored several books on systems analysis and design. Shoval has developed methodologies and tools for systems analysis and design, and for conceptual and logical database design.

Index